Y0-AGA-837

NORTHEAST CONFERENCE ON THE
TEACHING OF FOREIGN LANGUAGES

# TEACHING, TESTING, AND ASSESSMENT
## *Making the Connection*

**CHARLES R. HANCOCK, Editor**
**SYLVIA BROOKS-BROWN, Chair**
**1994**

National Textbook Company
a division of *NTC Publishing Group* • Lincolnwood, Illinois USA

# 1994 Board of Directors

Sylvia Brooks-Brown, *Chair*
Baltimore County (MD) Public Schools

Rebecca Kline, *Vice Chair*
The Pennsylvania State University

Martha G. Abbott, *Director*
Fairfax County (VA) Public Schools

Nancy E. Anderson, *ACTFL Representative,* Educational Testing Service

Julia T. Bressler, *Director*
Nashua (NH) Public Schools

Adrienne G. Cannon, *Director*
Prince George's County (MD) Public Schools

Celestine G. Carr, *Director*
Howard County (MD) Public Schools

James Crapotta, *Director*
Barnard College

José M. Díaz, *Past Chair*
Hunter College High School (NY, NY)

Richard Donato, *Director*
University of Pittsburgh

Robert Elkins, *Director*
West Virginia University

Eileen W. Glisan, *Director*
Indiana University of Pennsylvania

Charles R. Hancock, *1994* Reports *Editor,* The Ohio State University

Elizabeth L. Holekamp, *Executive Director,* Northeast Conference

André O. Hurtgen, *Director*
Saint Paul's School (Concord, NH)

Stephen L. Levy, *Consultant to the Chair and Local Committee Chair,* Roslyn (NY) Public Schools

Gladys Lipton, *Newsletter Editor,* University of Maryland–Baltimore County

Emily S. Peel, *Director*
Wethersfield (CT) Public Schools

Harry L. Rosser, *Director,* Boston College

Arlene F. White, *Recording Secretary,* Salisbury State University

Clara Yu, *Director,* Middlebury College

**1996 Printing**

Published by National Textbook Company, a division of NTC Publishing Group.
© 1994 by NTC Publishing Group, 4255 West Touhy Avenue,
Lincolnwood (Chicago), Illinois 60646-1975 U.S.A.
All rights reserved. No part of this book may be reproduced, stored
in a retrieval system, or transmitted in any form or by any means,
electronic, mechanical, photocopying, recording or otherwise, without
the prior permission of NTC Publishing Group.
Manufactured in the United States of America.

6 7 8 9 0 VP 9 8 7 6 5 4 3 2

# Contents

*Introduction*

**The average teacher tells.**
**The good teacher explains.**
**The superior teacher models.**
**The great teacher inspires.**

(author unknown)

When the 1994 chair of the Northeast Conference, Dr. Sylvia Brooks-Brown, selected *Teaching, Testing, and Assessing: Making the Connection* as theme of the conference, it was also approved by the Board as the theme for the Reports. The selection recognizes the need for a close linkage between the ways in which instructors teach, test, and assess their students. It also continues the Northeast's long tradition of selecting themes which treat important issues being faced by the foreign language teaching profession, even if some aspects of the topic are unresolved or controversial.

This volume of the Northeast Conference Reports is designed to explore ways in which foreign language professionals can effectively answer for themselves a key question: *Do my teaching, testing, and assessment match?* Both teacher and support personnel (e.g., department chair, supervisor, principal, curriculum coordinator) are headed into the next century with a view towards increased teacher empowerment. Thus, initiatives are to be valued that assist teachers in reflecting about professional priorities and that help them make informed decisions.

The 1994 volume of the Reports focuses on the relationship among teaching, testing, and assessment. Given the performance movement in the U.S. during the past decade, it is important for language professionals to reflect on the need to create a solid link between these important constructs in their own professional environment and to expand their use of alternative strategies in these three areas. Obviously, the desirable relationship among the three is a cohesive match between contextualized teaching and testing/assessing at the foreign language classroom level, but it is easier to talk about this match than it is to achieve it. Yet, few would disagree with the notion that, ideally, teaching, assessing, and testing should be correlated.

With this perspective in mind, the chapters of the volume all deal with aspects of the challenge of establishing a stronger bond among the ways we teach, test, and assess foreign language students. The difficulty of reaching this goal is obvious to any teacher whose focus is communicative language teaching but who is faced with large numbers of students and limited resources. How long should a teacher persist in emphasizing functional, practical use of the foreign language with students when s/he sees the faces of many students who do well in class work but whose test results are not good? Is there an internal conflict for the teacher who knows about validity and reliability as key factors which characterize good tests but who assigns grades based on other criteria? What is the incentive to use communicative testing strategies at the classroom level when standardized foreign language achievement tests (e.g., those coming from the Educational Testing Service and local college/university placement tests) seem destined to focus on discrete points of language? What is a *prochievement* test anyway?

And what about testing in the four skill areas (listening, speaking, reading, writing) and culture? Are there alternatives to conventional ways of assessing students' foreign language learning? And is there a difference between testing and assessment? How can portfolios be used in foreign language programs? Are portfolios limited to the writing skill? What innovative models for professional development and teacher education are on the horizon? These are the types of questions addressed by the authors of the 1994 Reports. Some issues were addressed even if there is no consensus within the profession at this point.

The first three chapters should be conceived as background for the rest of the volume. In the first chapter, Valette presents a conceptual model of what the relationship should be among teaching, testing, and assessment. She presents a new Five-Step Performance-Based Model of second language instruction to show how teaching, testing, and assessment are related. She draws an interesting analogy with football. The second chapter also deals with performance outcomes but presents a comprehensive profile from the national perspective on foreign language instruction and testing. In his chapter, Stansfield surveys major national and regional initiatives with a view toward identifying ways in which these independent projects can, in fact, be viewed as forming a coordinated effort which emphasizes the standards of knowledge, skills, and abilities that a student should have after studying a foreign language. In the third chapter, Wiggins, who is not a foreign language educator but who is well known for his work on testing and assessment, addresses the widespread need for authentic assessment. He argues that more emphasis on assessment and less on testing is called for as the profession continues to implment proficiency-oriented language programs. His chapter includes a set of nine criteria for judging the authenticity of a test.

The next three chapters are the "skills" chapters, dealing with listening, speaking, reading, and writing. The authors of these chapters worked from the perspective of a needed match among teaching, testing, and assessment. Boyles' chapter deals with oral production and shows the importance of incorporating a proficiency orientation; it offers sample testing formats that classroom teachers should find both reasonable and practical. The chapter co-authored by Long and Macián builds on the 1986 Northeast Conference Reports and describes more recent theory and research on the topic of listening skills. Their chapter also includes practical strategies for teaching, testing, and assessing listening in a coherent manner. They argue, however, that listening is a skill which still needs to be nurtured directly despite some recent gains in recognizing its importance in second language acquisition. Davis's chapter on reading and writing skills recognizes the interrelatedness of language skills. Although references are made to advanced level readers, the focus is on reading and writing in the beginning stages of language learning. His chapter centers on the notion that both reading and writing are interactive processes in which the foreign language student should concentrate on receiving and communicating messages, not on "decoding" particular aspects of the foreign language.

The final three chapters deal with culture, affective factors, and teacher education. Moore's chapter treats the topic of culture from the point of view of portfolio assessment of learners' knowledge of the foreign or second culture. She explores the concept of portfolio as a potentially powerful strategy for foreign language education and applies it specifically to assessing students' cultural learning. Barr-Harrison and Horwitz co-authored an important chapter dealing with affective student factors. The chapter centers on the special needs, concerns, and cognitive abilities of adolescents. Also included are details of a recently developed battery of proficiency-oriented language tests and student reactions to the tests. The final chapter in the Reports treats the topic of teacher education. Schrier and Hammadou co-authored this chapter written for both foreign language practitioners and teacher educators. The authors describe recent assessment instruments designed to evaluate teacher competencies and examine the potential benefits of portfolio assessment for preservice language teachers. It is argued that portfolios, while not a panacea, allow for a fair and principled assessment of teaching. Further, the authors demonstrate that the future demands increased opportunities for teacher involvement in the assessment of their competence.

The volume ends with several resources for the busy professional who needs to keep abreast of current thinking but who may not have time to head off to the local library. A glossary of selected terms is included both as a tool for interpreting chapters in this volume and simply as information. These terms have been defined by the editor as a helpful resource and not as a substitution for reading a more indepth treatment of the particular topic. Finally, the volume includes an annotated bibliography of selected, important articles researched by several current doctoral students who have described the gist of the article and offered a recommendation about its value. Both resources are new as part of the NEC Reports, and feedback is welcome.

Finally, as editor, I wish to thank all who participated in this ambitious volume, including the NEC Board and staff, the authors, The Ohio State University doctoral students, Kurt Müller who is an excellent editorialconsultant, others who read drafts and commented on manuscripts, and finally, my wonderful wife, Theresa, who continues to support me in ways too numerous to name.

Charles R. Hancock, 1994 Editor
The Ohio State University

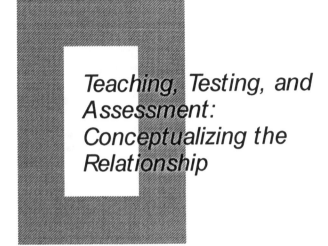

# Teaching, Testing, and Assessment: Conceptualizing the Relationship

Rebecca M. Valette
*Boston College*

In January 1993, the ACTFL/AATF/AATG/AATSP Students Standards Project was launched with the mandate of defining the desired outcomes of second-language instruction in the United States. If we view this new initiative in the recent historical perspective of similar standards projects undertaken by professional associations like the National Council of Teachers of Mathematics (NCTM), it becomes clear that once these student standards are established, they will be used by the National Assessment of Educational Progress (NAEP) to determine foreign language performance levels for students in grades 4, 8, and 12. In fact, NAEP has announced that it will begin assessing the progress of foreign language students in 1996 (Valette, 1993a).

Given this prospect, that within the next few years national attention will be focussed on how effectively American students can use the foreign languages they are studying in secondary school, it is appropriate that we reexamine the relationship between teaching, testing and assessment from this performance-based point of view. First, we will look at teaching and grading, the interplay between stated instructional outcomes and assessment measures, and the potential influence of the washback effect. Then we will propose a new Five-Step Performance-Based Model of second language instruction, and examine the role of testing and assessment within that model.[1]

# Teaching, Testing, and Assessment

When people acquire a second language in a natural environment, the focus is on the learner: it is the learner who progressively comes to understand more and more elements and features of the second language, who tests outs his/her comprehension through responses and questions of various sorts, and who informally and in natural situations assesses his/her ability to express personal ideas and participate in conversations. In this natural immersion environment, learning, testing and assessment are intimately interwoven, and the learner is the key player, the active participant.

In a school environment, the learner's language acquisition is structured and guided by the teacher. Whatever form this instruction takes (whether it is teacher-centered or student-centered, whether it is communication-based or grammar-focused, whether it utilizes the latest technology or pencil-and-paper worksheets, whether student progress is evaluated formally or informally), the learner's language acquisition is dependent on what happens in the classroom (the teaching) and is evaluated by an outsider (the testing and assessment). In the linguistically artificial school environment, the learner traditionally is one of a group of passive recipients, dependent on the teacher as both the source of what is to be learned and the instrument of evaluation.

It is perhaps appropriate at this point to define the terms that form the title of this chapter.

## Assigning Grades

Grades have traditionally been used to rank the students with reference to their classmates. In foreign language classes, these grades may be based on three types of evaluation:

| CLASS PARTICIPATION *evaluation of general work and behavior* | ACHIEVEMENT TESTING *tests based on material taught* | PROFICIENCY MEASURES *tests incorporating authentic assessment* |
|---|---|---|
| attendance / participation | lesson quizzes | oral interviews, oral testing in pairs |
| effort / attitude | dictations | understanding unfamiliar readings, videos, recordings, etc. |
| homework | dialog recitations | writing notes, letters, essays, etc. |
| special projects (skits, oral reports, compositions, posters, etc.) | recorded tests | |
| extra credit work | unit tests | |
| | *** | |
| | prochievement tests | |

Until the 1960s, most secondary schools taught foreign languages to "academically qualified" students in grades 9 to 12 and "covered" one textbook per level. Grades were based almost entirely on achievement tests that measured how well students had learned the material presented. Colleges were comfortable in equating two years of this type of secondary language instruction with one year of similar college instruction, and placed students accordingly.

In the last thirty years, however, as we have been striving to give all students the opportunity to learn a second language, our programs have come to reflect increasingly high levels of diversity. Some school systems have elementary school language programs, ranging from full and partial immersion programs to various types of sequential FLES programs and shorter exploratory programs. Similarly, at the middle or junior high level, different cities and schools offer foreign language courses of varying degrees of intensity. Even at the high school level, there is a great deal of tracking in foreign language classes, so that there is no way of equating a year of instruction with specific curricular content. Furthermore, as teachers have been working with students of various backgrounds and abilities, many have begun to rely more heavily on classroom participation than on achievement testing in assigning grades.

In the 1980s, the "proficiency movement" began to focus professional attention on how well students could actually use the language they were learning for interpersonal communication. Particular emphasis was placed on oral proficiency with the ACTFL Oral Proficiency Interview serving as a model for the type of performance skills to be developed in the classroom. Teachers still tended, however, to assign grades based on classroom participation and achievement testing, though the latter tended to become more contextualized and was often referred to as "prochievement" testing, that is, achievement testing in which items are presented in a proficiency-like context.

In the 1990s, we are seeing renewed interest in performance-based or outcome-based instruction. Schools are struggling to define what students should be able to do with the foreign language as the result of the instruction and then modify their curriculum so that these outcomes can be achieved. This new foreign language focus is looking closely at the "proficiency measures.

## Individualized Instruction vs. Performance-Based Instruction

In a sense, the current focus on outcome-based instruction is reminiscent of the "individualized instruction" movement of the 1970s with its emphasis on "behavioral objectives" or "performance objectives." However, there are major differences, as illustrated in Chart 1, below.

The "individualized instruction" movement wanted to define instructional outcomes and break them down into smaller components with the aim of enabling all students to achieve mastery of the new subject matter by making it more accessible to students of varying levels of ability. At the same time, these smaller performance objectives were carefully analyzed and classified according to taxonomies which ranked them in increasing order of complexity (see Valette and Disick, 1973). The main reason that the individualized instruction failed as a movement in foreign languages was that frequently teachers failed to focus enough attention on activities promoting interpersonal communicative language use. By stressing the mastery of the "bits and pieces" of the language, they and their students often lost sight of the whole picture.

| Chart 1. Goals of Individualized and Performance-Based Instruction | | |
|---|---|---|
| | *Individualized Instruction based on Performance Objectives* | *Performance-Based Instruction based on Outcomes* |
| Define goals... | in terms of limited attainable component skills or objectives | in terms of general proficiency-oriented performance goals |
| in order to... | individualize instruction | clarify instructional outcomes |
| so that... | all students can achieve mastery | students and teachers can be held accountable for achieving these goals |

The aim of performance-based instruction is to clarify the desired instructional outcomes in terms of broad proficiency goals, to enable teachers to focus on these goals more clearly and, in the eye of certain legislators, supervisors and parent groups, to enable them to hold schools accountable for the achievement of these objectives. The challenge facing the profession is to define these second language goals so that they are indeed attainable, and then to develop instructional programs whereby these goals can be achieved. In addition, the profession needs to inform legislators, supervisors and parents as to what these attainable goals are.

The long-range aim of performance-based instruction in the United States is to develop curricula which will enable students to meet "world-class standards" in the area of second (and third) language instruction. Such an ambitious goal will require first that we define these world-class standards by assessing the foreign language competencies of students in other countries. Even more importantly, it will require that we adopt the longer, articulated sequences of foreign language instruction so typical of the educational systems of developed countries around the world. The reader is encouraged to consult Stansfield's chapter for a fuller treatment of this topic.

## Transparency and Authentic Assessment

In a performance-based second-language curriculum, the desired outcomes of instruction are the development of proficiency in the skills of speaking, listening, reading and writing, and the concommitant development of cultural competence. As we look at how the attainment of these objectives can best be evaluated, we come face to face with the questions of transparency and authentic assessment.[2]

*Transparency*

Already in the mid-1970s, European language teachers and testers were discussing the question of *transparency.*[3] Their concern was how to make it readily apparent (i.e., transparent) to a student or parent what type of behavior or performance was being measured on a given test. It was also important that the student be familiar with the types of questions that would appear on the test and how they were to be scored. Clearly, requiring swimmers to demonstrate their ability to swim the crawl by having them complete four laps in the pool was considered to constitute a highly *transparent* test. Both the candidate and the evaluators could readily see what the test is measuring, and both could determine whether the performance was successful or not. In language tests, it may not always be possible to place the candidates in real-life linguistic situations, such as asking for instructions in Madrid or Buenos Aires, but to the extent that the behaviors measured on the test are seen by the candidate as imitating real-life linguistic situations, the test is considered transparent. In the writing tests, for example, one might ask candidates to write an actual letter in response to an actual ad that is reproduced in the test booklet. Such a test is transparent, whereas such would not be the case for a multiple-choice test in which students would read a similar letter and select the correct completions for missing words or phrases.

Currently the Council of Europe is focussing on the question of transparency and coherence in language learning programs. Researchers are exploring the possibility of a common European framework for reporting language competency by looking at the various scales of language proficiency that have been developed by member countries, as well as the ACTFL scale (Schärer and North, 1992; North, 1993). One of the proposed models omits the global scale and focuses on three main aspects of language use: understanding (one-way, receptive), interacting (two-way, live), and prepared production (one-way, productive). These are further subdivided as shown below in figure 1 (Schärer and North, p. 17).

*Authentic Assessment*

The current American interest in authentic assessment seems to parallel the European concern for transparency. Basically, the term *authentic assessment* is used to refer to language tests and measurement instruments that call on the types of linguistic performance which characterize real life usage.[3] Since performance-based second-language programs have as their goal the

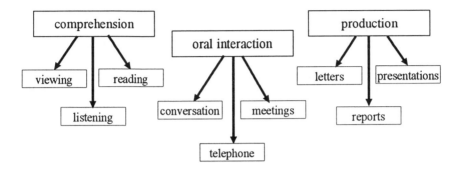

Figure 1. Schärer and North Model

development of language proficiency, it is necessary to evaluate how well students can use the language they are studying in authentic (or near-authentic) contexts. Chapter 3 of this volume includes an in-depth treatment of this topic by Grant Wiggins.

# Instructional Outcomes and the Washback Effect

Instructional outcomes reflect the goals of a formal teaching curriculum. These outcomes are of three sorts:

- the *desired or projected outcomes* of a course of instruction as described in the course framework,
- the *actual outcomes* as determined by what the students learn and what skills they acquire
- the *measured outcomes*, as determined by how well students perform on tests and other instruments designed to assess the desired outcomes.

## The Outcome-Based Language Program

In the ideal outcome-based language program, the desired outcomes, the actual outcomes and the measured outcomes are the same. The relationship between the three types of outcomes is conceptualized in figure 2, below.

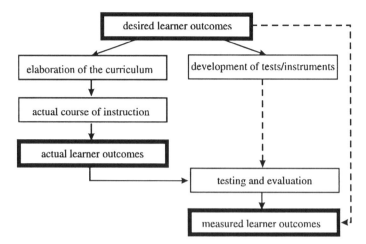

Figure 2. The Performance-Based Program

Theoretically, the model instructional program would evolve as follows:

1.  The course objectives and desired outcomes are defined.
2.  Appropriate tests and assessment measures are developed to reflect these outcomes.
3.  The syllabus/curriculum is designed as a function of the course objectives.
4.  The teacher activities are planned to help the learner acquire these outcomes.
5.  The learner participates in the class as instructed by the teacher.
6.  At the end of the course, the learner outcomes are evaluated and the results are analyzed to determine to what extent the learner has attained the objectives. Ideally, these measured learner outcomes are found to be identical to the desired learner outcomes elaborated in step (1), above.

In reality, however, there are often unexpected additional student outcomes which are not evaluated by the test instruments. In other words, the students learn or acquire things that were not described in the statement of desired outcomes. This is shown below in figure 3.

These additional unpredicted learner outcomes may be positive (e.g., students develop a love for the second culture and an eagerness to continue their study, although the statement of desired outcomes contained no affective goals) or negative (e.g., students acquire an anglicized pronunciation of the foreign language since the desired outcomes did not explicitly emphasize pronunciation).

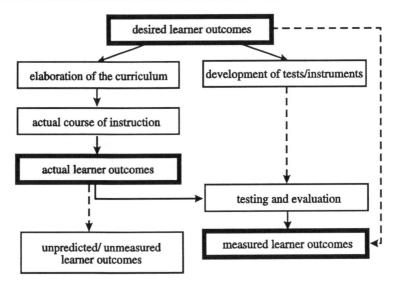

Figure 3. The Modified Outcome-Based Language Program

One of the key concerns of program evaluation is to identify these unpredicted learner outcomes and to take steps to correct those which are found to be negative. For example, the immersion programs in Canada were designed to produce fluent bilingual speakers of French. Recently, however, in analyzing the data, Swain (1992) has determined that many students are acquiring an inaccurate interlanguage, and that the program must be modified to strengthen their linguistic accuracy. This concern for more accurate language usage will presumably be reflected as new statements of desired learner outcomes are developed.

## The Washback Effect

Measurement specialists often refer to the *washback effect* which a testing program may have on the teachers and/or the learners. This washback effect is particularly strong in situations where the students' performance on a test determines future career options, such as university entrance. In such cases, teachers often feel obliged to "teach for the test," especially if their effectiveness as a teacher is in part evaluated by how well their students perform. In Japan, for example, where the English portion of the college entrance examination requires students to translate classical texts, classroom activities which focus on oral communication and creative language use are seen as a waste of precious time. In the United States, tests like the College Board

Achievement Tests, the AAT contests, and the New York State Regents examinations, and the Oral Proficiency Interview have over the years exerted their own washback effects.

Washback occurs when it is the testing instrument rather than the statement of desired learner outcomes that determines the nature of the curriculum and the course of instruction. The influence of the washback effect on a foreign language program is shown in figure 4.

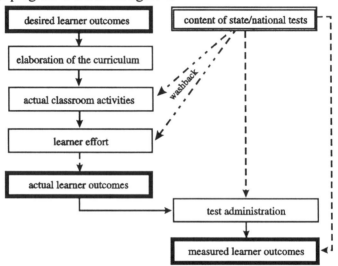

Figure 4. Language Program with Washback from Outside Tests

The washback from national or state tests is strongest on the teachers who organize their lesson plans so as to prepare their students to do well on the tests. There is also secondary washback on the student, who is more likely to study material that is seen as useful in scoring well on the outside test. If a new test or assessment instrument is seen as particularly valid, its availability may exert influence on the statement of desired outcomes and the elaboration of the curriculum.

The washback effect is also commonly found at the classroom level. The teacher may state course objectives in terms of desired learner outcomes, but students put in their learning effort on those elements and those skills that will be covered on the test or that will "count" for their grade. At the student level, this type of washback is often referred to as "studying for the test."

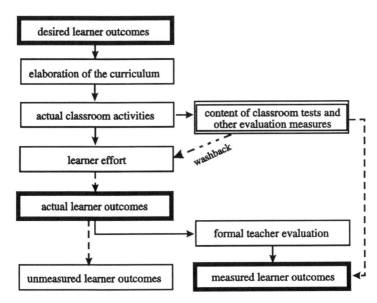

Figure 5. Student Effort Influenced by Washback
from Classroom Tests

At the classroom level, the creative classroom teacher can use the washback effect to great advantage by establishing a grading system that fosters the type of language learning which will promote the desired learner outcomes. For example, at Boston College all elementary French students must keep a "learning log" with entries for the dates and times that they study French, go to the language media lab (these visits are corroborated with a language lab stamp), or engage in French-related activities (such as seeing a French movie). In order to receive an "A," the learning log must have daily entries including daily listening practice. The focus on regular preparation and regular listening practice promotes the development of good language learning skills.

The clasroom teacher can also develop tests in a format that encourages learners to develop desired study habits. For example, the elementary French unit tests consist almost entirely of spoken cues, thus encouraging students to prepare by listening to tapes. Three recorded pronunciation tests per semester promote careful speaking practice, and two heavily weighted oral interview tests help students recognize the importance of oral interaction.

In addition to using formal grading criteria to promote positive washback, the teacher can watch for other learner outcomes that are not formally measured but nonetheless observable and thereby conduct an on-going informal assessment of how well students are progressing.

# The Five-Step Performance-Based Model of Oral Proficiency

The term "performance-based instruction" evokes, and perhaps appropriately so, the image of a sporting event, such as a football game.[4] Indeed, at the secondary school level, the one faculty member who is the most rigorously evaluated in terms of student performance or student outcomes is usually the football coach. Almost every weekend during the fall season, coach and players focus their attention on outcomes, or performance, namely on how well they will play in the "real" game against another school in their league. During the week, however, there is training and practice of various sorts.

In order to elaborate a model for performance-based instruction based on the football analogy, we must closely observe how young people learn to play football. At first, a child is happy to zigzag down the lawn carrying the ball. But soon the young player needs to learn what real football is by:

- watching actual football games,
- learning the rules of the game, and
- drilling the skills, such as throwing, receiving, blocking and running.

Furthermore, the young player needs to gain experience in:

- scrimmage practice , and
- participating in actual games.

Clearly a young player who cannot understand the game on television, who cannot catch a pass, and who does not know what is meant by "offside," may have fun "playing football" with friends, but certainly is not "proficient" at the game.

Of course, there are levels of performance in football, each with its corresponding levels of proficiency. Young players participate in the Pop Warner League. Then they may play junior high varsity and senior high varsity, before moving to university varsity, and perhaps even professional football. Each level becomes more complex and more challenging.

Common to all levels of football, however, is the emphasis on performance. The focus is on playing the game well, that is, responding creatively and effectively to situations as they develop on the field and initiating new moves and strategies as needed. Then during the following week, the performance in the previous game is closely studied and criticized. There is training and practice with much of the practice time spent on drills, building strength, and developing accuracy of execution of plays and routines. Daily workouts are not simply scrimmages followed by congratulations. Even the scrimmage sessions are followed by close critiques, in an effort to improve performance the next time.

Building oral proficiency in a foreign language is very similar to building proficiency in football. In the Five-Step Performance-Based Model[4] outlined below, the first four steps each contribute to preparing students for the last step which is using the language for actual communication with native speakers.

| *Steps* | *Oral proficiency* | *Football* |
|---|---|---|
| 1. Guided Observation | Listening to the spoken language | Watching actual football games |
| 2. Guided Analysis | Learning how the language works | Learning the rules of the game |
| 3. Guided Practice | Building the skills | Training: drill and practice |
| 4. Simulated Performance | Participating in guided conversations and role play | Scrimmage practice |
| 5. Performance | Speaking in real-life situations | Participating in actual games |

*Step 1. Guided Observation: Listening to the Spoken Language*

In Step 1, the students come into contact with the second language as it is spoken in authentic situations. At its most difficult, this means listening to conversations between native speakers, watching television, listening to the radio, etc. Listening to the second language in its most authentic manifestation is like going to a professional football game: people unfamiliar with the game have no idea what is going on, people with some notions of football follow the main movements of the game, avid fans know the players, the plays, the signals, and can analyze not only what did happen but what might have happened. At the highest level of comprehension, listening to authentic speech, like attending professional football games, requires an awareness and a sensitivity to cultural connotations and allusions.

The learner needs guidance in developing this initial skill of comprehension.

- At a beginning level, Step 1 consists of listening to the simplified but none the less real language of contrived and/or scripted spoken materials. This type of activity might include TPR (Total Physical Response) activities, listening to simplified narrations, watching videos scripted for language learners but filmed on location by native speakers. This activity is like attending a Pop Warner league game, where one can observe the main features of football in a less complex environment.
- At a more advanced level, this step will include listening to authentic material that has been specifically selected or edited so as to be more comprehensible. Usually this means listening to authentic material with the opportunity of stopping and replaying parts of a recording, perhaps even using captioned versions of a video to enhance comprehension. This is like watching a football game on television where instant replays and charts help clarify the action.

What the students understand from the material they are watching and/or listening to is often termed *comprehensible input*. With language learning as with football, the focus must be on moving from a general notion of what is going on to increasingly more accurate levels of comprehension and more precise appreciation of the complexities of the language.

The better a student understands a second language, the more effectively that student will eventually be able to participate in a conversation, just as the more a young player understands the game of football, the better that player will eventually be able to perform on the field.

*Step 2. Guided Analysis: Learning How the Language Works*

In Step 2, students learn how the second language is put together, how it works.

- At first, attention is focussed in isolated, individual elements, such as the sound system, snytax patterns, grammatical structures, and vocabulary. This is like learning the rules of football, such as what type of movements are considered "clipping" or "holding" and what penalty such calls carry.
- Then students are expected to recognize and understand the elements in the context of a spoken message: can they make phonemic distinctions, can they hear a gender marker and tell whether a noun is feminine or masculine, can they notice whether a verb is in the preterite or the imperfect, are they aware of the use of a subjunctive or the choice of a particular adjective and do they know how this affects the meaning of what is said. This is similar to the football

player or spectator recognizing an offsides movement when it occurs during a game without waiting for the referee to make the call.

Study of the language itself has traditionally been the focal point for second language instruction. Many types of techniques have been developed: inductive and deductive presentations, charts and paradigms, grammars of various sorts (e.g., classical, structural, transformational), mnemonic devices, illustrated vocabularies, flash cards, etc. In the context of the Five-Step Performance-Based Model, these activities constitute one of the five essential steps, but they must be viewed in the context reaching Step 5, which is the ability to use the second language in authentic oral communication situations.

*Step 3. Guided Practice: Building the Skills*

In Step 3, the students move from understanding and learning to actually manipulating elements of the spoken language.

- At first, students learn to handle short meaningful phrases, for example, giving their names, exchanging greetings, describing the time and the weather. Practicing these brief contextualized and meaningful phrases is like tossing the football and encouraging a young player to catch it and run.
- Then, students begin to drill and practice the second language more intensively, often by concentrating on specific elements in isolation. They may repeat verb forms, or practice difficult sounds like the French /y/, or mimic sentence intonations. They may identify colors, recite numbers, name objects on a transparency. These non-contextualized, word-level activities may be compared to the football team's pushups, blocking practice, and running drills.
- Finally there are the meaningful, contextualized activities where students respond to guided questions and various oral and printed cues to produce correct sentences. This is similar to drills where the football team runs through plays, with a focus on careful, accurate performance.

The above types of guided language-learning activities are not goals in themselves, but enabling outcomes. Their mastery enables learners to speak the language more effectively, just as precise drill and practice helps football players to perform more effectively during the game.

*Step 4. Simulated Performance: Participating*
*in Guided Conversations and Role Play*

In Step 4, students have the opportunity to use the new words, phrases and patterns they have learned in simulated conversational exchanges and role play situations. The emphasis is on self-expression and conveying information fluently in a meaningful context. Much as one might try to have these exchanges resemble real-life conversations, for example by using props to establish a café scene or a TV game show, teachers and students both recognize that the context is artificial. This type of language practice is similar to football scrimmage practice. In scrimmage, the players divide into two teams and play against one another: it may look like a real game from a distance, but everyone knows that it is not. Scrimmage gives the players the opportunity of running their plays in a game-like context where the focus is on performing effectively.

An important aspect of scrimmage practice is that although the coach allows the game to go on uninterrupted, he afterwards brings the team together to analyze weaknesses, criticize poor moves, and outline further drill and practice activities. The scrimmage practices may even be videotaped to allow the players themselves the opportunity of seeing how they performed and where they need to improve. Similarly, Step 4 activities in language classes can be rendered much more effective if they are followed up by analysis and individualized suggestions for additional practice.

*Step 5. Performance: Speaking in Real-Life Situations*

Step 5 represents the ultimate desired outcome of the Performance-Based Model of Oral Proficiency. This is the point where students have the opportunity to use the second language for real communication in an authentic situation. The type of situation may vary: e.g., the student is abroad or in an area where the language is spoken and uses the language to order food or ask for a service; the student has a casual conversation with an exchange student or with members of a host family abroad; the student makes a telephone call to request information. At this step, as one becomes increasingly proficient, it becomes important to be aware of the more complex aspects of communication, including cultural values and expectations, linguistic registers, and conversational characteristics such as turn-taking.

In real communication, as in the real football game, the "clock is running." One cannot start over, one must continue playing. The aim is to communicate as effectively as possible.

After the communication event, like after the game, the student can try to recall what went well and what caused comprehension to break down. Often the teacher is not available, and the "performance" was not recorded, unless the communication event was constructed as a test. In the latter case, there may be the opportunity for teacher and student to review the performance and use this diagnostic information to plan for other learning activities.

The five steps described above are not simply moved through once in sequential order. In second-language acquisition as in learning to play football, there is an evident upward spiraling as students improve their skills. In the course of their development, they grow to understand more complex speech, to learn about more difficult structures, to acquire a more extensive vocabulary, to practice these new linguistic aspects in more challenging activities and more complex simulated conversational exchanges. Each of the steps, however, continues to play an important role and none should be omitted.

It is particularly important to recognize that scrimmage practice is meaningless unless the players demonstrate during practice that the running backs know how to hold the ball, that the quarterback can pass the ball with some degree of accuracy, and that the pass receivers know how to catch it. Similarly, it is the role of the language teacher not to engage students in Step 4 (Simulated Performance) activities until they demonstrate at Step 3 (Guided Practice) that they can pronounce the language so as to be understood by native speakers, and that they have a reasonable control of the vocabulary and structures with the role-play activity will require.

In conclusion, one might reflect on the respective roles of the teacher and the coach. The good coach is constantly asking for more demanding and more precise effort from the players, but both coach and players know that they are working together to perform well in the next game. The coach is taskmaster, judge and trainer, as well as facilitator and provider of encouragement and praise. The coach knows that player self-esteem is linked to a job well done, a game well played. Similarly, the effective teacher in a performance-based language program must maintain high expectations, provide appropriate practice activities, and also motivate students to want to express themselves well.

# The Role of Reading and Writing in the Oral Proficiency Model

Reading and Writing are communication skills in their own right, and as such will be treated in the next section. However, for the more commonly-taught languages which use the Roman alphabet, instructional programs that stress oral communication frequently introduce students to printed texts and writing activities as a means of teaching the second language. If we review the Five-Step Performance-Based Model for Oral Proficiency, we can observe how reading and writing may play a supportive role in the first four steps in building the listening and speaking skills.

- Step 1. Guided Observation: Listening to the Spoken Language
  Listening comprehension can be enhanced by letting students read video captions or follow along the script of audio recordings or the lyrics of songs. To encourage more careful listening, teachers may ask students to transcribe the audio texts by writing down what they hear. The written transcription often facilitates a closer analysis of the spoken text.
- Step 2. Guided Analysis: Learning How the Language Works
  Reading (and writing) are often used in teaching students how the second language works. Visual-minded students in particular often find it easier to learn new vocabulary by seeing words printed, and even by copying and writing them.
- Step 3. Guided Practice: Building the Skills
  Often the cues for various drills and activities are given in written form. The use of written stimuli, whether in the textbook, on a worksheet or on an overhead transparency, act as a guide for language practice.
- Step 4. Simulated Performance: Participating in Guided Conversations and Role Play
  At this step also, the guidelines for role play activities are often printed rather than spoken so as to lessen the memory load and let students focus their attention on what they want to say.

At the performance stage of Step 5, where language is used in authentic conversational situations, students will usually utilize only listening and speaking skills. Occasionally, the conversation may revolve around authentic print material (such as a menu, a timetable, a listing of movies and film times) and thus require reading skills. In other instances, the conversation may require writing, such as taking down instructions as to how to get to someone's house. At this stage, however, the reading and/or writing do not play a supportive role in the acquisition of oral proficiency, but are instead examples of authentic reading and/or writing skills being used at Step 5 (Performance).

## Context and Contextualization

In performance-based foreign language courses, the primary focus is on teaching the students how to use the second language for communication: to express themselves orally and/or in writing and also to understand what they hear and read. Although some programs may give different degrees of emphasis to the four skills, the desired outcome is always to enable students to use the new language with a given degree of proficiency in an actual, true-life context.

*The Importance of Context*

The importance of *context* in a performance-based instructional model can be clearly seen if we return to the football analogy. The desired outcome or performance is playing the game (Step 5), but in order to reach this outcome, players must learn about the game and be trained to play it. In football, the activities in Steps 1 through 4 are almost entirely *contextualized*, that is, they reflect in as much as possible the context of the football game.

- Building familiarity with the *context* is the function of Step 1 (watching actual football games). Young football players know what a football game is and they enjoy watching games played by those who are more highly trained. So essential is Step 1, that is almost inconceivable to imagine football players in a scrimmage practice (Step 4) who do not know what a well-executed football play looks like.
- Step 2 (learning the rules of the game) is usually *contextualized*. Novice players are not given a book of official football rules and told to learn them in isolation. They acquire a knowledge of the rules within the context of the game, often as the result of watching others play, either in live games or on television (Step 1).
- Step 3 (drilling the skills) usually takes place in a *partial context*. Players do not simply practice running, they run while wearing their football uniforms. They do not simply go through plays in a grassy area, they run their plays on football field with ten-yard markers. When they engage in uncontextualized activities, such as weight-lifting, they nonetheless realize that these activities will help them perform better in the actual game.
- Step 4 (scrimmage practice) offers the players the opportunity to practice performing in a *simulated context*. The more "authentic" this simulated context, the more effective the scrimmage.

One of the reasons football players are willing to engage in grueling practice sessions is that almost all their training takes place in a football context. Not only is there a clear focus on the final outcome (playing the game), but the practice and training activities are contextualized in respect to that outcome.

*Context and Contextualization in*
*Foreign Language Instruction*

As we turn our attention to foreign language instruction, it is clear that context and contextualization play an important role in the five-step performance-based model of oral proficiency.

| Language Activity | Corresponding Context |
|---|---|
| Step 1. Guided Observation<br>Listening to the spoken language<br>• live conversations; broadcasts<br>• recorded/edited speech<br>• simplified/scripted speech | <br><br>• natural/real life context<br>• authentic context<br>• simulated context |
| Step 2. Guided Analysis<br>Learning how the language works<br>• individual elements/patterns<br>• elements/patterns in context | <br><br>• limited context or no context<br>• authentic or simulated context |
| Step 3. Guided Practice<br>Building the skills<br>• practicing elements in isolation<br>• contextualized activities | <br><br>• no context<br>• artificial/partial context |
| Step 4. Simulated Performance<br>Participating in guided conversations<br>and role play<br>• guided conversations | <br><br><br>• simulated context |
| Step 5. Performance<br>Speaking in real-life situations<br>• talking to native speakers | <br><br>• natural/real-life context |

Since students are expected at Step 5 to be able to engage in conversations in an authentic communication situation, it is important that they have ample opportunity to hear the language in authentic contexts spoken by native speakers. As they practice their oral language skills, these drills and activities will seem much more relevant if they too are contextualized in meaningful situations.[5] This is particularly important since students must learn to listen to what others are saying: the more they become involved in the context of the activity, the more likely they are to pay attention to what is going on. Just as the football players never lose sight of the fact that the training they do is preparing them for the game, so must language students realize that the aim of their classwork is to provide the training they need in order to communicate effectively in a second language. It is essential that they be constantly aware of the meaning of what they are hearing and practicing.

# Adapting the Five Step Performance-Based Model to Other Aspects of Second-Language Instruction

Although in its recent conferences and publications the foreign language profession has focussed a great deal of attention on developing oral proficiency, in part because of the availability and promotion of the Oral Proficiency Interview, the ACTFL Guidelines were originally also designed to define proficiency in listening, reading, writing and culture. In this section, we shall show how the Five-Step Performance-Based Model can be adapted to these other areas.

## Building Listening Comprehension

In language learning, as in football, it is possible to concentrate solely on developing one's comprehension skills; in other words, one can learn to understand a language without learning how to speak well, just as one can learn to appreciate football games without being proficient enough to play varsity ball. Thus, while the ability to understand what is being said in a second language is a crucial first step in the development of oral proficiency, the skill of listening comprehension can also be considered a goal of instruction in its own right.

The Five-Step Performance-Based Model for Listening Comprehension focusses solely on the listening skill:

| Chart 2. Listening Comprehension | |
|---|---|
| Step 1. Guided Observation | Listening to the spoken language |
| Step 2. Guided Analysis | Learning how the language works |
| Step 3. Guided Practice | Building the listening skills |
| Step 4. Simulated Performance | Guided listening for meaning |
| Step 5. Performance | Listening in real-life situations |

*Step 1. Guided Observation: Listening to the Spoken Language*

This step is the same as that for the Oral Proficiency Model.

*Step 2. Guided Analysis: Learning How the Language Works*

This step is the same as that for the Oral Proficiency Model.

*Step 3. Guided Practice: Building the Listening Skills*

In Step 3, students practice their listening skills in a variety of contextualized activities where the emphasis is on understanding what is said. These activities differ from those in Step 4 (Simulated Performance) in that either the language is contrived or the student response does not parallel a real-life listening situation. The emphasis is on building accuracy in listening.

One type of activity that comes under this step involves writing down exactly what is said.

- In a dictation (or partial dictation) the speaker pauses at appropriate times to enable the students to write down what they hear. To the extent that the text is read at a natural tempo, and the student text is corrected in terms of comprehensibility (rather than spelling features), this is a listening skill activity.
- In a transcription activity, the students are given an authentic spoken text on cassette and are instructed to work individually or in groups to write down the script. This is a more realistic task, since students have the opportunity to rewind and relisten as much as necessary. They may also consult dictionaries and other reference books if they wish.

Such activities may also be presented in multiple-choice formats where students hear a sentence and select which of three or four written versions or printed close options corresponds to what they have heard.

Another type of activity, one that often appears on tests, asks students to listen to a sentence or an exchange and determine where it might have occurred or to which situation it best refers. For example, they might hear: "I'll have the chicken with rice" and deduce that this sentence was probably said in a restaurant. Although the restaurant is a realistic context, the activity itself is artificial, for if one were actually to overhear such sentence, one would be in the restaurant and therefore know what the location was.

The listening skill can also be practiced with activities which require the students to select a continuation of a dialogue or to select the logical completion of statement. Typically the students hear the exchange, and then select the correct response among several printed options. This type of activity also frequently occurs on listening tests: again it practices the listening skill, and helps students build greater accuracy in listening comprehension. The recordings may be realistic-sounding, but the student response is not characteristic of a real-life situation.

As a preparation for engaging in exchanges with native speakers, it is also useful for students to master polite requests for clarification. They need to know how to indicate they have not understood, how to request a paraphrase or how to have a world spelled for them.

*Step 4. Simulated Performance: Guided Listening for Meaning*

Step 4 allows students to practice their listening comprehension skills in an authentic-type context. The focus is on understanding what is being said.

One type of activity at this step asks the students to transcribe the important elements of a recorded message. In a real-life context (such as listening to an answering machine), students would have the opportunity to rewind and replay portions of the message as much as needed to be sure that they understood properly.

Another type of activity places students in a simulated real-life context where they are looking for specific information, and then has them listen to a recording to get that information. For example, they may be calling to find out whether a certain movie is playing and what time the showings are. Or they may be at an airport listening to an announcement concerning their flight.

Students may also be told that they are in the target country together with a friend who does not speak the language. They are to act as interpreter and tell their friend what is being said. Here students demonstrate their listening comprehension by providing an English equivalent. The situations may vary widely from reporting what the hotel clerk said about room availability, to saying what the TV weather report is predicting or what two characters in a movie said to one another.

*Step 5. Performance: Listening in Real-Life Situations*

In Step 5 the students are on their own in selecting what they want to listen to. They may decide to watch a movie or listen to foreign language songs. If they have the opportunity to converse with native speakers, they will be able to negotiate meaning and ask for clarifications. Since the teacher is usually not present, the students themselves are the ones to assess their performance, that is, determine whether they have understood correctly or not. This ability to assess one's own performance in the area of listening comprehension is a skill that needs to be developed as part of the instructional sequence.

# Building Written Communication Skills

The Five-Step Performance-Based Model of Oral Proficiency with its football analogies was designed for the development of oral communication since both the game of football and the act of speaking call on psychomotor skills which take place in real time "with the clock running." Written communication is somewhat different because it involves primarily cognitive skills of reading and writing. Moreover, the written skills by their very nature allow for reflection. In the real world, one can often take as much time as one needs to write and edit a written text (such as a letter). Usually one has the opportunity to consult a dictionary for an unfamiliar word or use the spell-checker on the computer before printing out one's work.

The Five-Step Performance-Based Model for Written Communication is constructed as follows:

| Chart 3. Written Communication | |
|---|---|
| Step 1.  Guided Observation | Reading texts in the second language |
| Step 2.  Guided Analysis | Learning how the language works |
| Step 3.  Guided Practice | Building the skills |
| Step 4.  Simulated Performance | Guided writing for communication |
| Step 5.  Performance | Writing for self-expression |

*Step 1. Guided Observation: Reading Texts in the Second Language*

The first step in learning to write in a second language is learning to read in that language. In fact, for the students to produce writing that looks and reads like authentic written language, they have to know what authentic language is. In this sense, reading practice is a crucial element in the development of writing skills. If students do not possess a feeling for the second language, they tend to base their own writing on a word-for-word translation of their native language, producing sentences like *Je suis quinze* ("I am fifteen" instead of *J'ai quinze ans*) or *C'est joli intéressant* ("That's pretty interesting" instead of *C'est assez/vachement intéressant*).

In the more commonly taught languages which use a Roman alphabet and contain many cognate words, reading is a relatively accessible skill for students who are already literate in English. They can use their background knowledge to guess at meanings of unfamiliar words and expressions.

In Step 1, students learn to read authentic second-language texts of various sorts.

- An excellent source of authentic reading materials is a foreign language newspaper or popular magazine with its mix of types of readings, from very accessible items such as TV guides and birth announcements, to captions on illustrations, ads, headlines, sports columns, and then much more difficult pieces such as editorials and letters to the editor.

- Often in textbooks or readers, students are introduced to authentic reading texts that have been specifically selected or edited so as to be more linguistically accessible.
- Beginning students are usually given the opportunity to read stories and short selections written by native speakers precisely for a language-learner audience. When these are well-written, native speakers would consider them to be authentic materials.

The emphasis at this step is comprehension. In an authentic second-langauge environment, one can ask a native speaker what an unfamiliar word means, or else look it up in a dictionary. In readers and textbooks, comprehension can be enhanced in many ways ranging from side-by-side bilingual texts, to glosses and footnotes, and the addition of an end vocabulary. How the students arrive at understanding the text will vary due to different learner styles.

As students improve their reading comprehension, they will be able to go from mere searching for information (such as reading a menu) to reading for pleasure and ultimately reading for in-depth comprehension with an awareness of style and tone.

*Step 2. Guided Analysis: Learning How the Language Works*

This step is similar to Step 2 of the Oral Proficiency Model. In addition to the linguistic aspects mentioned with respect to the spoken language, attention here is focussed on spelling and/or the learning of different writing systems (for many of the languages less commonly taught at the secondary level) and on those linguistic conventions which are characteristic of the written form of the second language.

*Step 3. Guided Practice: Building the Skills*

In Step 3 students practice the skills they will need in order to express themselves in writing. These activities may include non-contextualized drill activities such as mastering declensions and conjugations or practicing vocabulary. At the word or phrase level students may practice writing by filling in blanks or completing sentences according to given instructions. Students may also practice a broad variety of more meaningful contextualized writing activities, such as answer questions, formulating guided sentences and transforming passages from one tense to another. Finally students practice writing guided paragraphs and letters.

*Step 4. Simulated Performance: Guided Writing for Communication*

Step 4 provides the opportunity for students to express themselves in writing. The parameters of the writing are set by instructor, but always are open enough to allow for student creativity. Beginning students may be asked to write shopping lists or notes to imaginary penpals. They may narrate the actions depicted in a comic strip or retell what happened in a video they watched. At a more advanced level, they may engage in pastiche writing, often with very readable results. Just as the scrimmage practice looks like a real game, so can guided creative writing read like an original composition.

In the real world, most writing activities take place in an open environment where the writer can consult a dictionary or ask a friend how to spell a word. To the extent that simulated performance at this level imitates the real-world context, students should be given similar freedom to use a dictionary or a grammar appendix to check their work.

*Step 5. Performance: Writing for Self-Expression*

Step 5 represents the desired outcome of the Performance-Based Model of Written Communication. At this point students initiate their own writing in a natural authentic context. For example, they may send a note to a French friend, write a letter applying for a job, prepare an essay on a topic of interest, or compose an original poem or essay. As in Step 4, above, they are free to consult dictionaries and grammar handbooks as they edit their writing.

## Building Reading Comprehension

Just as a second-language learner can concentrate on learning to understand the spoken language without speaking it, so the development of the reading skill can for some students be a desired outcome of instruction. Most people, in fact, use their reading skill in another language much more frequently than their writing skill.

The Five-Step Performance-Based Model for Reading Comprehension focusses solely on the reading skill, as shown in Chart 4, below.

*Step 1. Guided Observation: Reading Texts in the Second Language*

This step is the same as that for the Written Communication Model.

*Step 2. Guided Analysis: Learning How the Language Works*

This step is the same as that for the Written Communication Model.

| Chart 4. Reading Comprehension | |
|---|---|
| Step 1. Guided Observation | Reading texts in the second language |
| Step 2. Guided Analysis | Learning how the language works |
| Step 3. Guided Practice | Building the reading skills |
| Step 4. Simulated Performance | Guided reading for meaning |
| Step 5. Performance | Reading in real-life situations |

*Step 3. Guided Practice: Building the Reading Skills*

In Step 3, students build their reading skills through a variety of activities: they learn to recognize cognate patterns, to use context to guess the meanings of unfamiliar words and phrases, to read for the general message, to look for supporting details, etc. Some teachers and students may prefer working with glossed texts or bilingual readers, while other may prefer unglossed material. The choice of approach depends on the language being learned, and the learning styles of students. Students also learn how to use both monolingual and dual-language dictionaries.

Students first practice reading at the word and sentence level (perhaps using contextualized realia), and then advance to the paragraph and narrative level. The main focus is on accuracy of comprehension.

Depending on the language under instruction, students may also need to learn how to read handwriting. This is particularly important if they wish to exchange letters with a penpal or if they plan to be in a situation where they need to read handwritten notes.

*Step 4. Simulated Performance: Guided Reading for Meaning*

In Step 4, students are reading in a simulated real-life situation. At the elementary level, they may be given a newspaper and asked to find when and where a certain film is playing, or which TV program they would prefer watching at 8 p.m. They may read through several recipes and decide which one they would like to prepare. At a more advanced level they may read several newspaper articles on a given topic and compare the positions of the writers. As with listening comprehension, the students may be told that they are to explain the content of a letter or a written message to a friend who does not understand the target language.

Depending on the context, it might be realistic to allow students to consult dictionaries or work in pairs helping one another with the reading activity.

*Step 5. Performance: Reading in Real-Life Situations*

At Step 5, the students themselves select what they want to read— they may read for information or simply for pleasure. At this point, they will be the ones judging how effectively they are able to read the foreign language, and they will need to be able to find assistance if there are passages they do not understand.

# Developing Cultural Competence

While second-language teachers strive to make their students *bilingual*, that is, to bring their students to the point where they can perform near-natively in the second language orally and/or in writing, most programs do not set out to make their students *bicultural*. In other words, students are not expected to replace their native values, food tastes, sexual roles, etc., with those of another culture. Rather, the ultimate outcome of instruction in the area of cultural competence is usually defined as the ability to appreciate and fit into a second culture while maintaining one's own cultural identity. The aim is to enable students to perform in a culturally acceptable manner.

In reality, very few second-language programs have as a goal to prepare students to function in a foreign culture. The development of a degree of cultural competence is primarily only the concern of programs which are preparing to send a group of students to the target country for an exchange visit or an extended homestay. On the other hand, most language programs have as a stated outcome the development of cultural awareness and cross-cultural understanding.

The following chart describes the Five-Step Performance-Based Model for Cultural Competence.

| Chart 5. Cultural Competence | |
| --- | --- |
| Step 1. Guided Observation | Observing the second culture |
| Step 2. Guided Analysis | Understanding how the culture functions |
| Step 3. Guided Practice | Requiring cultural behavior patterns |
| Step 4. Simulated Performance | Participating in simulated cultural situations |
| Step 5. Performance | Living in the target culture |

*Step 1. Guided Observation: Observing the Second Culture*

Since the aim of a performance-based program is to prepare students to be able to live and integrate in the target culture, it is essential that they first learn to observe that culture. For most American students studying a second language, this means observing the culture second-hand, via authentic documents such as films, videos, photographs and printed documents. It is not enough merely to "read about" the culture. One can be told that French young people greet one another with *une bise*, but students only really understand what this kiss on the cheek is if they have the opportunity to see many different young people on video greet one another in this traditional way.

Just as a person who sees a football game for the first time will not be able to understand what is happening on the field, so too will the second-language learner need guidance in observing authentic documents in order to appreciate on the meaning of unfamiliar aspects of the target culture.

*Step 2. Guided Analysis: Understanding How the Culture Functions*

In Step 2, students learn about how the target culture works. With this knowledge comes increased cultural understanding together with an awareness of cross-cultural differences. To the extent possible, this study of the target culture will be contextualized through the observation of cultural patterns which characterizes Step 1. By developing greater familiarity with the features of the new culture, students begin to acquire an appreciation of how these aspects represent and are determined by cultural values and attitudes which may differ from those of the students' native culture.

*Step 3. Guided Practice: Acquiring Cultural Behavior Patterns*

In Step 3, students learn to imitate and begin to acquire cultural behavior patterns. For example, by watching videos of young Italian speakers interacting naturally with one another, students learn to mimic differences in body language and gestures. After watching films clips of young French people having a meal at home, students practice appropriate ways of handling silverware. This contextualization of culture behaviors through the medium of film is very important, for much as one might try to explain behavior patterns verbally, not all details can be covered. Behaviors at this step can be evaluated via video by filming students as they practice new behavior patterns.

Cultural behavior patterns also determine the way people speak to one another, how they take turns, how they react to different registers of language. Here, too, students can practice imitating models which they hear or see on videocassette.

*Step 4. Simulated Performance: Participating
in Simulated Cultural Situations*

For Step 4 to be effective, the simulated cultural situations must be as realistic as possible. Students need a great deal of training at Step 3 before they are able to interact with a native or near-native speaker in a culturally accurate role play situation. (Role play activities that are not culturally authentic are best avoided, for they tend to give students erroneous impressions about the target culture and fail to prepare them for the real-life performance of Step 5.)

*Step 5. Performance: Living in the Second Culture*

Whereas the difference between Step 4 and Step 5 is very small in the Performanced-Based Model for Written Communication, it constitutes a giant leap in the area of cultural competence. Simulated cultural situations are extremely artificial and in the back of their minds students know that they are, after all, still in their native culture. Actually living and being integrated into a second culture is quite a different challenge, and frequently presents problems of culture shock and anomie, even for students who felt very comfortable at Step 4.

# The Role of Testing and Assessment in Performance-Based Second-Language Instruction

In performance-based second-language instruction, the role of testing and assessment is to promote the attainment of the desired outcomes of instruction. Ideally the match between the stated objectives (i.e., descriptions of student performance) and what is tested is so close that any washback effect is harnessed to encourage the type of teaching and the type of learning needed to reach those objectives.

## Desired Outcomes and Enabling Outcomes

Although we have up to now been examining desired outcomes of instruction, it is appropriate at this point to make a distinction between desired outcomes and enabling outcomes.

- The *desired outcomes* are those end-of-program outcomes that describe what students will be able to do as the result of instruction. In the Five-Step

Performance-Based Model, the ability to perform at Step 5 (Performance) constitutes the desired outcome (just as in the football analogy, the desired outcome is winning the game). Given the fact that many students may not have the opportunity to use the second language in the context of the target culture, many schools may need to consider Step 4 (Simulated Performance) as the desired outcome, at least for elementary and intermediate levels of instruction.

• In the complete model, Steps 1 through 4 constitute the *enabling outcomes*. They represent types of things that students need to be able to do in order to perform well at Step 5. They constitute an important component of the instructional program, although they do not represent the final goal of the course. In situations where Step 4 (Simulated Performance) is considered the desired outcome, then Steps 1 through 3 are the enabling outcomes.

Traditionally, language instruction focussed on the enabling objectives, especially Step 2 (Guided Analysis) and Step 3 (Guided Practice). Classroom time, school tests, and even standard tests evaluated how well and how accurately students could handle these enabling objectives. In fact, the enabling objectives became the desired objectives. Step 4 (Simulated Performance) was usually omitted, and Step 5 (Performance) was the privilege of those who were able to participate in an exchange program.

What distinguishes performance-based instruction from traditional language instruction is precisely its attention to *performance*—whether real or simulated. Performance-based instruction emphasizes the need for students to master the enabling objectives but constantly focuses on the desired outcome, namely the ability to use the language in real-life situations as evaluated via authentic assessment.

## Formative and Summative Evaluation

In measurement parlance, *formative testing* is the type of assessment that takes place as the students are learning the new skills. It is often closely related to the instructional program and may take the form of quizzes and chapter tests. Its results are often used in a diagnostic manner by teachers to modify instruction so that students can attain the desired outcomes.

*Summative testing*, on the other hand, is the type of assessment that occurs at the end of a period of study. It goes beyond the material of specific lessons and focuses on evaluating general course outcomes.

In a performance-based curriculum, formative testing would focus on how accurately students can handle the various aspects of the second language in classroom contexts while summative testing would evaluate how well students can function linguistically in authentic situations.

## A Comprehensive Testing Schema

While other chapters in the volume will develop in detail certain aspects of the assessment of students' control of the skills of listening, speaking, reading, and writing, it is appropriate at this point to look at all the types of testing and assessment that have a role to play in performance-based second-language instruction. The interrelationship of these various types of evaluation techniques is graphically depicted in Chart 6.

In a performance-based program where the key focus is on oral proficiency, the primary desired outcome will be Step 5 (Performance): the ability to speak with native speakers in an authentic natural context. In this case, Steps 1 through 4 are considered enabling outcomes. Summative testing is carried out at Step 5, and formative testing is used to evaluate the enabling outcomes.

Chart 6. Comprehensive Testing Schema for Five-Step Performance-Based Foreign Language Programs

| Step | Oral Proficiency | Written Expression | Cultural Competence |
|---|---|---|---|
| 1 Guided Observation | understanding authentic spoken language; [beginners] understanding native speakers on tapes/videos designed for learners | understanding authentic written language; [beginners] understanding texts written for language learners by native speakers | understanding the significance of cultural aspects of an authentic document: film, video, photograph, poster, written text, etc. |
| | Criterion: accuracy of comprehension | | |
| 2 Guided Analysis | in isolation, sentences, and natural spoken context, hearing and identifying language elements, e.g., words, structures, patterns, sounds | in isolation, sentences, and authentic written context, reading and identifying language elements, e.g., words, structures, patterns, graphemes | in authentic contexts, observing and identifying cultural elements, e.g., kinesic patterns, behaviors, linguistic references, values and attitudes, visual aspects |
| | Criterion: accuracy of identification and analysis | | |
| 3 Guided Practice | responding orally to classroom-type cues, e.g., reading aloud, answering questions, identifying or describing pictures, manipulating structures | responding in writing to classroom-type cues, e.g., filling in blanks, completing sentences, transforming patterns, identifying or describing pictures | modelling culturally appropriate body language and gestures; demonstrating culturally appropriate responses to verbal and visual cues |
| | Criterion: accuracy of response | | |

| Step | Oral Proficiency | Written Expression | Cultural Competence |
|---|---|---|---|
| 4<br>Simulated Perfor-mance | speaking in a simulated "authentic" context, e.g., guided interview, role-play situations, monologue | writing in a simulated "authentic" context, e.g., a postcard, letter, description, narrative, report | acting in a simulated "authentic" context, e.g., greeting people, casual conversations, reacting to unexpected situations |
| | Criteria: success of communication (degree to which student is understood)<br>• level of linguistic sophistication (appropriateness, originality, etc.)<br>• accuracy of expression (syntax, structure, vocabulary; accent/spelling)<br>• [speaking, in dialogue context] ability to understand other speaker<br>*(Samples of student performance may be collected for portfolio assessment)* | | Criteria:<br>• success of cultural interaction<br>• ability to react to cultural cues<br>• level of cultural sophistication<br>• accuracy of expression: cultural appropriateness |
| 5<br>Perfor-mance | speaking with a native speaker in an authentic natural context | writing to a native speaker in an authentic natural context | functioning in an authentic cultural situation; interacting with native speakers |
| | Criteria:<br>• success of communication (degree to which student is understood)<br>• level of linguistic sophistication (appropriateness, originality, etc.)<br>• [oral proficiency] ability to understand the native speaker | | Criteria:<br>• success of cultural interaction<br>• ability to react to cultural cues<br>• level of cultural sophistication |

Chart 6. Comprehensive Testing Schema for Five-Step Performance-Based Foreign Language Programs (cont'd)

Chart 6. Comprehensive Testing Schema for Five-Step Performance-Based Foreign Language Programs (cont'd)

| Step | Listening Comprehension | Reading Comprehension |
|---|---|---|
| 1 Guided Observation | understanding authentic spoken language; [beginners] understanding native speakers on tapes/videos designed for learners | understanding authentic written language; [beginners] understanding texts written for language learners by native speakers |
| | Criterion: accuracy of comprehension | |
| 2 Guided Analysis | hearing and identifying language elements (e.g., words, structures, patterns, sounds) in isolation, in sentences, and in natural spoken context | reading and identifying language elements (e.g., words, structures, patterns, graphemes) in isolation, in sentences, and in authentic written context |
| | Criterion: accuracy of identification and analysis | |
| 3 Guided Practice | demonstrating comprehension via dictation or transcription; answering questions on what was heard; selecting appropriate completions for exchanges | demonstrating comprehension by answering questions, defining specific words or phrases, deciphering native handwriting; using a dictionary appropriately |
| | Criterion: accuracy of response | |

Chart 6. Comprehensive Testing Schema for Five-Step Performance-Based Foreign Language Programs (cont'd)

| Step | Listening Comprehension | Reading Comprehension |
|---|---|---|
| 4<br>Simulated Performance | listening to natural language in "authentic" contexts, e.g., taking a phone message, listening to recordings; acting as interpreter<br><br>Criteria:<br>• success of comprehension (degree to which student can understand material)<br>• level of linguistic interpretation (sensitivity to connotations, implied messages)<br>• accuracy of interpretation (sensitivity to syntax, structure, vocabulary) | reading native texts in "authentic" contexts, e.g., reading a postcard, letter, newspaper, short story |
| 5<br>Performance | in an authentic natural context, listening to native speech, live or recorded<br><br>Criteria:<br>• success of comprehension (degree to which student can understand material)<br>• level of linguistic interpretation (sensitivity to connotations, implied messages) | in a natural context, reading authentic materials, e.g., letters, ads, stories, newspapers |

Frequently, however, in the early levels of some language programs constraints are such that the desired outcome of instruction is defined as Step 4 (Simulated Performance): the ability to speak in a simulated "authentic" context. Here, Steps 1 through 3 become the enabling outcomes. The summative (end of term) tests will evaluate the students' abilities to function at Step 4, and formative tests throughout the term will evaluate the enabling objectives (Steps 1 through 3).

When final examinations or end-of-program assessment measures evaluate only or predominantly the mastery of the enabling outcomes (especially Steps 2 and 3) rather than desired performance outcomes, the latter are no longer seen as constituting the focus of the course. Both teachers and students will tend to concentrate their attention on elements of language in artificial and/or meaningless contexts and fail to attain the desired outcomes of meaningful language use. The washback message is that although the course may claim to be developing language proficiency or skill-using, in reality the emphasis is exclusively on drill and skill-getting.

## Accuracy and Fluency

In a performance-based second-language program it is important to develop both accuracy and fluency (see Hammerly 1991; Valette 1991, 1992, 1993). To return to the football analogy: the coach expects precise ball control during passing practice while realizing that not all passes will be completed under the pressure and more complex environment of the actual game. However, the more accurately the players run the plays and handle the ball in practice, the more likely the team will be to win the game. So, too, the language teacher must encourage correct language usage at the level of the enabling outcomes so as to increase the probability that students will be effective in understanding and using the language with an acceptable degree of accuracy in authentic natural situations.[6]

To the extent that teachers fail to use appropriate formative tests to promote accuracy and hesitate to provide feedback on role play activities in terms of correctness as well as creative language use, the washback message sent to the students is that sloppy linguistic performance is tolerated. In a balanced performance-based program, formative and summative tests must be designed so as to encourage and promote high quality performance, and this focus on true linguistic proficiency is immediately evident to the students.

# A Cohesive Approach:
# Teaching, Testing, and Assessment
# in a Performance-Based L$_2$ Program

In order to build a cohesive performance-based second-language program, it is essential to lay the proper groundwork.

First, it is necessary . . .

- to define the desired outcomes of instruction, and
- to develop summative tests and assessment instruments to measure those outcomes.

Then, it is equally important . . .

- to define the enabling outcomes in terms of the steps that are essential in reaching the desired outcomes, and
- to develop formative tests and assessment instruments to evaluate to what degree the enabling outcomes are being attained.

Finally, it is necessary . . .

- to provide a syllabus or framework within which teachers and students can work together to attain both the enabling and the desired outcomes.

## Program Implementation

In implementing the Five-Step Performanced-Based Model in their second language program, teachers may want to consider the following questions.

1. Given the parameters of the program/course, should the desired outcomes be set at Step 5 (Performance) or Step 4 (Simulated Performance)?
2. Is adequate emphasis placed at Step 1 (Guided Observation)?
   Do students have ample opportunities to listen to the target language in authentic meaningful contexts (video, film, tapes, teacher talk) so that they can develop a sense of "what the game is all about"?
   Similarly, do they have opportunities to read authentic texts and observe authentic cultural contexts?
3. Are students at Step 2 (Guided Analysis) learning how the language works and how the culture functions?
   Are these learning activities contextualized as much as possible?

Are students encouraged to go from general to more precise understanding?

Does formative evaluation promote accuracy of comprehension?

4. Are students given enough time at Step 3 (Guided Practice) to learn
to handle elements of the language and imitate corresponding body
language?

To the extent possible, to these activities take place within meaningful
contexts?

Does formative evaluation encourage accuracy at this level?

5. Is there a clear and apparent focus on activities at Step 4 (Simulated
Performance) so that students are consistently encouraged to use the
target language creatively in role play situations and writing activities?

Are students given ample opportunity for authentic listening and reading practice?

Is appropriate feedback given so that students are encouraged to improve the quality of their performance?

6. Is a significant part of the student's grade based on performance at
Step 5 (or Step 4, if appropriate)?

Do students, parents and administrators all realize that the ability to
use the target language for communication is the desired outcome of
the language program?

# Program Evaluation

Once the outcomes, the testing instruments, and the syllabus are in place,
on-going evaluation will enable teachers to determine to which degree the
second-language program is working effectively. The bottom line is the extent
to which students are attaining the desired outcomes for each level of instruction. If these outcomes are not being attained by a large majority of the
students, it is necessary to determine whether this is because the outcomes
were too ambitious, or whether the enabling outcomes are not being met.
Figure 6 indicates one way in which problems can be diagnosed.

Once the problem areas have been pinpointed, modifications can be made.
As the new program is implemented, it, too, is scrutinized to determine how
well it is working in producing the desired outcomes.

The implementation of a cohesive performance-based program provides
an exciting challenge to a foreign-language department, stimulating them to
work together in attaining a common goal: a "winning team" of students who
are able to use their second language in authentic linguistic and cultural
contexts.

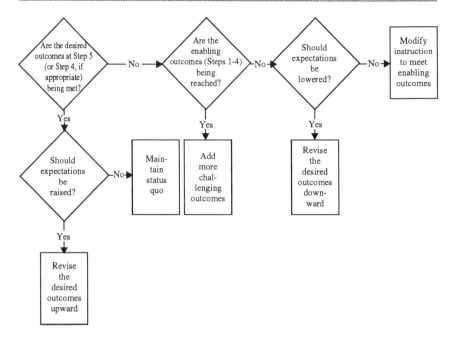

Figure 6. Evaluating the Five-Step Performance-Based Program

# Notes

[1]This Five-Step Performance-Based Model of Second-Language Instruction was in-itially presented at the Orientation Workshop for Teaching Fellows organized by the Department of Romance Languages, Boston College, August 1992, and was described, in a simpler, version in Valette and Valette (1993, p. 7).

[2]The concent of *authentic assessment* is developed by G. Wiggins in Chapter 3 of this volume. Other chapters will detail how authentic assessment can be introduced in the areas of Speaking, Listening, Reading and Writing.

[3]In 1978, one of the plenary sessions of the Lucerne meeting of the Fédération International des Professeurs de Langues Vivantes (FIPLV) focussed on the question of transparency; see Valette (1978). That this interest in transparency is still of major concern is evident in the title of the Intergovernmental Symposium at R_schlikon, Switzerland, held in November 1991: "Transparency and Coherence in Language Learning in Europe: Objectives, Assessment, and Certification."

[4]I have used the football analogy rather extensively throughout this chapter to highlight the distinctions between the five steps of the performance-based model and to clarify the role of context and contextualization. Although there are obvious differences between playing football and communicating in a second language, we as second language teachers can put our classroom teaching, testing and assessment practices into a more effective performance-based framework is we observe with a critical eye the practices of the football coaches. (In this context, it is interesting to note that a drawing of a football player was used to illustrate G. Wiggins' article "A True Test: Toward More Authentic and Equitable

Assessment" when it first appeared in the *Phi Delta Kappan*, May 1989, p. 703.)

I have also found that the football analogy, imperfect though it may be, has been most useful in explaining the interrelationship of the five steps of performance-based language model of second-language instruction to educators, parents, and students. (However, I would like to invite readers who have not been nurtured on American football simply to skip the analogies and focus directly on the model itself.)

[5]In 1975, *French for Mastery* was the first major foreign language textbook in the United States to contextualize all its exercises. The Teacher's Edition described this feature as follows:

> Contextual presentation of exercises. To elicit the students' active participation in the learning process, all exercises of *French for Mastery*, including those on the tapes and in the *Workbook*, are set in a situational context. The situations are sometimes practical (planning a trip, answering an ad in the newspaper, selecting dishes from a menu) and sometimes merely humorous (cutting class, playing the role of the devil). The purpose of these contextualized exercises is to induce the students to use French for communication and self-expression rather than as a mere response to artificial drill stimuli." (Valette and Valette, 1975, p. T3)

[6]In their research on the effects of study abroad on the acquisition of Russian, R. Brecht and D. Davidson discovered that the higher the American students scored on a reading/grammar qualifying test, the more likely they were to show significant improvement in their speaking skills as the result of an academic program in Russia. They conclude: "As far as we know, this is the first broad-based empirical evidence for the common conviction that communication skills are most effectively built upon a solid grammar/reading base" (Brecht and Davidson, 1992, p. 98). In other words, a strong command of the enabling skills of Step 1 to 3 facilitates the acquisition of performance skills of Step 5.

# References

Brecht, R., and Davidson, D. Language acquisition gains in study abroad: Assessment and feedback. In E. Shohamy and A. R. Walton (Eds.), *Language assessment for feedback: Testing and other strategies*. Dubuque, IA: Kendall/Hunt Publishing Co., 1992.

Council of Europe. *Transparency and coherence in language learning in Europe: Objectives, assessment, and certification*. Intergovernmental Symposium at Rüschlikon, Switzerland, November 1991. Strasbourg: Council of Europe, 1992.

Hammerly, H. *Fluency and accuracy: Toward balance in language teaching and learning*. Clevedon/Philadelphia: Multilingual Matters Ltd., 1991.

North, B. *The development of descriptors on scales of language proficiency*. Washington, DC: National Foreign Language Center Occasional Papers, April 1993.

Schärer, R., and North, B. *Towards a common European framework for reporting language competency*. Washington, DC: National Foreign Language Center Occasional Papers. April 1992.

Swain, M. Using assessment information in French immersion programs. In E. Shohamy and A. R. Walton (Eds.), *Language Assessment for Feedback: Testing and Other Strategies*. Dubuque, IA: Kendall/Hunt Publishing Co., 1992.

Valette, J.-P., and Valette, R.M. *Discovering French—bleu: Extended teacher's edition*. Lexington, MA: D.C. Heath, 1993.

Valette, J.-P., and Valette, R.M. *French for mastery 1, teacher's edition*. Lexington, MA: D.C. Heath, 1975.

Valette, R.M. Objective evaluation and transparency. In R. Freudenstein (Ed.), *Language learning: Individual needs: Individual needs, interdisciplinary co-operation, bi- and multilingualism*. [The Lucerne Congress Report of the Fédération Internationale des Professeurs de Langues Vivantes (FIPLV)]. Brussels: AIMAV, 1978.

Valette, R.M. Proficiency and the Prevention of fossilization—An editorial. *The Modern Language Journal*, 1991, 75, 325–28.

Valette, R.M. Proficiency and accuracy: Enemies or allies? In J. Alatis (Ed.), *Georgetown University round table on language and linguistics 1992*. Washington, DC: Georgetown University Press, 1992.

Valette, R.M. Making foreign languages part of NAEP—Advantages and dangers. *Newsletter of the Northeast Conference on the Teaching of Foreign Languages*, 1993 (a), *34*, 21–13.

Valette, R.M. The challenge of the future: Teaching students to speak fluently and accurately, *Canadian Modern Language Review*, 1993, *50* (1), 173–78.

Valette, R.M., and Disick, R.S. *Modern language performance objectives and individualized instruction*. New York: Harcourt Brace Jovanovich, 1973.

# Developments in Foreign Language Testing and Instruction: A National Perspective

Charles W. Stansfield[1]
*Center for Applied Linguistics*

## Introduction

A merican schools have come under increasing criticism from business persons, politicians, and parents over the past decade and a half. The charge has been made repeatedly that American schools are not preparing students adequately, i.e., schools are not providing students with the skills they will need to function, perform, and compete in a changing and increasingly complex world. An emphasis on accountability and on "performance" has characterized the movement to reform and improve American education. During the 1980s, many states revised their curriculum to better reflect what they thought students should know. In recent years the focus has shifted to the national level. State governors and President Bush joined together in 1989 to establish the National Education Goals and initiate activities that could lead to the development of national standards in major areas of the curriculum.

Tests, and their place in the overall scheme of education, are being used by politicians, educational policy makers, and those involved in the current reform movement to reshape teaching and to effect learning in the schools.

Traditionally, educators have viewed the use of tests to affect learning, curriculum, and instruction as undesirable. However, in recent years, tests, and the knowledge, skills and abilities (KSAs), with which tests are closely linked, have become the focus of educational reform initiatives. The implementation of these KSAs into the curriculum and into teaching methodologies is the challenge that educators are now facing.

The issue of the influence of tests and the use of associated KSAs to drive educational reform is a complex and often controversial one. Tests, which traditionally have been used to make decisions about students, are powerful instruments within the educational system. Because of concern about this power, the use of tests to affect curricular and instructional matters has traditionally been considered inappropriate. However, New York has long been involved in such testing through its Regents Examinations, and today state education agencies from Texas to Connecticut are using tests to affect curricular and instructional change, and ultimately, to affect learning and to achieve desired educational goals. The same observation applies to regions within states and to local school districts.

Foreign language instruction has also been recently affected by this emphasis on performance, although the profession was already moving in this direction due to the influence of the proficiency movement. This paper presents an overview of the National Education Goals and seven initiatives that are underway to develop standards, curriculum, and better assessment and placement measures in foreign language education. The initiatives are: the ACTFL Standards Project, the National Assessment for Educational Progress, the College Board's Pacesetter Program, the Articulation and Achievement Project, the Ohio Collaborative Articulation/Assessment Project, the SOPI tests developed by the Center for Applied Linguistics (CAL), and the Texas Oral Proficiency Test. We will describe briefly these initiatives, which although independently designed and executed, have certain characteristics that place them within the context of the current educational reform movement. These initiatives attempt to link standards, assessment, curriculum, and instruction in a way that brings about improved learning and rewards the development of real-life foreign language skills. Valette's conceptual chapter in this volume provides further information on these linkages.

# The National Education Goals

Since the passage of the Elementary and Secondary Education Act in 1965, the principal focus of federal assistance to education has been the creation of educational equity. Generally, Americans have agreed with this focus. However, by the late 1970s there was growing concern that the quality of education in the public schools was declining. This decline, which began in 1965 and continued until 1984, was evidenced in the gradual slide of mean scores on the Scholastic Aptitude Test (SAT) among college bound high school students. The decline signaled problems in the education of not only disadvantaged minority students, but in the education of college bound majority students as well. Indeed, SAT scores and results from the National Assessment of Educational Progress showed that while minorities were making slight gains in achievement (a result of the federal focus on school equity), majority student achievement was continuing to decline.

The level of concern about this situation entered a new phase with the publication in 1983 of *A Nation at Risk*, which was the report of a presidential commission on educational excellence. *A Nation at Risk* said that the quality of education in American public schools had dropped to the point where we were facing an educational crisis. The report stated that our schools were not turning out students who could handle even moderately challenging intellectual tasks. Because graduates would enter the work force without the skills needed by employers, the report said that the nation's economy and its future were both at risk.

The concern about declining standards in the schools continued throughout the 1980s. The quality of schools became an issue in the 1988 presidential election, at which time then candidate George Bush stated that he hoped to become known as the "Education President." Following his election, President Bush called for an Education Summit involving the nation's governors, the President, and the Secretaries of Education and Labor. During this Summit, held at the University of Virginia in September 1989, President Bush and the governors made a commitment to common education goals for America and a timeline for achieving them. Subsequently, in February 1990, six National Education Goals were announced by the US Department of Education. The goals seek to raise the performance of American students and schools to "world class" levels by developing voluntary national educational standards. In order to implement the Goals, in July 1990, the National Education Goals Panel (NEGP) (composed of eight governors, four members of Congress and two presidential appointees) was created. The NEGP is charged with monitoring and reporting progress toward realization of the Goals, which are expected to be achieved by the year 2000. This monitoring, if it is to be effective, requires that a system of achievement measures and indicators relative to each goal be developed.

Of the six goals that were promulgated, Goal 3 seemed most readily applicable to foreign language education.

> By the year 2000, American students will leave grades four, eight, and twelve having demonstrated competency in challenging subject matter including English, mathematics, science, history, and geography; and every school in American will ensure that all students learn to use their minds well, so they may be prepared for responsible citizenship, further learning, and productive employment in our modern economy. (National Education Goals Panel, 1992, p. 82)

While foreign languages have normally been considered "challenging subject matter," they were not mentioned in the Goals. This became a major point of dissention for foreign language educators. Under the guidance of the Joint National Committee for Languages, many professional language teaching associations wrote letters complaining about the failure to include foreign languages among the subjects mentioned in the goal. Thus, when the National Education Goals Panel developed five objectives to accompany Goal 3, one stated "the percentage of students who are competent in more than one language will increase." (National Education Goals Panel, 1992, p. 82) This inclusion as an objective only partly corrected the problem.

As hearings were held at different locations throughout the U.S., foreign language educators continued to protest the failure to incorporate their discipline directly in the Goals. The problem will be fully remedied if the Goals 2000: Educate America Act (H.R. 1804) is passed. This act amends the National Education Goals to include foreign languages as a subject area. As of July 1993, the act has been approved by committees in both the House and the Senate, and is ready for consideration on the floor of each body.

The National Education Goals seek to raise the performance of American students and schools through the adoption of voluntary national educational standards. Subject-matter, student performance, and opportunity-to-learn (local educational system) standards are to be developed. Subject-matter standards are being developed for each field by its professional association, with funding from the U.S. Department of Education and other sources. The ACTFL Standards Project is part of this program. Subject-matter standards have already been completed in Mathematics and Geography, while standards are currently under development in the Arts, Civics, English, History, and Science ("Guide," 1993, pp. 16–17). Upon completion, the voluntary subject matter standards are to undergo certification by the National Education Standards and Improvement Council (NESIC), a broad-based panel appointed by the President, Congress and the National Education Goals Panel. After certification, national standards will be available for use by states as guides or models for improving their own standards. States will also be free to develop their subject-matter standards independently and have them certified by NESIC, so long as they are as rigorous and demanding as the national standards (Committee on Education and Labor, 1993, pp. 43–44).

The Goals 2000: Educate America Act recognizes that the establishment of content and performance standards will not create appropriate measures for determining whether the standards are being met. Therefore, Goals 2000 authorizes the US Department of Education to make grants to states and districts to defray the costs of developing, field testing, and evaluating assessment systems. If this provision is retained by both houses of Congress and the bill is signed by the President, it will create new funds ($100 million) for the development of new performance tests. Such funds could represent a boon to foreign language test development.

# ACTFL Standards Project

On January 8, 1993, Secretary of Education Lamar Alexander announced that the U.S. Department of Education was awarding a grant of $211,494 to ACTFL for the first year of a three-year grant from the U.S. Department of Education and the National Endowment for the Humanities to develop and disseminate voluntary national content and performance standards for foreign language students in grades kindergarten through 12. These student standards will serve as the basis for the development of appropriate measures for monitoring the performance outcomes of foreign language study in the schools. The American Association of Teachers of French (AATF), the American Association of Teachers of German (AATG) and the American Association of Teachers of Spanish and Portuguese (AATSP) joined ACTFL to form a consortium to guide the National Standards in Foreign Languages Project (ACTFL, 1993a).

Following funding, ACTFL and the AATs spent the first months setting up the organizational structure and recruiting people to serve on the Standards Project. The project's Board of Directors consists of the permanent officers of the four collaborating organizations: Lynn Sandstedt of the AATSP, Fred Jenkins of the AATF, Ed Scebold of ACTFL and Helene Zimmer-Loew of the AATG. The Board also includes Robert LaBouve representing the Texas Education Agency, and Jane Barley from the New York State Department of

Education representing the less commonly taught languages.

An Advisory Council consisting of representatives of government, business, parents, educators and second language professionals is cochaired by Protase Woodford, retired from the Educational Testing Service, and A. Graham Down, President of the Council for Basic Education. The Standards Project is being directed by Dr. June K. Phillips, a member of the ACTFL Executive Council. Christine Brown is the chair of the student standards task force. The four organizations (ACTFL, AATF, AATG, AATSP) are seeking supplemental funding to develop standards for students at the college level, standards for entry level teachers, and standards for experienced teachers (ACTFL, 1993a).

The first meeting of the student standards task force was held on June 11–13 in St. Louis, MO. During this meeting, a statement of beliefs about the value of foreign language study was drafted, as was a series of difficult questions such as how to address issues of age, program variations, native speakers, and whether foreign language study should be required of all students. The questions were put into a project newsletter that was sent to all ACTFL members in August. The questions raised in the questionnaire are being discussed at state and regional conferences.

A second meeting of the task force took place August 16–20 in Cape Cod, MA. At this meeting, the group adopted an operating rationale based on the beliefs statement, reviewed standards developed by other organizations and the advice received from these organizations, and made a decision to focus its work initially on learner outcomes at grade 12. The group reached agreement on the components of the process of learning a foreign language in the schools. These are the four skills, sociolinguistic aspects of language usage, foreign languages within interdisciplinary studies and in the broader school curriculum, and knowledge of the foreign culture. An initial attempt was made to draft some standards. Members will work independently on these and bring them to the next task force meeting which will be at ACTFL 93 in San Antonio.

A basic issue that the standards group had to confront early in the project was whether they would design minimal competencies, high level competencies, or multiple levels of competencies. Initially, the consensus of the group is to develop standards that reflect an ideal, rather than a minimal set of competencies for high school graduates. They believe that with the support of the US Department of Education, such "world class" standards could affect curriculum and sequencing, so that students would begin language study earlier and continue it longer. However, the group is committed to an ongoing dialogue with the profession and the public on its general approach and all particulars.[2]

Plans call for the standards to be drafted during year one and then reviewed extensively. Reviewers will include teachers at all levels, individuals with special expertise (such as urban or rural schools, elementary or middle schools), representatives of other disciplines, the general public, and the business community, and key individuals in the major foreign language associations. Following successive revisions, the standards will be pilot tested in districts with a long sequence of instruction during year two. During year three, the final version of the standards will be field tested and validated and assessment strategies will be designed.

According to W.S. Cody (1993), Executive Director of the National Education Goals Panel, the foreign language standards will serve as the foundation for developing new curriculum guides, new forms of instructional materials and textbooks, revised teacher education programs and new forms of assessment.

# The National Assessment of Educational Progress

Popularly known as the "Nation's Report Card," the National Assessment of Educational Progress (NAEP) was created by an act of Congress in order to measure the educational achievement and progress of our nation's students. Funded through the National Center of Education Statistics at the U.S. Department of Education, NAEP administers tests to a national sample of students to provide educators and policy makers with accurate and useful information about the state of our nation's schools.

Since conducting its first assessments in 1969, NAEP has broadened its scope. NAEP's original mandate specified that it measure student achievement in Reading, Writing, Science and Mathematics. Since then, assessments of student performance in Art, Citizenship, Civics, Computer Competence, Geography, Literature, Music, Social Studies, U.S Government and Politics, and U.S. History have also been conducted.

Conducting examinations biennially, NAEP administers tests to over 120,000 students. Tests are administered at three age levels: ages 9, 13 and 17; and since 1983 in grades 4, 8, and 12 as well.

NAEP reports, called "report cards," have revealed serious shortcomings in the performance of American students. As Emerson J. Elliott, Commissioner of Education Statistics, wrote in the Foreword to NAEP's 20-year summary of findings:

> ... our present education performance is low and not improving. The achievement of 17-year-olds in reading, mathematics, science, history, and civics represent only modest performance ... large majorities of these students—81 percent to 96 percent—have rudimentary interpretative skills; they can make generalizations, solve one-step problems, and understand basic science. Only 5 percent to 8 percent of our 17-year-olds, however, demonstrate those skills we usually associate with the ability to function in more demanding jobs in the workplace or the capability to do college work. These students can carry out multiple-step problems, synthesize, draw conclusions, and interpret (Mullis, Owen & Phillips, 1990, p. 3).

The development of the six National Education Goals has strengthened the need for NAEP. Although NAEP tests were not designed with the goals in mind, and the content of NAEP tests is not oriented toward the new standards being created, NAEP data does provide some information on how the nation is progressing relative to the goals. Thus, interest in and funding for NAEP is increasing.

NAEP has tried to satisfy the increased need for information regarding educational performance in America. In addition to measuring student performance, NAEP also collects information on students' background and home environment, and on teaching practices and school facilities through questionnaires for the school principal that accompany NAEP tests. This information has provided a clearer picture of what goes on in our nation's classrooms, and allows for the examination of the impact of various factors on student achievement.

Another need that NAEP has moved to satisfy is the need for information about educational achievement at the state level. Originally, NAEP was designed to permit the appraisal of change over time at the national level. The results did not allow states to receive information on how they changed over time or how they compared with each other. After Congress authorized NAEP to conduct cooperative assessment programs with states by enlarging the sample within a state, the response by states was enthusiastic. The publication of the results of these state assessments caused a flurry of articles in the press nationwide as states compared their performances in math and other subjects. There is even some indication that this information is being put to good use. Georgia's state Superintendent announced that a task force would examine schools and classrooms after Georgia received poor rankings in the 1992 assessment (Wisniewski, 1993).

NAEP has also attempted to meet the need for more information with plans to conduct assessments more frequently and in additional subject areas. NAEP's Governing Board adopted a proposal to begin conducting assessments in three subject areas every year, and approved the development of assessment frameworks for Civics, Economics, Foreign Languages and World History. The first foreign language test was to be conducted in 1994–95. However, because NAEP is located within the Office of Educational Research and Improvement (OERI), and the legislation which authorized the creation and functions of OERI is currently being reauthorized (rewritten), the status of a the foreign language assessment is in doubt. The version of this legislation currently being considered by the Congress implements funding in cuts for NAEP recommended by the Clinton Administration. As a result the Math and Science assessments planned for 1994–95 have been postponed until 1996–97. Unless these cuts are restored, the earliest a foreign language assessment could take place would probably be 1998–99.[3] NAEP remains interested in conducting a foreign language assessment, but cannot do so without Congressional authorization and funding. The need for a national assessment in foreign languages is great. As Rodomar (1990) noted in testimony before the House Subcommittee on Elementary, Secondary, and Vocational Education, "while there is some data on 'process' variables, such as enrollments, 'seat time,' the number of foreign language teachers and so on, we know little at the national level about the proficiency of the students who graduate from these language programs (2)." She argues that a national assessment in foreign languages will lead to improvements in foreign language education not only by informing educators and reformers, but "by spotlighting the importance of foreign language education to the nation and sending a clear signal that foreign language needs to be a core element in the curricula of our nation's schools (2)."

While NAEP has not begun work on designing foreign language tests, it is possible that NAEP would assess productive skills. Traditionally, NAEP employed multiple choice tests exclusively. However, due to the increasing demand for performance measures, in recent years NAEP has administered direct tests, including open-ended responses and the use of writing samples. These tests are clearly in line with proficiency standards emphasizing creative and productive language use.

Because NAEP is considering a foreign language assessment, it is appropriate to make a few recommendations here.

Since NAEP assessments are only administered to students in grades four, eight and twelve, it would make most sense to administer the foreign language assessment to students in grade 12. The majority of foreign language enrollments are at the high school level. Furthermore, an assessment at grade twelve would serve as an "outcome" assessment, allowing the appraisal of foreign language skills of students leaving high school.

In a foreign language assessment, deciding which skills to assess (listening, reading speaking and writing) is important. Listening and reading could be easily assessed through objective means, and then the results could be interpreted in terms of the ability to comprehend real life listening and reading tasks. A subset of students could be tested for speaking and writing skills. This would make for a very cost effective assessment.

NAEP will also have to make decisions regarding which languages and levels to assess. Due to funding constraints, though it is clearly desirable to test as many languages as possible, it makes sense to assess them in the order in which they are most frequently studied by American elementary and secondary school students: Spanish, French, German and Russian. The matter of grade or course level is also important. It would be most informative to focus the assessment on students who have completed three years of instruction. It is after such extended exposure to a foreign language that students begin to develop skills that can be regained in later life when needed. Students should also be asked how long it has been since they completed their study of the language. Additionally, some provision will have to be made for distinguishing between students who speak the language at home, students who have been exposed to the language outside the classroom, and students whose only exposure is in the classroom.

The foreign language assessment could be accompanied by questionnaires for principals and teachers. Questions posed to principals could inquire about the languages taught in the school, the enrollment at each level, etc. A questionnaire for teachers could deal with their background in the language, teaching experience, work load, and the emphasis given to the various skills at each level in their courses, etc. Such a questionnaire could tell us much about the delivery of foreign languages instruction nationally. Information from both questionnaires would be especially useful as educators and the public begin to assess the extent to which we are meeting any opportunity-to-learn standards that are established for foreign languages as part of the National Education Goals.

# The College Board's Pacesetter Program

For decades the College Board has offered the Advanced Placement program, which allows students enrolled in advanced courses at the secondary level the opportunity to earn college credit if they can demonstrate college level attainment. While the Advanced Placement program has grown increasingly popular, it still remains a program for the relatively small proportion of students who are enrolled in college level courses. Such courses are usually taught by teachers who are willing to follow a generic course description in the teaching of a course whose content is parallel to that typically offered at American colleges.

The College Board wholeheartedly joined the educational reform movement when it announced its "Pacesetter" initiative in May 1992. Pacesetter is an integrated program of standards, teaching, and assessment for educational reform at the secondary school level. The program seeks to establish high standards for what students should know in mathematics, English, science, Spanish, and world history; and then to develop curricula to help students attain those standards. The Pacesetter program will then offer schools a coordinated package of course curricula, student assessment, and teacher development opportunities.

The Pacesetter program is based on five premises: (a) higher educational goals can be met only if teachers and subject matter experts are actively involved in the development of those goals, (b) educational reform must begin with definitions of specific student outcomes necessary to compete in the workplace, (c) student outcomes must be defined before it is decided how to measure progress, (d) teachers must be prepared to assist students in developing the skills specified in the student outcomes, and (e) assessment should be conducted by a variety of methods, including performance based tasks (College Board, 1992).

Following from the above five premises, each Pacesetter course is intended to include: (a) an outline of course content and student outcomes; (b) course materials; (c) a strong professional development program for teachers linked to course content outlines, including in-school assessment techniques, summer workshops, institutes and publications illustrating successful teaching techniques; (d) classroom assessment that permits teachers to monitor and shape instruction while providing feedback to students; (e) a variety of end-of-course assessments measuring achievement and proficiency; and (f) a system for determining end-of-course achievement that would allow comparisons on state, regional and local levels (College Board, 1992).

The College Board has solicited the help of educators and professional associations to guide the development of its Pacesetter courses. ACTFL is involved in the development of the Spanish Pacesetter program. Actual writing is done by writing teams consisting primarily of teachers of Spanish in public and private secondary schools.

The goal of the Spanish task force is the development of a Pacesetter "capstone"[4] content-based Spanish course for high schools. The Spanish task force, cochaired by Lynn Standstedt, executive director of the AATSP, and Myriam Met, foreign language coordinator for Montgomery County Public Schools, has already identified the three main student outcomes of the program. The first is the use of Spanish to acquire new knowledge in any appropriate area. The second outcome specifies some of these areas, such as the student's own culture and other cultures.[5] This is to be accomplished by having students inquire about other cultures and their perspectives on various issues and to compare those perspectives with the perspectives of their own culture. The third student outcome is a proficiency goal: using and understanding oral and written Spanish in a culturally acceptable manner in order to participate effectively in everyday situations at home and abroad. (Valdes, 1993, p. 14)

As of October 1993, the Spanish writing team had drafted five of six units in the curriculum. Piloting of the program is to begin in fall 1994. While nothing has been finalized, some elements of the Spanish Pacesetter course are becoming apparent.

In contrast with the course descriptions that the College Board developed for French, German, and Spanish Advanced Placement language courses, which recommend a number of textbooks that could be used in the course, the task force is developing completely new course materials for Pacesetter. The course materials will be significantly different from anything else on the market (L. Sandstedt, personal communication, 6 July 1993). One of the goals of the Pacesetter Spanish course is to provide content-based instructional materials to further language acquisition while promoting interdisciplinary understanding. Information will be presented and manipulated in nontraditional ways. Students use the information presented to undertake activities and projects in order to create oral and written products.

The Pacesetter course will follow a unit-module system. There will be six, six-week units, each of which will be divided into three modules. Each module will conclude with a "culminating activity" designed to test as many of the four language skills as possible. The culminating activities of the modules will be an integral part of the assessment system. Since many of these activities will be product-oriented, there will be many different ways in which they may be assessed. In addition, the task force is looking into using student portfolios as part of the assessment package as well as some way to test the oral proficiency. Plans call for a standardized end-of-course assessment, linked with the curriculum. Scoring would be done on the district, state or regional level and be managed by the Educational Testing Service, which is the test development arm of the College Board. No final decisions regarding assessment measures have been made, except that multiple measures of desired outcomes will be used.

While proficiency is one of the curriculum's stated student outcomes, the task force is uncertain whether this outcome will be defined as the attainment of a specific level on the ACTFL Proficiency Guidelines. The ACTFL Proficiency Guidelines are being kept in mind during the development of the Pacesetter course, but the Guidelines are not being used as the "guiding force" because they offer little direction on instructional strategies for achieving particular proficiency levels. Task force members also question whether the Guidelines are an appropriate evaluation instrument for year-long courses on the high school level, since the Guidelines are not sensitive to short term progress or small gains in proficiency (M. Met, personal communication, 9 July 1993).

# The Articulation and Achievement Project

The project entitled Articulation and Achievement: The Challenge of the 1990's in Foreign Language Education Project (Articulation and Achievement Project or AAP) is a joint effort by the College Board, the American Council on the Teaching of Foreign Languages and the New England Network of Academic Alliances in Foreign Languages and Literatures. Supported by a three year grant from the U.S. Department of Education's Fund for the Improvement of Postsecondary Education, the AAP seeks to articulate student standards and achievement levels in grades 7–14 and to develop matching classroom assessment strategies. The results of the AAP project will be formally disseminated via a series of professional development workshops and publications, and will be considered in ACTFL's effort to develop national standards. The AAP is directed by Claire W. Jackson, who founded the New England Network of Academic Alliances in Foreign Languages and Literatures.

While the Articulation and Achievement Project began in the fall of 1992, the project has already made considerable progress. A provisional draft of the student outcomes (standards) was completed in the spring of 1993, and significant headway was also made in developing assessment measures. The provisional draft is divided into five stages. At the early stages, assessment measures are often specific to the function taught. At the higher stages, more comprehensive and integrated assessments are used. According to Jackson, the AAP has found authentic and performance assessments to be the most productive. The AAP is focusing its efforts on four assessment strategies:

portfolio assessment, developing a modified Oral Proficiency Interview, holistic evaluation, and integrated assessment.

In order to make portfolio assessment more manageable, the Articulation and Achievement Project has been beta testing the Electronic Portfolio, which is being developed by Scholastic, Inc (740 Broadway, NY, NY 10003). Designed for use with Apple Macintosh computers, the Electronic Portfolio can store key-entered samples or scanned handwritten samples of student work. Audio samples can be recorded and played back with CD quality. Short video samples can also be recorded. The Electronic Portfolio is a tool to help teachers collect and manage student products.

The Articulation and Achievement Project is also working on the development of a practical oral assessment measure for classroom use called the Modified Oral Proficiency Interview (MOPI). Like the OPI, the MOPI is a face-to-face interview, but it differs from the OPI in several important ways. Most significantly, it measures student performance relative to course outcomes rather than overall proficiency. The MOPI is topic and content specific, is much shorter than the OPI, and teachers can be trained easily to administer and score the interviews using their own criteria. The MOPI can be administered as often as desired, but within the context of the AAP it is given four times a year. The MOPI can be used as a measure of both performance and progress, since sections of student interviews are recorded for comparison.

The AAP is also developing integrated assessment measures. Integrated assessments provide a thematic context in which students are asked to perform tasks that involve a variety of language skills and cultural knowledge. In the Spring of 1993, Jackson field tested the integrated assessments as final exams in third level French, Italian, Spanish and Russian courses at Newton (MA) South High School. The test was conducted over a four-day period of standard 50-minute classes. In one thematic context, students were given several brochures about different summer camps. They had to decide which one they wanted to apply to for a job as a camp counselor. Their first task was to use the phone to call the "Director," a teacher in another classroom, to ask questions about the camp and request an application. The next task was to fill out the application and write an essay on why they wanted to work at the camp they chose. The final task was a job interview with the "Director." These interviews were taped and, along with the other material produced over the week, evaluated according to preestablished criteria. Other thematic context for integrated assessments were exchange programs, travel abroad, class reunions, and job applications. Jackson notes that the integrated assessment model can easily be adapted to other languages.

Both teachers and students were pleased with the results of the final exam. When asked on a questionnaire how the integrated assessment test compared with a more traditional final exam, one 10th-grade student in a 3rd-level Spanish class responded: "I think it is much more effective. I was very glad to find that you were testing our cumulative knowledge and we didn't have to memorize things all over again that we would forget later. You also tested all areas of our learning." Both the outcomes and assessment measures are being piloted in 14 schools (10 secondary and 4 postsecondary) during the 1993–94 school year (C. Jackson, personal communication, August 15, 1993).

# The Ohio Collaborative Articulation/Assessment Project

The Collaborative Foreign Language Articulation/Assessment Project (CAAP) is a joint effort between Ohio State University (OSU), Columbus Public Schools and Columbus State Community College. Supported by a three-year grant from the Fund for the Improvement of Postsecondary Education, CAAP is focusing on the transition from high school to university level foreign language instruction. With better articulation of curricula and early assessment of students, CAAP hopes to provide students with the opportunity to study foreign language and culture in a continuous, efficient sequence from the secondary through the postsecondary level. While Diane Birckbichler of OSU is the principal investigator, the project is guided by a steering committee representing participating public school, community college, and OSU departments. The project was initiated in August of 1992, and work is still underway on all of the project's components.

CAAP has five goals. The first is the development of a functional articulation relationship encompassing the perspectives of the project's three partners: a large urban public school system, a community college and a university. The second goal is the articulation of a coherent long-term sequence of language instruction for the thousands of French, German and Spanish students involved in the project. The third goal is the development of an early assessment program to provide feedback to both students and their teachers while the students are still in high school. The fourth is the creation of uniform and valid measures for the placement of large numbers of language students upon entrance at OSU and Columbus State Community College. The fifth goal is for the institutions to develop a functioning relationship for articulation and assessment that can be replicated in other settings across the nation (Birckbichler et al., p. i).

Like many universities, OSU found that many incoming students who studied a foreign language in high school fail to place into intermediate-level courses. Therefore, these students enroll in entry-level courses where they repeat basic grammar and vocabulary instruction. There is concern that this repetition of courses constitutes a waste of the students' time and valuable resources. Instructionally, it is difficult to manage classes that are divided between true beginners and students who are repeating material. True beginners become frustrated and disadvantaged when placed in courses with students who are repeating material, while repetition of material deadens student motivation. CAAP hopes to remedy this situation with better articulation of language sequences, early assessment of high school students, and better placement measures (Birckbichler et al., pp. 5–6).

Instructors from the three institutions participating in the CAAP Project have developed an effective working relationship. Initial fears that meetings of high school, community college and university level instructors would lead to unproductive complaining sessions where the groups viewed each other with mutual suspicion have proved unfounded. Once there was a common goal and product to produce, the groups became effective at working together. Although work has not yet been completed on articulation of the language sequences, the relationship and discussion between the project's partners has already led to some improvements. One such improvement is the possible implementation of a common final exam in language courses in the Columbus Public Schools (CPS). When the CPS foreign language teachers discovered that their students were not placing at anticipated levels, they became concerned that they were straying from their own curriculum standards. They are considering a common final exam to evaluate how well they are accomplishing the objectives of their own curriculum.

CAAP is developing an early assessment college level placement test for high school students and hopes that early assessment and feedback will help improve the transition from secondary to postsecondary language instruction. Students who take the early assessment test at the end of their third year of instruction will find out what course level they would place into at OSU. This will provide feedback to both students and high school teachers. The CAAP project directors hope that the test will motivate high school students to perform better and to continue taking foreign language courses in their final year of high school.

CAAP hopes to replicate the success of the Early Mathematics Placement Testing Program in Ohio. Developed by the OSU Mathematics department, the test is given to high school juniors, who receive information about the strengths and weaknesses in various math skills and into what classes they would place at several Ohio universities. High school senior math enrollments have climbed while enrollments in remedial math classes at OSU has dropped. CAAP staff hope that the early assessment test will have a similar effect on foreign language enrollments.

While CAAP has not completed development of the early assessment test, they plan to use multiple measures and want to test listening, speaking, reading and writing skills. Some of the tests will probably be multiple choice, but a portfolio component is also being considered. CAAP plans to train high school teachers to administer and rate the oral exams. In this way, the teachers will gain valuable diagnostic information on their students and become a vital part of the testing process. The early assessment will not be directly tied to the curriculum, but CAAP staff expect that it will have a washback effect on secondary and postsecondary curriculum and instruction. Thus, the washback will link testing, curriculum and instruction.

CAAP staff also hope that the early assessment test will have a "frontwash" effect on student placement testing at OSU. OSU currently uses number of years of high school language study and scores on computer-adaptive tests to place incoming French, German, and Spanish language students. (Larson, 1989) One complaint the high school language teachers have is the absence of an oral section in the current OSU placement test. It is not done because of time and financial constraints involved in conducting oral assessments when trying to place thousands of students during the first few days of the semester. The CAAP project directors hope that the early assessment test (especially if it does include an oral component) will serve the dual functions of providing early information to high school students on how they compare with college level students of the language, and that it will serve as an alternate placement measure for local incoming university students at OSU.

CAAP has produced a working relationship between community college, high school and university level instructors which has been very fruitful. "There have been a lot of changes just because teachers at the different levels are communicating with each other" (D. Birckbichler, personal communication, June 28, 1993).

# The CAL SOPI tests

The Simulated Oral Proficiency Interview (SOPI) is a semi-direct tape recorded speaking test modeled on the Oral Proficiency Interview (OPI). The SOPI was developed at the Center for Applied Linguistics (CAL) in the mid 1980s in an effort to create a way to obtain an oral proficiency rating in situations where a trained or certified interviewer is not available to conduct a face-to-face interview. The SOPI consists of a warm-up and 15 speaking tasks/situations that are prerecorded on a test tape. The examinee also uses a test booklet containing pictures and the written description of each task heard on the tape. The examinee listens to the description of each task/situation and, after organizing his or her thoughts during a timed pause, responds in the target language to a native speaker who has made a statement or asked a question. The SOPI can be administered to an individual through the use of two cassette tape recorders (one plays the test questions while the other records the questions and the student's responses) or to groups (in a language laboratory setting).

Research reveals that there is a strong correlation between the SOPI and the face-to-face OPI at the Intermediate through Superior levels. Across a series of studies, when trained raters are used, the SOPI has shown high parallel form reliability, high inter-rater reliability, and high concurrent validity with the OPI. Indeed, the SOPI generally correlates with the SOPI as highly as the OPI correlates with itself, thus demonstrating that it can serve as a surrogate of it. (Stansfield and Kenyon, 1992)

Since the 1980s, SOPIs have been developed in Arabic, Bengali, Chinese, Hausa, Hebrew, Hindi, Indonesian, Japanese, Portuguese, Tamil, and Tibetan. To help expand the users of the SOPI, the National Foreign Language Resource Center at CAL with support from the US Department of Education has developed two-day workshops in Arabic, Chinese, Japanese, and Portuguese, that train teachers to administer and score the SOPI using the ACTFL Proficiency Guidelines. During the past three years, the NFLRC has offered over 20 workshops (without charge) to teachers of these languages, with the greatest number of workshops offered in Chinese. These workshops have allowed teachers of the less commonly taught languages to learn about proficiency concepts, to discover ways to implement them into their teaching, and, subsequently, to measure proficiency through a reliable and valid measure that produces scores that are widely understood in the foreign language teaching community. The workshops are offered each year in April at the Eastern Michigan University Conference on Languages for Business and the

Professions and by special request.

The success of the SOPIs in the less commonly taught languages led to frequent requests for the development of such tests in the commonly taught languages. As a result, CAL received a $400,000 grant from the US Department of Education in 1992 to develop SOPIs in French, German, and Spanish. The Spanish SOPI is now being field tested at universities in the Washington, DC area and at Middlebury College. Three parallel forms of each test will be developed. As with the other SOPIs, one form will be used at workshops, while the other two will be reserved for secure testing situations.

In addition to developing the French, German, and Spanish SOPIs, a rater-self-training kit will be produced. We have developed and field tested a similar kit for use by universities in Texas and have found that, for most raters, the kit works as well as the face-to-face training that one receives in a workshop (Kenyon and Stansfield, 1993). This kit will consist of a rater training tape containing examples of performance at each level on the ACTFL scale for each of the 15 SOPI speaking tasks. The kit will also contain a rater training manual, which will explain in detail how to administer the SOPI, provide a profile of typical performance at each level for each task, and include a key and a written justification for the rating assigned to each performance on the rater training tape. The kit will also contain copies of the rater notes sheet, which the rater uses to make notes on the examinee's performance while listening to the tape.

In addition, the kit will include a rater testing tape, which the rater may use to assess his or her skill at assigning accurate ratings. The kit will be made available at cost to high schools and universities that wish to use the SOPI for oral proficiency testing. Subsequently, teachers may administer and score the SOPI without incurring any test fee. These SOPIs and the rater training kit will provide teachers with a user-friendly means to implement oral proficiency testing in their instructional program.

As indicated above, the SOPI is designed for students who have reached at least the Intermediate-Low level of oral proficiency. This limitation poses a problem for its use in secondary schools, since many secondary students are at the Novice level of proficiency. At CAL, we have developed two solutions to this problem. The first is a Preliminary (lower level) SOPI, available in Japanese as the Preliminary Japanese Speaking Test, or PRE-JST. This version of the SOPI consists only of tasks at the Novice and Intermediate Levels. The second solution involves re-structuring the current SOPI format. This re-structuring will allow low-level examinees to respond only to Intermediate and a few Advanced level items. When this format is followed, the warm-up (which is at the Novice level) is scored. This format of the SOPI is suitable for examinees at the Novice High through Advanced levels. The French, German, and Spanish SOPIs under development are structured to permit this possibility by allowing examinees to stop the test after the seventh item. Thus, the French, German, and Spanish SOPIs will be applicable to both the secondary and tertiary levels.

Finally, we are also working to develop and publish a manual to help language teachers develop their own SOPIs. The manual will detail for teachers how the regular and the Preliminary SOPI are developed. It will include advice on item writing, developing SOPI prompts, designing forms for collecting pilot test data from examinees and raters, recording the test, working with an artist, etc. With the aid of the SOPI test development manual, teachers will be able to create additional forms of the SOPI for use in their program or to devise a SOPI that is most appropriate to the level of proficiency of their students. The information in the manual will also assist teachers in creating other semi-direct tests tailored to the instructional outcomes of their program.

# Texas Oral Proficiency Test (TOPT)

Throughout the 1980s, foreign language teachers in Texas demonstrated strong support for oral proficiency testing and requested the Texas Education Agency to begin testing the oral proficiency of teachers. Texas educators felt strongly that this would ensure high standards among those entering the teaching profession, and that it would send a clear message to universities preparing teachers about the importance of developing students' oral language skills. As a result of this pressure, the Texas Education Agency contracted with the Center for Applied Linguistics in March 1990 to develop multiple forms of a SOPI in French and Spanish to be used as part of the teacher certification process in Texas. This test, called the TOPT, is now administered three times per year in seven cities across the state. Two weeks after the administration, the examinee response tapes produced by these teacher certification candidates are rated in Austin at a group rating session involving from 20 to 50 raters. Each tape is evaluated by two different trained raters using the ACTFL scale. If there is a disagreement as to whether the performance is passing, the tape is rated by a third rater. In all, approximately 2,000 French, Spanish, and Bilingual Education teacher certification candidates take the TOPT each year.

CAL has developed a *TOPT Test Preparation Kit* for students, which includes a manual that describes the functions that are assessed on the TOPT, a complete practice test, and test tape. After familiarizing themselves with the TOPT by studying the manual, students may take the test for practice, and record their responses on another tape. The reverse side of the test tape contains sample responses to the same TOPT items at each proficiency level on the scale. By comparing their responses with those on the test tape, students can assess their strengths and weaknesses and derive a score themselves. They can use this information to determine if they are ready to sign up for the official TOPT.

CAL also developed a rater self-training kit that was distributed without cost by the Texas Education Agency to professors at the state's 67 universities. By using the kit, professors at universities can train themselves to score the TOPT test form included in the TOPT Test Preparation Kit and determine the student's level of proficiency. In addition, the professor can make a diagnostic assessment of which language functions the student needs to master in order to reach the passing level (ACTFL Advanced) on the test. The rater can also note any particular structures or topics with which the examinee may need more instruction and practice. Again, such information can be used for advising the student appropriately.

The effects of the TOPT have been just as was imagined. Texas universities have held two state-wide meetings to discuss how they can better develop their students' oral proficiency so they can reach the Advanced level and thus pass the TOPT. Universities have begun offering more courses designed to develop oral proficiency and upper level courses that have traditionally been taught in English are coming under special review. Faculty are recognizing that even literature classes present opportunities for students to develop speaking skills. Special study abroad programs have been created to provide a language immersion experience for students who are about to take the TOPT. These programs focus on developing the functional language skills that are the basis of the ACTFL Guidelines and the TOPT.

Because of the need to learn more about the language functions tested by the TOPT, universities have assumed the cost of sending faculty to Austin to participate in the TOPT scoring. Upon returning, the faculty are better able to advise their colleagues on changes needed in the curriculum or in teaching methods in order to prepare students for the test.

The influence of the TOPT extends to the secondary level as well. In 1986, a representative committee of teachers completed work on a proficiency-based curriculum known as *Essential Elements for Languages*. This curriculum was approved by the Texas State Board of Education and implemented throughout the state. Subsequently, ESEA Title II funds were used to provide inservice training to teachers to upgrade their spoken language proficiency and to teach them methods appropriate for implementing the curriculum.

In 1991 and 1992, the Texas Association of Language Supervisors, which had become familiar with the SOPI, underwent a two-day workshop in order to learn how to develop semi-direct tests like the PRE-SOPI. As a result, some districts formed teams of teachers to create proficiency-based speaking tests that will be scored at the district level.

More recently, the Texas Education Agency has contracted for the development of listening and speaking tests for use at the secondary level. An advisory committee consisting of teachers of the major foreign languages taught in the public schools has been established to advise on the specifications for the tests. The speaking test will involve meaningful and contextualized language tasks like those on the TOPT. Some initial field testing of speaking tasks for the Spanish test was done in May 1993. It is hoped that the test will be available for voluntary use by districts in the spring of 1994. The results of the testing will provide baseline data on the language proficiency of students in the district. Although plans have not been finalized, it is hoped that the test can be implemented throughout the state in 1995–96. One possible outcome of this project is to reward students who perform well on the test by designating a proficiency level on their transcript.

## Summary

This article has reviewed several current national, regional and state initiatives. Although these initiatives are independent and no organized coordination between them is presently in place, they share several common features. Each initiative is a response, in some way, to the current national effort to reform educational practice. Each attempts to begin the reform effort with a focus on the knowledge, skills, and abilities that a foreign language student should have. Each initiative consists of multiple components. These usually include statements of desired content standards, statements of desired performance standards, tests, articulation, feedback to the student, feedback to the teacher, curriculum development, and teacher training. All of these components are combined in the implementation of the project, and the implementation depends on collaboration at different levels of the educational system.

It is significant that these initiatives reflect a more favorable view of testing than has been the case in the past. Previously, concerns about the potential deleterious effects of testing on the curriculum have prevented testing from true integration into the curriculum. This complaint was often justified, since in the U.S., standardized tests have relied on the multiple-choice format since the 1930s. The exclusive use of multiple-choice tests has limited the ability of testing to serve the curriculum and instruction, since these tests generally do not influence either in any direct way. The reliance on multiple choice tests is psychometrically and economically efficient, but such tests do not support the development of skills and abilities that are needed to succeed in life or to progress in a specific discipline. By incorporating productive skills tests and tests based on authentic tasks into the curriculum, testing progresses beyond an evaluative role to a supporting role in the educational system.

Given the new view of testing reflected in the initiatives reviewed here, and in the national agenda reflected by the National Education Goals, it is appropriate to end this article by listing some tenets that underlie the contribution that tests can make to educational reform.

1.  Tests can affect curriculum and learning.
2.  Tests can provide feedback on learning.
3.  Tests can help implement content and performance standards.
4.  Tests can influence the methodology teachers use.
5.  Tests can motivate teachers and students.
6.  Tests can orient students as to what is important to learn.
7.  Tests can help orient needed teacher training.
8.  Tests can help implement articulation.
9.  Tests can help implement educational reform.

# Notes

[1] I wish to express my appreciation to my excellent research assistant, Richard Lein, for the assistance he provided in collecting and organizing the information contained in this article and for the preparation of drafts for several of the sections. Thanks are also due to my colleagues Nancy Rhodes and Craig Packard for comments on a draft of this article.

In the course of writing and revising this article, I received information and helpful comments from Nancy Anderson, Diane Birckbichler, Christine Brown, Rick Donato, Charles Hancock, Claire Jackson, Mimi Met, Lynn Sandstedt, and from Mary Crovo and Mary Lyn Borque of NAEP.

[2] One of the problems that those working on the ACTFL standards will encounter is the request that they follow the standards developed by the National Council of Teachers of Mathematics and by other groups. These standards identify skills acquired at three grade levels: grades 4, 8, and 12. These grade levels correspond to those tested in the NAEP. However, because foreign language is an elective in the American education system, it is rarely taught as part of a twelve-year sequence of studies. Thus the utility of standards

developed for a twelve-year sequence is questionable.

The ACTFL standards group made an initial effort to alleviate this problem by envisioning three sequences of study. The first would begin at grade 3 and continue 30 minutes per day until grade 6; then it would continue 50 minutes per day in grades 7–12. This is the only sequence that would involve grades 4, 8, and 12. The second sequence would begin at grade 5 and continue 30 minutes per day through grade 6 and then continue at 50 minutes per day in grades 7–12. The third sequence would begin in grade 9 and continue 50 minutes per day through grade 12. It would involve a total of 600 hours of instruction (ACTFL, 1992). Even this last sequence is followed by only a few students, and hardly any follow the first or second sequence. Therefore, it will be interesting to see how the staff of the standards project solve this problem. The problem represents a dilemma for the Standards group and for the profession: do we produce standards that reflect current and historical realities, or do we propose standards that ignore realities and represent an ideal?

[3]The OERI reauthorization legislation also withdraws the authority of the NAEP Governing Board to approve the conduct of assessments in areas other than the core subjects. Depending on the interpretation of this legislation, foreign languages may not be subject to assessment under NAEP. Or, the legislation may be interpreted to mean that only those subjects mentioned in the National Education Goals could be assessed, in which case foreign languages could be, if they remain in Goal 3, as currently proposed.

[4]The College Board uses the term "capstone" to refer to the *culminating* course that a high school student would typically take in a discipline. This Spanish course will be approximately equivalent to a Level III course.

[5]It should be noted that the focus on culture directly addresses one of the five specific objectives of National Education Goal 3: "all students will be knowledgeable about the diverse cultural heritage of this nation and about the world community."

# References

ACTFL. ACTFL, AATs to develop foreign language standards. *ACTFL Newsletter*, 1993a, *5* (2/3), 1, 3.

ACTFL. *Standards update*, 1993b, (mimeograph).

ACTFL. Standards for foreign language education. *ACTFL Newsletter*, 1992, *5* (1), 7–10.

Birckbichler, D.W., et al. *The collaborative foreign language articulation/assessment project*. [Project proposal and narrative for the Fund for the Improvement of Postsecondary Education]. Columbus, OH: The Ohio State University, Columbus Public Schools, Columbus State Community College, n. d.

Cody, W.S. Foreign languages and the national education goals. *ACTFL Newsletter*, 1993, *5* (2/3), 14–15, 20.

College Board. *Pacesetter: An integrated program of standards, teaching, and assessment*. New York: Author, 1992.

Committee on Education and Labor, United States House of Representatives. *Committee report on H.R. 1804, Goals 2000: Educate America Act*. Washington, DC: U.S. Government Printing Office, 1993.

Guide to national efforts to set subject-matter standards. *Education Week*, 1993, *12* (38), 16–17.

Kenyon, D.M., and Stansfield, C.W. *Evaluating the efficacy of rater self-training*. Paper presented at the 14th International Language Testing Research Colloquium, Cambridge, UK, 2–3 August 1993.

Larson, J.W. S-CAPE: A Spanish computerized adaptive placement exam. In W.F. Smith (Ed.) *Modern technology in foreign language education: applications and projects.* (pp. 277–89). Lincolnwood, IL: National Textbook Company, 1989.

Mullis, I.V.S., Owen, E.H, and Phillips, G.W. *Accelerating academic achievement.* (Report no. 19-OV-01). Princeton, NJ: NAEP and ETS, 1990.

National Education Goals Panel. *The national education goals report: Building a nation of learners.* Washington, DC: U.S. Government Printing Office, 1993.

Rodomar, D.G. *The need for a national assessment of educational progress in foreign language competence.* [transcript of testimony before House Subcommittee on Elementary, Secondary, and Vocational Education, June 7, 1990], (mimeo).

Stansfield, C.W., and Kenyon, D.M. Research on the comparability of the SOPI and the OPI. *System*, 1992, *20* (3), 347–64.

U.S. National Commission on Excellence in Education. *A nation at risk: the imperative for educational reform: a report to the nation and the secretary of education.* Washington, DC: U.S. Government Printing Office, 1983.

Valdes, G.M. The Pacesetter initiative. *Florida Foreign Language Association Newsletter*, February 1993, p. 14.

Wisniewski, L. State may form math task force to pull up ranking: Specialists blame outdated teaching. *The Atlanta Constitution*, April 9, 1993, p. D1.

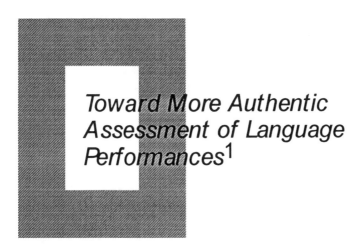

# Toward More Authentic Assessment of Language Performances[1]

Grant Wiggins

*Center on Learning, Assessment, and School Structure*

**W**hen an educational problem persists despite the well-intentioned efforts of many people to solve it, a safe bet can be made that the problem is improperly framed. Assessment in education has clearly been such an issue when everyone agrees that simplistic indirect tests shouldn't drive instruction but their number and influence remain. And we still seem not to see the harm of indirect, generic and mechanical test of human performance—where realistic performance challenges and context-sensitive human judgment of performance are deliberately by-passed in the name of statistical precision and economy.

We haven't moved beyond mere laments because we typically fail to stop and ask some essential questions. Just what are tests meant to do? Whose purposes do they and should they serve? As I argue in my recent book, tests have traditionally served the interests of psychometricians and policy-makers and not those of students and teachers.[2] We routinely sacrifice validity for reliability, to put it in measurement terms: we go after precise scores on less that worthy tasks. Most importantly, we forget that the student ought to be the primary client of assessment information. Assessment should improve performance, not just audit it.

We thus won't get far with these questions until we ask the most basic one: what is a genuine challenge, a true test? I propose a radical answer, in the sense of a return to the roots: we have lost sight of the fact that a true test of intellectual ability requires exemplary tasks, set in authentic contexts and constraints.

Lauren and Daniel Resnick proposed a different way of making this point: they have argued that Americans are the "most tested" but the "least examined" group of students in the world.[3] As their epigram suggests, we rarely honor the original meaning of the word "test." The original "testum" was a porous cup for determining the purity of metal, later generalized to the procedures for determining the worth of a person's effort. To "prove the value" or "ascertain the nature" of a student's understanding implies that mere appearances—of student answers, as of metal—can deceive. A correct answer can hide the most thoughtless recall; an error can be quickly self-corrected, a slip obscuring a thoughtful understanding, or not even an error at all *when the answerer's reasoning or re-statement is heard.*

We can put the matter of better "examining" in different language. We need more assessment and less testing. As the root of the word "assessment" reminds us, the assessor must "sit with" the learner in some sense to be sure that the student's answer *really* means what we think it means. Does a correct answer hide thoughtless recall? Does a wrong answer hide thoughtful understanding? We can only know by responding with further questions, seeking more explanation or substantiation, requesting a self-assessment, or by soliciting the student's response to the assessment.

Assessment should be designed and conducted to *improve* performance, not just audit it. We need to ask: What kinds of challenges would be of most educational value to students (and to teachers concerning the abilities of their students)? How will the results of this test be used to help students know their strengths and weaknesses on essential tasks? What kinds of evaluating will provide the best incentives and aims, thus enabling students to raise their own standards? How can a school adequately objectify, justify and communicate its standards to interested outsiders so that standardized tests become less necessary and influential?

# The Implications for Foreign Language Assessment

In foreign language instruction this view no longer appears as odd or soft as it once did. The commitment to a proficiency-based view of language learning has taken root in most schools and colleges. But far too often teachers still rely on unending short-item tests of words, verb tenses and syntax out of context. We have not yet figured out how to keep our eye on the ultimate performance of effective communication when designing tests and exams, particularly for novices. We forget that novice speakers, listeners, readers, and writers work with dictionaries and phrase books while trying to use the language in context. Reform begins, then, by treating each and every test we design for what it is: it should *teach*; it is central to, not an add-on to instruction; not a set of drills or exercises, but equivalent to the "game" of performance in context. We need to ensure that students are taught by their tests how language challenges are typically encountered in the world. In short, we must aim for authenticity in *all* our language assessment.

Most school tests make the complex simple by dividing it up into isolated, decontextualized and simplistic chores—as if the student need not regularly practice the test of performance, of putting it all together. But to efficiently and effectively empower the novice language students we must help them make progress in handling complex "whole" language-related tasks. (Note that this is the norm in performance-based activities: the novice athlete, musician, and actor is always engaged in the "same" challenges facing the professional, even as a novice.) The "logical" approach of testing simple elements of language, out of context, leads to tests that mislead the student about progress at the criterion performances. And a heavy dose of such drill-tests provides very little incentive for the student to learn the language in an effective, graceful way. How different the problem of language learning seems when one is in a foreign country, as I found out last March in a visit to Germany, given my limited ability to use the language. My one former course in it, with tests of words instead of situations, seemed hopelessly inappropriate.

Implicit in this view of assessment is the need for the challenges we put before the student to better replicate the *interactive* challenges and standards of performance typically facing would-be language users in the field as they "do" their communication. Implicit here is the idea that legitimate assessment—unlike a test—is appropriately responsive to the (perhaps idiosyncratic) student, and the situational and school context. We need to be able to diverge from a protocol if necessary if we sense that a student has misunderstood our question in a way that is self-correcting when we re-ask or re-frame the question, just as in natural discourse. Evaluation is most accurate and equitable when it entails human judgment and dialogue so that the person tested can clarify questions and answers if necessary and properly personalize the problem to be solved. A genuine test of intellectual achievement doesn't merely check "standardized" work in a mechanical way. A good test teaches the student, revealing the actual challenges and constraints facing the would-be communicator in the field instead of being a contrived exercise to shake out a score.

That is why most so-called traditional "criterion-referenced" tests of language or other subjects are typically inadequate. The problems are contrived and the cues artificial: they are like the cakes in Wonderland that say "eat me": the student need only plug in the correct phrase or sentence on cue. They thus co-opt what is central to intellectual competency and effective use of language in context: using one's judgment and wits to solve communication problems. Authentic challenges are inherently messy, and not at all about plug-in behavior. As a senior ETS researcher has said:

> Most of the important problems one faces are ill structured, as are all the really important social, political and scientific achievement test . . . Efficient tests tend to drive out less efficient tests, leaving many important abilities untested and untaught. . . . All this reveals a problem when we consider the broader conception of what a test is.[4]

When teachers treat tests as something to be done as quickly as possible after "teaching" has ended in order to shake out a final grade, they succumb to the same logic employed by the test companies (with far less statistical justification of the results). When testing is what you do "after" teaching and learning are over, you ensure that testing is driven by time and expense consideration, and test formats that are quick and indirect come to predominate. Such acquiescence is only possible when the essential links between learning and feedback are lost. If tests serve only as audits, short-answer, "objective" tests— an ironic misnomer[5]—will do (particularly if I teach 128 students and have only one day to grade their final exams). If, however, a performance challenge is seen as the heart and soul of the educational enterprise—as it would be if we understood our aims clearly, namely equipping performers—reductionist shortcuts in testing (not to mention absurd student-teacher ratios and dysfunctional schedules), or the farming out of test design to strangers in companies would be seen as intolerable.

Instructively, schools and teacher-coaches do *not* tolerate the same thinking in athletics, arts, and clubs. The needs of the game, recital, play, debate, or science fair are clear and determine the use of time, personnel, and money. Form follows function when we are clear about performance goals: far more time, often one's spare time as a "coach," is usually allotted to insure adequate practice and success. So too with allocation of adults: even in the poorest schools, the ratio of interscholastic coaches to players is about 12 to 1.[6] The "test" demands it; "coaching" requires it where "teaching" somehow does not. And no one complains about "teaching to the test:" in performance-based activities teaching to the test of performance is the coach's passion and *raison d'etre*.

## What Is Performance? What Is Authenticity?

To "perform," as the dictionary reminds us, comes from the word for "consummate" or accomplish. When we perform we try to "execute a task or process and to bring it to completion." Our ability to perform with knowledge therefore can only be assessed by our having to produce some work of our own, using a repertoire of knowledge and skills while responsive to the particular tasks and contexts at hand. (The use of the plural is important: we assess "performance" through many different "performances" in diverse settings and situations, whether we are considering professional athletes or doctors.)

One way to see the difference between drilled skill and performance ability is through an anecdote from my soccer coaching career. It is common practice in soccer and other sports to do drills in practice related to gaining numerical advantage on offense (since, in theory, that is a sure-fire way to score, if one can execute the moves). So, every coach routinely does what are called "2 on 1," "3 on 2," or "4 on 3" drills, namely, where the offense has the ball and a numerical advantage to exploit. But mastery of the drill does not translate into game mastery, as the following tale reveals. One time, early in a season, one of my better players had a series of opportunities to exploit such a numerical advantage. So, I yelled from the sidelines "2 on 1!" She actually stopped dribbling the ball and yelled back at me, "I can't *see* it!"

That incident sums up in a nutshell the problem with testing by indirect items. Items are the equivalent of drills: deliberately simplified and decontextualized events, designed for isolating and practicing discrete skills. But the sum of the drills is never equal to fluid, effective and responsive performance, no matter how complex or varied the items. As all good athletes and foreign language students know, adaptive judgment and "anticipation" (perception of the unfolding situation) are essential elements of competence, so much so that players who are able to "read" the game can often compensate for skill deficiency. Yet if we look at almost every major test or set of problems in the back of language textbooks they are drill-tests, not performance tests.

Even when teaching rank novices, we must keep asking: What is the equivalent for testing in foreign language of the game? What does the "doing" of language use in context look and feel like, and how can our tests better replicate the challenges and conditions, not just isolated tasks or drill-exercises of authentic challenges? If we want later competent performance, we need to introduce novices to target performance from day one. Only a deep and ancient prejudice about academic learning keeps us thinking that intellectual competence is achieved by accretion of knowledge and movement through simple logical elements to the complex whole—instead of movement from a crude grasp of the "whole" performance to a sophisticated grasp of the "whole."

What are the actual performances that we wan students to be good at? Let us design them and worry about a fair and thorough method of grading them as a secondary problem. Do we judge our students to be deficient in writing, speaking, listening, following or asking directions? Let even beginning tests then ask them to write, speak and listen in the target language—using dictionaries and phrase books just like I did in Germany last March. We would, for example, develop scoring systems that distinguish between reference-book dependence and independence in performance. We might also develop rubrics that describe different levels of language use, judged in terms of how much English vs. the target language was used.

This reversal in thinking (whereby we immerse the novice student in tests of fluency) will appropriately make us devote more attention to what we mean by evidence of "understanding" and progress. Mastery is never about producing pat answers on cue. Thoughtful and effective understanding and communication in context implies being able to do something effective, transformative, or novel with a complex situation. An authentic test" enables us to watch a learner tackle, pose and solve open-ended and context-bound problems.

Traditional tests, as arbitrarily-timed, superficial exercises (more like the drills than the game) given only once or twice, leave us with no way of capturing the students' ability to make progress, over time, at the "same" important test. We typically learn too much about the student's short-term recall and little about what is most important: the student's *habits of mind*. As the word "habit" implies, if we are serious about students displaying thoughtful control over ideas, one "test" is inadequate. We need to observe students' *repertoires*, not wooden catechisms in response to pat questions.

The most important habit *we* need to break is testing with "secure" tests. Secrecy is antithetical to performance assessment. If the true test is so central to instruction, it must be known from the start and repeatedly encountered because it is both central and complex, equivalent to the (known) game to be played or the (known) musical piece to be performed. The true "test" of ability is to perform consistently well in performance(s) where the tasks and criteria are known and valued. By contrast, when standardized test questions are kept "secure," hidden from students (and teachers), we contradict the most basic conditions required for learning.[7]

## Criteria of Authenticity

Let me then propose a set of criteria by which we might distinguish authentic from inauthentic forms of testing. Here is my latest version of a much-revised set of criteria for judging the authenticity of a test.[8]

Authentic tests of intellectual performance involve:

1. engaging and worthy problems or questions of importance, in which students must use knowledge to fashion performances effectively and creatively; tasks are either replicas of or analogous to the kinds of problems faced by professionals in the field, or adult citizens and consumers

2. faithful representation of the contexts facing workers in a field of study, or the real-life "tests" of adult life; formal *options, constraints and access to resources* are apt as opposed to arbitrary; particularly, the use of excessive secrecy, limits on methods, the imposition of arbitrary deadlines or restraints on the use of resources to rethink, consult, revise, etc.—all with the aim of making testing more efficient—should be minimized and evaluated

3. non-routine and multi-stage tasks; real problems; recall or "plugging in" is insufficient or irrelevant; problems require a repertoire of knowledge, hence, good judgment in determining which knowledge is apt when and where; and skill in prioritizing and organizing the phases of problem clarification and solution

4. tasks that require the student to produce a quality product and/or performance

5. transparent or de-mystified criteria and standards; the test allows for thorough preparation, as well as accurate self-assessment and self-ad-

justment by the student; questions and tasks may be discussed, clarified and even appropriately modified, etc. through discussion with the assessor and/or one's colleagues

6. interaction between assessor and assessee; tests ask the student to justify answers or choices, and often respond to follow-up or probing questions

7. involve response-contingent challenges where the *effect* of both process and product/performance (sensitivity to audience, situation and context) determine the quality of the result; thus, there is concurrent feedback and the possibility of self-adjustment during the test

8. *trained* assessor judgment, in reference to clear and appropriate criteria; an oversight or audit function exists: there is always the possibility of questioning and perhaps altering a result, given the open and fallible nature of the formal judgment

9. the search for patterns of response, in diverse settings, under differing constraints; emphasis is on the consistency of student work—the assessment of habits of mind in performance

Authenticity also implies that test design should involve knowledge use that is forward-looking. We need to view tests as "assessments of enablement," in Robert Glaser's terms. Rather than merely judging whether students learned what was taught we should "assess knowledge in terms of its constructive use for further learning . . . [we should assess reading ability] in a way that takes into account that the purpose of learning to read is to enable them to learn from reading."[9] All tests should *initiate* students into the actual challenges, standards, and habits needed for ultimate success in the disciplines or workplace: original research, analysis of others' research in the service of one's own, critical argument and synthesis of divergent viewpoints. A real test replicates, within reasonable and reachable limits, the authentic intellectual challenges facing a person in the field. (Those tests are usually also the most engaging tasks).

## Some Examples of Authentic Tests

Let us examine some tests and rubrics, devised to honor this idea of assessing authentic performance. The first set come, perhaps surprisingly, from the State of New York. Here is an example of the foreign language testing that has been required in the state during the past few years:

---

**Speaking Tasks are provided in four categories:**
socializing
providing and obtaining information
expressing personal feelings
getting others to adopt a course of action

Sample speaking task:

[Student initiates]. Teacher says, "You are in a store looking at clothes. I am a salesclerk. You are going to tell me what you are looking for. You will start the conversation."

Sample note-writing prompt:

"You are looking for your friend . . . He is not at home. Write him a note in [target language] so that you can meet him later."

---

Again on a state-wide level, Connecticut a few years ago implemented a range of performance-based assessments in foreign language (as well as other academic and vocational areas) using experts in the field to help them develop apt performance criteria and test protocols. The foreign language staff was able to adapt the ACTFL guidelines for a more fine-tuned assessment of young novice performers in language. Below is an excerpt from the manual that describes the foreign-language performance criteria.[10] On the written test, students are asked to draft a letter to a pen pal. The four levels used for scoring are: Novice, Intermediate, Intermediate High and Advanced. They are differentiated as follows:

N   Use of high-frequency words, memorized phrases and formulaic sentences on familiar topics. Little or no creativity with the language beyond memorized patterns.

I   Recombinations of learned vocabulary and structures into simple sentences . . . Choppy sentences with frequent errors in grammar, vocabulary, spelling. Sentences will be very simple at low end of intermediate range . . . often reads very much like a direct translation of English.

IH   Can write creative sentences, sometimes fairly complex ones, but not consistently. Structural forms reflecting time, tense or aspect are attempted, but the result is not always successful. An emerging ability to describe and narrate in paragraphs . . . papers often read like academic exercise.

A  Able to join sentences in simple discourse . . . has sufficient writing
vocabulary to express self simply although the language may not be
idiomatic. Good control of the most frequently-used syntactic structures . . . a sense that student is comfortable with the target language
and can go beyond the academic task.

Put simply, what the student needs is a truly valid test—valid in the sense
of corresponding to the ultimate criterion of performance, not just other
indirect tests—in the case of language use, communication in context. In a
truly authentic and criterion-referenced education, far more time is spent
teaching and testing the student's ability to understand and internalize the
criteria of genuine competence. What is often so harmful about current testing
(and the teaching that follows from it) is that evaluation often unwittingly
reinforces the lesson that mere right answers, put forth by going through the
motions, are adequate signs of competence. Again, this is a mistake rarely
made by coaches who know that their hardest and most important job is to
raise the standards and expectations of their students.

Obtaining rigor in a performance-based assessment system is not the im-
possibility claimed by the detractors of assessment reform. As I think most
readers know, the American Council on the Teaching of Foreign Languages
(ACTFL) foreign-language proficiency guidelines show that performance can
be rigorously and reliably assessed without sacrificing validity; all student
assessment should strive to emulate this approach. For each language and
mode of communication there are detailed descriptions of each successive
level of performance sophistication, from novice to superior. In the scoring
descriptors the judgments and any scores made thus reflect *empirically-
grounded traits* about the speaker's performance, irrespective of the per-
former's age or experience, based on years of categorizing particular performances into levels of competence.

The guidelines identify typical successes and errors for each stage of
language performance to aid in the judging. For example, the mistake of
responding to the question *Quel sport preferez-vous?* with the answer *Vous
preferez le sport tennis.* is noted as "an error characteristic of speakers" at
the mid-novice level, where "Utterances are marked and often flawed by
repetition of an interlocutor's words . . ."[11] These are the kinds of descriptors
for use in school and college assessment of foreign language.[12]

# Toward Meaningful Reform

The problem can be cast in broader moral terms, however. The problem is not the good or bad intentions of test designers but the morally problematic aspects of generic indirect tests. The test is insensitive by design. Mass testing as we know it treats students as "like" objects, as if their education and thought processes were similar and as if the reasons for their answers were irrelevant. Test-takers are not, therefore, treated as human subjects whose peculiar responses and feedback are essential to the accuracy of the assessment. The standardized test is thus inherently "inequitable" because it is unresponsive. (I am using the word "equity" in its original philosophical meaning, incorporated into the British and American legal systems in the office of the chancery or equity courts. The idea is a common-sense but profound one: blanket laws, policies or, in this case, standardized tests are inherently unable to encompass the inevitable idiosyncratic cases to which we ought always to make "exceptions to the rule." Aristotle put it best: "The equitable is a correction of the law where it is defective owing to its universality."[13]

Put in the context of testing, equity requires that we insure that human judgment is not overrun or made obsolete by a merely efficient, mechanical scoring system. Externally-designed and mandated tests are dangerously immune to the possibility that a student might legitimately require a re-phrasing of the question or the opportunity to defend an unexpected or "incorrect" answer, even when the test questions are "well-structured" and the answers multiple-choice. How many times, as teachers, parents or employers, have you had to alter an evaluation on the basis of having the person explain an answer or action? Sometimes all the students need is a hint or rephrasing to recall and use what they "know." We rely on human judges in law as in athletics because judgments cannot be reduced to rules. To gauge understanding we must explore an answer: there must be some possibility of dialogue between the assessor and the assessee to ensure that the student is fully examined. What is so striking, for example, about many of the test protocols used in British performance testing in the 1980s in the Assessment of Performance Unit (APU) is that the assessor is meant to probe, prompt, and even teach, if necessary, to be sure of the student's actual ability and to enable the learner to learn from assessment. In many of these tests *the first answer or lack of one is not deemed a sufficient insight into the student's knowledge.*

The scoring system works as follows:

1. unaided success
2. success following one prompt from the tester
3. success following a series of prompts
4. teaching by the tester
5. an unsuccessful response; tester did not prompt or teach
6. an unsuccessful response despite prompting and teaching
7. question not given
8. unaided success where student corrected an unsuccessful attempt without help

Successful responses were combined into two larger categories called "unaided success" and "unaided plus aided success" with percentages given for each.[15]

At stake here is a vital question, now unconsidered due to test questions that require right answers in one attempt: How should we think of error, particularly the errors of a novice? Are the first responses a person makes, if in error, necessarily their ultimate answer? Miscue analysis in elementary language development suggests otherwise. And as elementary teachers have learned in encouraging "invented" spelling, sometimes a spelling error is tolerated in the name of language development and use because the student takes the risk of using more sophisticated vocabulary in their writing. Why not apply the same logic to foreign language? The issue is not counting up mistakes, but gauging the growing effectiveness of the communication: some mistakes are more important than others in performance. Let's develop scoring rubrics that give credit for sophisticated errors. Let's give credit for work that reveals a thoughtful attempt to communicate with limited tools. Let's immerse novices in immersion problems and see how they perform without judging them on the number of "mistakes" they make. Let's see how well they self-correct before judging their mistakes, just as we now do in elementary reading through miscue analysis.

Teacher autonomy, typical school-test unreliability, and the "subjectivity" of human judgment are often cited as reasons to retain "objective" tests (the design of which is usually quite "subjective"). But higher standards in schools depend on how to uphold them. Reliability is only a problem when judges operate in private and without shared criteria. In fact, multiple judges, when adequately trained to assess actual student performance using agreed-upon criteria, display a high degree of inter-rater reliability. In the Connecticut foreign language test described above, two judges using a 1–4 scoring system agreed on a student score 85% of the time out of of the thousands of tests given.[16] Nor, when the test has essay questions, are there typically criticisms of the reliability of AP test scores, only of the cost. The issue is thus not "testing technology" but the will to invest the time and money in authentic assessment and collaborative standard-setting (from which adequate reliability would follow).

To let students "show off what they know and are able to do" is a very different business than the fatalism induced by error counting on contrived questions. Since the standardized tests are designed to highlight differences, they often end up exaggerating those differences (by not including pilot questions which everyone gets right) to gain a useful "spread" of scores.[17] And since the tasks are designed around hidden, often arbitrary questions, we should not be surprised if the test results end up having too much to do with native language ability or cultural background, instead of the best fruit of their efforts.

There are no easily identified villains in the testing mess. As I have elsewhere noted, teachers fail to understand their own unwitting role in the growth of standardized testing.[18] The influence of such tests has grown in proportion to the schools' failure to set clear, justifiable, and consistent standards. It remains possible for a student to pass all his or her courses and be functionally and culturally illiterate: school transcripts tell us nothing about what a student can actually do.[19] An "A" in English 3 may mean merely that a student was dutiful and able to fill in blanks on worksheets about juvenile novels. There is therefore some merit in having tests (or any other "standard" indicators) that enable us to make comparisons. No matter that standardized tests now merely compare schools to each other instead of to genuine intellectual standards: Until schools offer adequate evidence of their standards and efficacy in meeting them, the tests will exert influence by providing some measure of accountability.

# Conclusion

As I said at the outset, we need a return to the roots, a new philosophy of assessment in this country that never loses sight of the student. We might start by adopting the manifesto in the introduction of the recent national assessment report in Great Britain, a plan which puts the students' (and teachers') interests first:

> Any system of assessment should satisfy general criteria. For the purpose of national assessment, we give priority to the following four criteria:

- the assessment results should give direct information about pupils' achievement in relation to objectives: they should be criterion-referenced;
- the results should provide a basis for decisions about pupils' further learning needs: they should be formative;
- the grades should be capable of comparison across classes and schools . . . so the assessments should be calibrated or moderated;
- the ways in which criteria are set up and used should relate to expected routes of educational development, giving some continuity to a pupil's assessment at different ages: the assessments should relate to progression.[20]

The re-design of assessment is thus inexorably linked to the "restructuring" of schools. Authentic restructuring depends on continually asking: What new methods, materials *and schedules* are required to test and teach "habits of mind" well? What structures, incentives and policies will insure that a school's standards will be known, reflected in teaching and test design, coherent school-wide and high enough but achievable by most students? Who will monitor for teacher failure to comply, and with what response? How schools frame diploma requirements, how the schedule supports school aims, how job descriptions are written and hiring done, how syllabi and exams are designed, how the grading system reinforces standards and how teachers police themselves are all inseparable from reform of assessment.

Authentic tests must come to be seen as so essential that it is *worth* disrupting the habits and expenditures of conventional school keeping for them. Otherwise standards will only be aped or idealized, not made tangible and realizable. There are, of course, legitimate reasons for taking the intellectual pulse of a student or system through standardized tests. But mass testing through matrix sampling and other less intrusive methods can and should more readily be implemented.

We need to recognize that the obstacles to lasting assessment reform are thus more "ecological" (political, structural, and economical) and psychological than technical. The resistance to tackling them will only be overcome by making a powerful case to the public (and to our colleagues habituated to short-answer tests as an adequate measure of ability) that a standardized indirect test of intellectual ability is a contradiction in terms. The task is to show that "monitoring" tests are so irrelevant (even harmful) to genuine intellectual standards that their cost to student learning and teacher professionalization is too high, despite the efficiently-gained data and short-term financial savings.

Only a more intellectually valid approach to evaluation can give us the credible and useful insights we need to ensure progress toward student intellectual fitness. As long as simplistic monitoring tests are thought to be adequate models of and incentives for reaching intellectual standards, the flaccidity, in current overall student performance and in our thinking about assessment, will remain.

# Notes

[1]Parts of this chapter originally appeared in *Phi Delta Kappan*, May 1989.

[2]See G. Wiggins (1993).

[3]Resnick, D., and Resnick, L. (1985).

[4]Fredericksen (1984), p. 199.

[5]See Stiggins (1988) on the inadequacy of teacher tests and the training they (do not) receive in classroom testing.

[6]In all performance-based education, as Peter Elbow points out, the teacher goes from being the student's adversary to the student's ally. See Elbow (1986).

[7]This point is developed at length in Chapter Three of Wiggins (1993).

[8]See Wiggins, "A True Test."

[9]Glaser (1988), pp. 40–42. Cf. Glaser (1986).

[10]Manuals are obtainable from the Office of Research and Evaluation, Connecticut Department of Education. Test design and result information is available in a paper entitled "Performance Testing in Connecticut: Examples from Science, Drafting, and Foreign Language." For further information on ACTFL Guidelines, see ACTFL (1982) and Higgs (1984).

[11]From the ACTFL Provisional Proficiency Guidelines for French, American Council on the Teaching of Foreign Languages (1982), ACTFL Provisional Proficiency Guidelines. Yonkers, New York, NY, 10701.

[12]Note that the British scales mentioned above and the scales used in many states for performance testing do not resolve this problem. The rubrics use vague, general language that invariably leans too heavily on relative comparisons—a 5 is "less thorough" than a 6 paper, for example. There is, thus, no criterion-reference standard at work. Look at state writing assessment rubrics used for different grade-levels: they are almost indistinguishable, showing that the "standard" is relative to the anchor papers they choose, not embedded in the language of the rubric.

[13]*Nichomachean Ethics*, 1137, pp. 25–30.

[14]Similar work on a research scale is being done in this country as part of what is called "diagnostic achievement assessment." See Snow (1988) and Brown and Burton (1978).

[15]From *Mathematical Development, Secondary Survey Report #1*, Assessment of Performance Unit, Department of Education and Science, Great Britain, 1980.

[16]As told to me by Joan Baron, Director of CAEP Assessment for Connecticut.

[17]See Oakes (1985), pp. 10–12.

[18]Wiggins (1988).

[19]The Vice President of the College Board recently echoed this view in responding to criticisms of the influence of SATs by asking rhetorically, "Don't colleges have the right to ask for independent confirmation that the kid can do the work?" (as reported by Ted Fiske in the education column of the New York Times, December 18, 1989). That does not explain, of course, why the student should pay for the service.

[20]Paragraph 5 of TGAT (1988).

# References

American Council on the Teaching of Foreign Languages, ACTFL *provisional proficiency guidelines.* Hastings-on-Hudson, NY: ACTFL Materials Center, 1982.

Alverno College Faculty. *Assessment at Alverno College,* Revised Edition, Milwaukee, WI: author, 1979/1985.

Alverno College Faculty. *Analysis and communication at Alverno: An approach to critical thinking,* 1984.

Archibald, D., and Newmann, F. *Science at age 15: A review of APU survey findings 1980–1984.* Assessment of Performance Unit, Department of Education and Science. London: Her Majesty's Stationery Office, 1988.

Aristotle, *Nichomachean ethics,* 1137, Buffalo, NY: Prometheus Books, 1987.

Bloom, B., Madaus, G., and Hastings, J.T. *Evaluation to improve learning.* New York: McGraw-Hill, 1981.

Brown, J.S., and Burton, R.R. Diagnostic models for procedural bugs in basic mathematical skills, *Cognitive Science,* 1978, *2,* 155–92.

Callahan, R. *Education and the cult of efficiency: A study of the social forces that have shaped the administration of public schools.* Chicago: University of Chicago Press, 1962.

Connecticut Department of Education. Toward a new generation of student outcome measures: Connecticut's common core of learning assessment. Hartford, CT: State Dept. of Education, Research and Evaluation Division, 1990.

Department of Education and Science and the Welsh Office, *National curriculum: Task group on assessment and testing: A report.* (TGAT Report). London, England: Dept. of Education and Science Publications, 1988.

Educational Testing Service, *Learning by doing: A manual for teaching and assessing higher-order thinking in science and mathematics* (A Report on the NAEP pilot of performance-based assessment: Report #17-HOS-80), 1987.

Elbow, P. *Embracing contraries: Explorations in teaching and learning,* New York: Oxford University Press, 1986.

Frederiksen, N. The real test bias: Influences of testing on teaching and learning, *American Psychologist,* 1984, *39,* (3), 193–202.

Glaser, R. The integration of instruction and testing, *The redesign of testing for the 21st century,* 1985 ETS Invitational Conference Proceedings, Princeton, NJ: ETS, 1986.

Glaser, R. Cognitive and environmental perspectives on assessing achievement, *Assessment in the service of learning,* 1987 ETS Invitational Conference Proceedings, Princeton, NJ: ETS, 1988.

Gould, S.J. *The mismeasure of man,* New York: Norton, 1981.

Grant, G., Elbow, P., et al. *On competence: A critical analysis of competence-based reforms in higher education.* San Francisco: Jossey-Bass, 1979.

Haney, W. Making Testing More Educational, *Educational Leadership,* 1985, *43,* 2.

Higgs, T. (Ed.). *Teaching for proficiency, the organizing principle,* Lincolnwood, IL: National Textbook Company, 1985.

Resnick, D.P. and L.B. Standards, curriculum and performance: A historical and comparative perspective, *Educational Researcher,* 1985, *14,* (4), 5–21.

Snow, R. Progress in measurement, cognitive science and technology that can change the relation between instruction and assessment, *Assessment in the service of learning,* 1987 ETS Invitational Conference Proceedings, Princeton, NJ: ETS, 1988.

Stiggins, Rick. Assessment literacy, *Phi Delta Kappan ,* 1991, *72,* 1, 534–39.

Stiggins, R. Revitalizing classroom assessment, *Phi Delta Kappan,* 1988, *69,* 5.

Tyack, D. *The one best system: A history of american urban education,* Cambridge, MA: Harvard University Press, 1974.

Vermont Department of Education, *Vermont writing assessment: The portfolio,* Montpelier, VT: author, 1989.

Wiggins, G. *Assessing student performance: Exploring the purpose and limits of testing,* San Francisco: Jossey-Bass Publishers, 1993.

Wiggins, G. Creating tests worth taking, *Educational Leadership,* 1992, *49,* (8), 26–33.

Wiggins, G. Standards, not standardization: Evoking quality student work, *Educational Leadership,* 1991, *48,* (5), 18–25.

Wiggins, G. A True Test: Toward More Authentic and Equitable Assessment, *Phi Delta Kappan,* 1989a, *70,* (9), 703–13.

Wiggins, G. Teaching to the (authentic) test, *Educational Leadership,* 1989b, *46,* (7), 41–47.

Wiggins, G. Creating a thought-provoking curriculum, *American Educator,* 1987, *11,* 4.

Wiggins, G. Rational numbers: Scoring and grading that helps rather than hurts learning, *American Educator,* 1988, *12,* (4), 20–48.

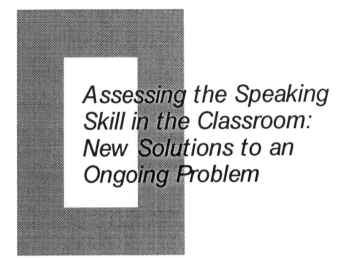

# Assessing the Speaking Skill in the Classroom: New Solutions to an Ongoing Problem

Peggy Boyles

*Oklahoma City Schools*

## Introduction

Good foreign language teachers are like good disc jockeys. They both offer a variety of "good music" to their audience in order to keep them tuned in to the program! It can be a mix of their favorite oldies-but-goldies, but the newest songs with more meaningful lyrics for the 90's generation also need to be played. Teachers can no longer assume that their students will automatically find interesting the same things they enjoyed, or that students will enjoy the same activities and topics that young people liked in the past. And unfortunately, as every experienced teacher knows, what worked with students the first thing in the morning may be completely different than what works with students right after lunch!

Consequently, those who are playing the "same old song" hour after hour, and year after year, soon discover that their students are selecting the mute option on their student controls during class or are switching to another station at the semester! As Forbes (1973) points out, "gone are the happy days in which a teacher could spend a whole period on his favorite poem if he wanted to" (p. 134).

Assuredly, if students were to write a Top 10 List of the reasons for studying a foreign language, the love of learning subtle (albeit important) nuances between the imperfect and preterite tenses is not likely to make the list. The popular reason for studying another language given by students in survey after survey is to be able to speak the language. As Rivers (1973) warns, "we can so easily kill, or at least considerably dampen, the enthusiasm of a foreign language learner by preferring accuracy of detail" above sincere student efforts (p. 19).

It is the purpose of this chapter to emphasize the importance of incorporating a proficiency orientation into regular classroom testing for the speaking skills, and to offer samples for speaking tests that are reasonable for teachers to administer on a regular and frequent basis, even to large numbers of students at the same time. Models for testing formats that can be easily coordinated with current foreign language texts, as well as models for scoring proficiency-oriented tests is an additional concern that will be addressed. Lastly, the integration of technology as an assist in the administration of such testing procedures will be discussed.

In the summer of 1990, the author attended the MLA Professional Development Institute in Middlebury College. Her project for the institute was to design materials and testing formats to assist teachers in giving their students opportunities to demonstrate their speaking. As part of the process of defining her goals, she reflected back over her years in the classroom. In the beginning years, her teaching fell into a very predictable, repetitive pattern. Her testing program was automatic and presribed solely by the book. However, with the advent of the proficiency movement, she began to change her her teaching style to a more communicative approach. Her impatience with the testing program prompted her to investigate different possibilities for assessment.

During that era she dreamed that her classes would be filled with "wannabe" language students. They would be comfortable in her classes and they would be willing to take risks. They would eagerly "sing the melody" of language before having to know the individual notes. But every morning reality set in and she was faced with what she really knew. She knew that many times kids feel helpless in a foreign language classroom. She knew that kids were reluctant to perform in front of their peers. She knew that both teachers and students need incentives for change. And she knew that aligning her teaching with her testing was imperative. Most importantly, she knew that teachers were the most important factor in providing opportunities for success.

# The Contexts of Teaching
# and Testing Speaking

As any veteran teacher knows, the best way to send messages of importance to students is to put them on the test. When a student waves his hand in the middle of her finest communicative activity and asks, "Will this kind of stuff be on the test?", the teachable moment may be gone but the teacher's credibility in on the line. Because teachers know that the out-of-textbook experiences are often the most meaningful to students, they will have to be prepared to answer the student's question in the affirmative. If not, they can have the same results as the 5th grade science teacher described by Frank Medley. (1985) When the 5th graders made notes about their experiment with growing beans in the classroom, they were excited after the first few signs of progress. The green leaves gave them encouragement, and students eagerly reported positive results. After a few days, the beans started to show a few brown tips around the edges. Undaunted, the kids eagerly entered the classroom the next few days, only to find that the plants were becoming more leggy and tentative. Finally, the inevitable conclusion of the classroom was that beans won't grow in the classroom.

Foreign language teachers too will have "dead beans" in their classroom, despite the initial nourishment of proficiency-oriented activities if they don't follow up with proficiency-oriented testing. If students are asked to participate in communicative, open-ended activities every day in the classroom, then it is hypocritical to assess their progress with traditional discrete point grammar tests.

Both teachers and students are brought up in an educational culture where one is rewarded with a certain grade for mastering a designated amount of material. Ever since elementary school, students are used to receiving a list of spelling words on Monday that will be tested on Friday. This tradition has carried over into the foreign language classroom. In many level one classes, students are given a vocabulary list at the beginning of the chapter, and are tested on this same list later in the week.

In many instances, these are the kind of tests students prefer. In one class a few year ago, a second year student pleaded with the author to give the semester final "like his other Spanish teacher did last year." When asked for more details, the student reported that his first-year teacher had each student select five slips of paper from a shoebox, and then conjugate those verbs in three different verb tenses. He was decidedly more comfortable with conjugating verbs than in using the language in any communicative way. Some students are, of course, as resistant to change as some adults.

Just as athletes learn to develop a game face for the rival team, students have mastered a "game face" for teachers while asking questions about an upcoming test. With the most demanding tone, they ask for absolute clarification on the number of pages the test will cover in the book. Teachers brace themselves for the proverbial question at the end of the test review. "So, Mrs./Ms./Mr. Brown, if I know everything on pages 49–65 by tomorrow, I'm guaranteed a 100% on the test, right?" It is during moments like these in the classroom where we must wrestle with the question of "whether 'tis nobler in the mind to suffer the slings and arrows" of outraged students, or "to take arms against a sea of troubles" and persist in a new direction in testing.

If students are assured that mastery of a prescribed number of pages in the book will ensure success on an upcoming test, the students are studying for an achievement test, which tends to be based on what has been taught. In proficiency-oriented testing, students are eliciting language they have acquired in a variety of contexts and are using them in real life situations. As Terry (1986) states, "creative testing encourages students to perform at their own level of ability through the use of logical and appropriate reactions or responses involving those structures and vocabulary items that they have acquired" (p. 523). Valette dicusses this extensively in chapter one of this volume.

Certainly, testing speaking ability in the target language has not been regularly included as part of our testing programs. As Terry (1986) observes, "Although lip service is paid to proficiency-focused instruction, many tests still reflect a sole preoccupation with grammatical accuracy" (p. 521). Students need to know that their teachers believe that to be able to communicate in the language in real life situations is an important outcome for language learning. As Gonzalez Pino (1989) points out, "those who wish to be pedagogically fair by testing what they teach are incorporating the speaking skill into the regular tests that their students take. To do otherwise is to send the wrong message to students" (p. 487). The best way is to put it into the regular classroom testing program where it should be part of learning a second language.

# Teachers' Reflective Questions

Why do we test at all? What do our tests say about our teaching? These questions are being addressed in both foreign language research, as well as in classrooms across the country. According to a survey of teacher concerns (Cooper, 1985), testing and evaluation led the list as the most pressing question facing teachers in the foreign language classroom. Teachers are often concerned about how best to test the speaking skills. According to Cooper, this is a healthy sign, for it indicates that "teachers are examining what the real objective of their courses are, and that they are taking an active role in establishing these objectives, rather than passively accepting what the so-called experts dictate about testing" (p. 24).

Do we test simply because we are told to test? Do we test because we believe it is the only way to get kids to learn? Do we test out of habit? Do we test as a punitive measure to hold students accountable? It is important for teachers to reflect and to ask themselves questions like these.

Is testing an essential part of the learning process? Can we, as Wilga Rivers (1973) suggests, view testing as a natural activity? That is the challenge of designing proficiency-oriented speaking tests for the classroom. Can it become something other than a discouraging barrier for students to face or a hurdle they have to jump at prescribed points?

Many of our tests appear to have an image problem. They are dreaded and looked upon by students as a hoop that must be jumped through before going on to the next chapter. In many cases, students view testing as a rather meaningless and impersonal routine, or at its worse, a rather threatening and punitive ordeal. So, how can we make our test more user-friendly? Can tests be a positive challenge rather than an ominous barrier?

Surely one of the most disturbing realities of adding a speaking test to the regular testing program is the issue of scoring and evaluating a speaking sample. Initially, it appears to be a very subjective task. How can you measure a kiss? How do you grade a person's laugh? Although at first we might say that these types of things are impossible to measure or assess, we do just that on a regular basis in real life.

We judge a person's laugh as either sincere or artificial based on our own standards established through the years. We evaluate a kiss as merely proforma or outstanding based on years of experience or on comparisons to past performances. Perhaps these very real and very practical methods of evaluation can be helpful in establishing guidelines for both designing and evaluating a student's performance in speaking a foreign language. Even in the first weeks of beginning to study a language, students need to get used to the message that they are accountable for speaking the language too. Since the ACTFL guidelines tell us that novice learners can say only a few memorized words and phrases in the beginning stages of language use, and that these words can not yet be used spontaneously, we need to use those guidelines and incorporate them into a novice/entry-level speaking test.

For example, after studying clothing vocabulary in a beginning text, many students could achieve 100% mastery if asked to spell 15 lexical items. But when asked to use the vocabulary in a communicative context, many times these same words are pronounced in an unrecognizable manner.

Before beginning to administer and evaluate speaking assessments at an early stage of her Level I classes, the author often found the students' attitude toward pronunciation to be indifferent. "Yeah, whatever!" was the typical response when given a friendly reminder about the correct pronunciation. So, it was clear that something needed to be done about the problem of encouraging and assessing speaking skills.

## Sample Testing Formats

In designing the *Picture Prompt* speaking test, the author wanted to create an experience for students to use the limited vocabulary they had learned in the first weeks of class. It was important that a more meaningful context be created than merely to have students recite a memorized list of vocabulary.

In this test, students are asked to supply single words or phrases in the context of a very simple narrative. They hear a story with missing words symbolized by "picture prompts" (e.g., a line drawing of a sweater or a shirt), as seen in Figure 1. The format used in this test is very similar to the format used in many children's magazines for teaching pre-reading skills. The person reading the story will pause at each picture, waiting for the child to supply the necessary word to continue the story. In the *Picture Prompt*, students supply the missing word at the sound of a beep on a pre-recorded tape. Students know that they receive 2 maximum points only if they pronounce the word so that it is clearly recognizable. The "yeah, whatever" syndrome starts to disappear.

Certainly *Picture Prompt* is only a small step away from the traditional "end of the chapter" vocabulary quiz. However, the assessment takes place *in a context* which provides picture clues as to the correct word or phrase, which is a characteristic of a more communicative test. As Canale (1981) points out, a "test is in fact not so much an objective tool for collecting data

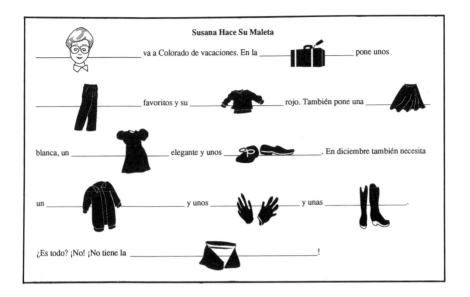

Figure 1.

as it is a complex event for creating data" (p. 43). With this small sample of student talk, a teacher can begin to create data for a student's portfolio during the first weeks of language learning, and it continues throughout the language learning experience.

As students begin to move away from simple memorization of isolated words and high-frequency phrases, they start to understand and answer direct questions which include cognates and are supported by visuals. The *Teddy Bear Test* [1] is a natural follow-up to the *Picture Prompt* test. As students begin to recycle what they have learned, albeit with virtually no variation from the way it was initially learned, they can start to respond to direct questions in a more creative and personalized way.

Oral descriptions of visuals comprise probably the most appropriate conversation stimulus at the novice level, not only because they provide a psychological prop, but because they facilitate listing and identifying tasks for the students.

In the *Teddy Bear Test*, students see several different pictures of bears at work and play. Accompanying the illustrations shown in Figures 2, 3, and 4 are three questions for each picture. The first two questions are specific, objective questions about the picture. The third question attempts to personalize the situation for the student. Students attempt to answer each question tape or in the time provided by the teacher if the questions are not recorded.

[Picture of bear at a Senate office desk, working and eating a sandwich]
Note: copyright restrictions preclude reproducing the original illustrations.

Example 1

1. Où travaille cet ours?
2. Qu'est-ce qu'il mange pour le déjeuner?
3. Qui est ton sénateur?

[Picture of bear at easel, painting portrait of two other bears]

Example 2

1. Was ist der Bär von Beruf?
2. Was macht der Bär?
3. Fur welchen Beruf interessierst du dich?

[Picture of bears making Christmas cookies in the kitchen]

Example 3

1. ¿En qué mes estamos?
2. ¿Dónde están los osos?
3. ¿Cuál es tu mes favorito?

Clearly there are no "right" or "wrong" answers to the last questions in each sequence. There are even ways to circumlocute for legitimate responses to questions concerning the location or actions of the bear. This is a refreshing change for students to be assured teachers don't know all the answers. There are myriad possibilities for appropriate answers. As Rivers (1973) suggests, "the individual learner must have the opportunity to express himself through the language in terms of his own personality" (p. 13).

The purpose of the *Teddy Bear Test* is to provide a thematic context for synthesizing novice-level vocabulary in a proficiency-oriented test and to provide an opportunity for students to personalize answers in a testing format. If the teacher frequently uses teddy bear visuals in her class to have students talking about generic topics such as clothing, weather, emotions, likes and dislikes, etc., then students will be prepared to respond to similar questions about similar pictures on the test. Students are not simply memorizing the answers to "twenty bear pictures."

Students gradually begin to prefer this more creative and open-ended way of testing. They realize that they are given more control in a spontaneous and autonomous situation, and can show the teacher what they know and can even avoid situations which might cause them to show what they don't know. A direct, positive benefit to students in a proficiency-oriented testing environment is that they get points for what they do know, and are not always penalized for what they don't know.

According to Canale's (1981) checklist for validity, the tests should "involve unpredictability and creativity in form and message" and should encourage student responses that are not "contrived utterances" (p. 44). The pictures and questions on the *Teddy Bear Test* are not identical to the pictures and questions used in paired and small group "teddy bear" activities in the class.

As Canale (1981) admits, we can not eliminate all factors that effect validity "anymore than we can eliminate such factors as IQ, world knowledge, personal values, and personality from authentic communication" (p. 49). We can begin to design tests that encourage students to recombine what they have learned by actively participating with them in proficiency-oriented activities during the week. Test items should be derived from daily activities and practices in the classroom. As Bartz (1991) points out, "students should never be faced with a testing situation that is completely unfamiliar to them" (p. 80) Consequently, collecting thematic calendars with colorful visuals illustrating each month can provide teachers with visuals for both classroom activities and tests.

When a proficiency-oriented approach is emphasized in testing, many teachers feel that their efforts in the classroom are affirmed and their professional judgement is confirmed by colleagues. For example, after developing an oral-proficiency testing program in Campbell Union High School District in suburban San Jose, California, many teachers reported feeling "professional validation for what they have been doing in their classrooms" and that the proficiency-testing program added a sense of direction to the foreign language program in the district (Huebner, 1992, p 105).

Those teachers who did not feel this same affirmation reported feeling a need to modify their teaching practices to some extent in the classroom in order to incorporate more proficiency-oriented activities. In underscoring this recurrent them of aligning our daily teaching with our testing, Rivers (1973) points out that we cannot teach for "creativeness in language use with functional comprehension and comprehensibility as the ultimate criteria and then test for mere accuracy of detail, as most standard tests seem to do at present" (p. 15). Teachers might also be resistant and even fearful that they will have to start teaching to a new kind of test.

This notion of the influence of tests on teaching, or backwash, is a very common concern. The phenomenon is usually associated with the negative influence of tests on teaching. Alderson (1992) thinks this hypothesis assumes "that teachers and learners do things they would not necessarily otherwise do because of the test" (p. 6). Seen in a positive light, this might mean that teachers will abandon their favorite verb conjugation worksheet in favor of a paired information-gap activity. Based on their activities, the teachers in the San Jose study did not feel threatened by the new kind of testing but did have to dramatically reevaluate what they considered important (Huebner, 1992).

Foreign language teachers are at different points along the continuum of the paradigm shift to more creative and "real-life" testing. Some say that they do not need to formally test the speaking skills because they already assess the speaking ability of their students on a daily basis and do not feel that separate tests need to be given. They stress that they frequently award "participation points" to students in their classes, and that these points are reflected in the overall grade. However, as Duncan (1987) states, participation grades reflect less of oral proficiency and serve more as an index of attendance, attitudes, and behavior. A prescribed number of checks in a grade book does not equate to a progressive assessment of speaking tasks. In coaxing students to move from achievement testing to proficiency testing, gradual steps must be taken to familiarize them with new formats. Students feel successful if they are able to synthesize what they have learned and to use it in a purposeful way. Testing should require students to rely on integrating what they have learned up to a particular point in time, rather than on simply proving that they have mastered prescribed amounts of material. Of course, the success of the students directly relates to how many speaking activities students have had during the regular class routine.

The bottom line to all the new proficiency-oriented curricula is the question that Bartz (1991) poses: "Does the teacher really know if students are achieving what is intended by the newly designed curriculum, materials, and instructional goals?" (p. 69). Proficiency-oriented testing is the most effective means of determining the success with which a student carries out certain functions within various everyday contexts. Encouraging kids to use the language creatively within a personal context requires a creative and personalized kind of testing.

# Additional Ideas for Teaching, Testing, and Assessing Creatively

The purpose of the *Snapshot Similarities Test* is to provide a more global, integrative approach to testing communicative skills. In this testing format, students are given a set of pictures which have settings such as friends meeting at a restaurant, watching TV at home, or studying for a test. As students look at each picture, they will hear a description of a similar picture, but which has very distinctive differences. Students must describe orally how their picture is different from the description they hear on a pre-recorded tape or by the teacher in the classroom. As shown in Figure 5, students would correct the following state-ments to corre-spond to the picture illustrated.

Instructions: You will hear five sentences that de-scribe each of the pictures you have at your desk. Each picture being de-scribed on the tape is very similar to your picture, but there are some dif-

Figure 5

ferences. At the end of each sentence, there will be a pause. In the time provided on the tape, describe how your picture is different for that particular detail.

1. Una chica lee una revista. (Pause)
2. Il y a trois personnes dans la piscine. (Pause)
3. Der kleine Junge schwimmt. (Pause)

There is a variety of acceptable answers. At the early stages of language learning, the teacher might accept simply changing the sentence into a negative statement. Ex: The girl is reading a magazine" could be replaced with "The girl is not reading a magazine." Later, the expectation might be that the student says something such as "The girl is in the water," or "The boy is pushing the girl off the raft." The type of response depends upon what the student is able to do with the language he or she has learned up until that point. Each test item should elicit potentially different answers from each student in the class taking the exact same test. "There are three people in the pool," might be simply changed into "There are four people in the pool," or more creatively changed into "The two girls are flirting with the teenage boy, while the little boy watches." In designing these types of proficiency-oriented tests, one makes them adaptable to all levels of instruction. They should be challenging for both the advanced and beginning students. The pictures simply provide the vehicle for communication, and the test format provides a broad palette upon which to create language.

The visuals used in the test for novice-level students could be from a group of pictures that the students have previously used in class, since these students are functioning on the basis of memorized material. However, it would be reasonable for the more advanced students to use different pictures from those used in the classroom but that have a recombination of the same vocabulary item. No matter what textbook the students are using, certain lexical items are likely to be covered in virtually all first-year texts: common action verbs, weather expressions, clothing, physical descriptions, food, places, colors, family.

A source of visuals can be the teacher's personal slides and photos, since these are usually of great interest to students. Additionally, the author found that students enjoyed using pictures in classroom activities and tests that were borrowed from the yearbook teacher, since these reflected their own lives. Of course, the boxes full of magazine pictures that all teachers have cut out which have "potential" written all over them, now have a *raison d'être*. If teachers frequently work with these visuals to provide speaking opportunities for various classroom activities, their performance on a similar speaking test will be a reflection of how they are synthesizing what they are learning. As Terry (1986) points out, "we should use the same types of tasks in testing as we use in language-practice activities in order to enable us to test what our students have been practicing. Any good teaching strategy should have equally good validity as a testing strategy." (p. 523) Certainly, the payoff for designing these new types of tests should be that they will contribute to higher student achievement in language learning. As teachers, we can of course evaluate the attainment of this latter goal.

An important facet in writing proficiency-oriented tests is taking into account what Terry (1986) refers to as the distinction between "learned" and "acquired" knowledge, and the ways in which they are typically assessed in the classroom. Learned material is often called for on the traditional unit or chapter tests, whereas acquired knowledge must be used on tests where "grammar and vocabulary have been internalized by the students and can be evoked spontaneously when needed in unexpected situations that call for potentially divergent answers" (p. 522). The *Look Who's Talking Test* provides students opportunities to complete successfully a given situation by performing realistic communicative acts.[2] This testing format requires that students put together all the acquired bits and pieces of language they have learned, and tie them into a specific function such as making excuses, providing instructions, giving advice, expressing concern, voicing a complaint, convincing others, etc. These tests provide a vehicle for students to begin to create with the language and to begin to wean themselves away from only memorized material. On the intermediate level, teachers may use these testing formats to provide role-play for functioning in a "survival situation" in which they might encounter in a real life situation. As Canale (1981) suggests, valid communicative tests always have a purpose and should be interaction based.

In the *Look Who's Talking Test*, each student receives a set of situation cards on which are listed role-playing instructions for the students. Each card corresponds to a particular picture, and students are given the latitude to choose one of two role-playing situations listed on the cards. As seen in Figure 6, students choose to engage in one of two very real-life situations:

A. When you see two of your friends at the mall, you decide to invite them to your party. Tell them when and where it is, what you will do at the party, how many people will be there, what they should wear, and any other details you think they would be interested in knowing.

or

B. Your parents just gave you $500 for your birthday. You want to spend it all. When you run into two of your friends at the mall, you describe to them what you are going to buy with the money.

Figure 6

This test was designed to see if the students could go beyond the structure and context of classroom instruction. It requires that both teachers and students get their heads out of the textbook and worksheets and into the real world. As Liskin-Gasparro (1987) points out, it is very easy to forget that the vocabulary items and points of structure are not ends in themselves, but rather parts of the larger picture of language use. This type of test puts students into situations where they must carry out communicative, real life tasks with the linguistic and grammatical ammunition that they have in their personal arsenal of language learning. This type of test verifies to students that teachers believe that "getting across a message" in the target language is just as important as accuracy of grammar.

Certainly situational diversity needs to be a concern to those developing testing formats to be used in the classroom. As Genesee (1984) suggests, "it cannot be assumed that competence in one situation is associated with competence in other situations even those that might be situationally similar" (p. 139). It is therefore important that students be assessed in a variety of different ways throughout a school year. Limiting the speaking test to the standard one-on-one interview is not adequate to produce a necessary composite of a student's overall speaking ability. As Terry (1986) states, "a single, all encompassing proficiency rating cannot be assigned on performance on any one in-class test" (p. 522).

The *Leave a Message at the Beep Test* is designed to give students a real-life, culturally authentic task. The test items are encased in a realistic contest, rather than as isolated items. The cultural universality of the telephone answering machine is the vehicle for the test design. Although the "recorded message" that the students hear before leaving their message may be different according to the target culture, the premise of leaving a personal message for a friend is a realistic communicative task likely to be encountered in another culture. Even in the Russian version of the test, the student will leave a message with a neighbor or storekeeper who has the nearby telephone.

At the beginning of this speaking test, each student receives a set of student message cards written in English. The student hears a recorded message on the "answering machine" and then waits for the familiar beep to begin recording the message specified by the card. For example, the recorded message the students hears to "set up" the response might be:

Perdona! Soy un desastre. Otra vez no puedo contestar el teléfono. Por favor, deja tu recado a la senal.

or

Pour l'instant, je ne peux pas répondre à votre appel. Laissez un message avec votre nom, l'heure de votre coup de fil...et, si possible, un peu d'orginalité, s'il vous plait!

or

Im Moment kann ich das Telefon nicht beantworten. Hinterlassen Sie Ihre Nachricht, Ihren Namen, und die genaue Zeit.

Even if students are unable to understand each word in the recorded message, it gives the task the feeling of reality that is needed for the task. The students are then asked to give certain information in their recorded message. The requested information is given in English in order to avoid giving too many vocabulary clues in the target language. Additionally, the main focus of the task should be in the student's oral response, rather than in translating the instruction on the card. As Canale (1981) points out, "the more time a testee is given to focus on individual, discrete aspects of the language, the less such tasks correspond to authentic language-use demands" (p. 47).

The communicative tasks outlined by the student message cards will vary according to the level of proficiency. As soon as students learn the novice level functions of introducing themselves and of supplying simple physical descriptions, or of expressing simple likes and dislikes, they are ready to perform effectively in the *Leave a Message at the Beep* setting. The task can be altered according to the level of the students, but even beginning level students should be able to supply the following information in his recorded message:

#1
1. Ask the person where he is.
2. Leave your name and the time you called.
3. Tell the person where you are going tonight.
4. Tell the person when you'll be back home.
5. Tell the person you'll see him or her tomorrow at a particular place and time.

or

#2
1. Don't leave your name. Imply that you're a secret admirer.
2. Describe yourself physically.
3. Describe an aspect of your personality.
4. Describe what you like to do.
5. Describe your mood and tell him to call you.

Certainly a viable alternative would be for students to invent their own messages without the guided-prompt cards. The teacher would simply request that the students leave at least five different pieces of information and/or identification on the message. To allow students to have direct input into the kind of situations they will encounter on the test is to empower them to participate and be responsible for their own learning. In practical terms, this is a direct message from the student which helps teachers provide suitable tests. Individualized instruction can lead to individualized testing without the time consuming process of the teacher himself having to write several different test items.

So why don't teachers eagerly embrace this new testing philosophy and begin to design tests and assessments that would appear to be the logical next step to a proficiency-oriented approach to teaching? Perhaps the current over-dependence on textbook tests is due to convenience rather than conviction. It may be that tests of this kind are not readily available, and that they are time consuming to grade. It may be, as Bartz (1991) suggests, that the classroom teacher must first be convinced that the effort involved in developing these types of tests will contribute to the "realization of higher achievement in language learning" (p. 77). Even subconsciously, teachers may shy away from giving their students speaking tests "…for fear of poor results, and the associated guilt, shame or embarrassment…" that goes along with their students' poor test performance. However, as E. Phillips (1988) points out, when teachers become convinced of the ease and appropriateness of classroom activities that encourage the development of oral proficiency, they then consequently convince themselves and their students of both the importance of oral work and the need to evaluate it regularly.

Students used to be guaranteed success on tests if they had mastered discrete points of languages, and teachers felt a quiet sense of accomplishment if the prescribed numbers of chapters were completed by the end of the year. Everyone knew the point value of an accent mark and a correct verb ending. However, in the 1990's teachers need to view themselves in the broader context of instructional leaders and test designers, rather than as a mere consumers of the ideas of the others.

Unfortunately, many classroom teachers feel uneasy and/or unqualified to evaluate a student's speaking sample. They fear that without sanction from the "experts", their evaluation would be inadequate. They fear that someone might question their judgement. Even some recent studies seem to validate those fears and apprehensions. In his study, Levine (1987) concludes that while the teachers assessing students' oral performance were not accurate, they were predictably *consistent* in their overestimation of pupils' oral abilities.

# Testing and Grading of Speaking Assessments: Some Practical Points

According to Canale, (1981) there are five factors that influence test scores: mode, response type, administration procedures, environment and scoring procedures. He also emphasizes that the validity of a test depends on *what* the test tries to measure and *how* it tries to measure it.

According to the work done by Gonzales-Pino (1989) with regular classroom teachers, there is a basic decision teachers must make about establishing a system of grading for speaking tests. The integration of the speaking tests within the full course grading structure must be determined. Gonzalez Pino suggests three oral tests each semester, and each test is worth 10% of the course grade.

In the author's grading structure, all speaking tests constituted at least 25% of the overall grade of any chapter test or end of the grading period assessment. Most teachers with whom the author piloted her tests encouraged the author to develop an "on the spot grading" for students. In order to effectively assign a grade to any given speaking sample in the "on the spot" manner called for by these teachers, the classroom teacher had to be able to concentrate on only one or two components of the student communication at one time. The author looked at grading systems from other test designers in the field to begin to formulate what worked best for her situation in a secondary school setting (Gonzalez-Pino, Bartz). A system was developed where teachers addressed only two issues at a time when assessing a sample of student speaking. The descriptions of grading the tests described in this chapter are meant to be examples of how to use such categories as comprehensibility, amount of communication, fluency, and effort to communicate can be made manageable for teachers to grade.

In both the *Picture Prompt Test* and the *Teddy Bear Test*, the scoring procedure was one that was most familiar to students. It was the least subjective and therefore the easiest type of scoring to begin with when initiating speaking tests. Students were given points for either clear pronunciation and/or fluent responses. In the *Picture Prompt Test*, students were given 0–2 points for each word in the narrative. One point was given if the student provides a correct word, but the pronunciation impedes understanding. A full two points were given for the correct word with understandable pronunciation. In the *Teddy Bear Test*, one point is given if the answer to each direct question concerning the pictures is correct, even if mispronunoucned. The full two points are given for a correct answer with unhesitating, correct pronunciation. No points are awarded if the content is incorrect and the utterance is mispronounced.

Of course, it is imperative that teachers model for students what is meant by an "unhesitating response." The author showed her students that a "jump start" response such as, "Yo, ah, ... yo tiene, no, yo tengo, etc" would not receive full credit. The important thing for teachers to remember is that their criteria for grading be consistent for each student. It is *not* as important that the criteria for one point or two points used by the Russian teacher be the same criteria used by the German teacher across the hall giving the same type of test. In very practical terms, the decision reached by a practicing classroom teacher in his/her classroom is an altogether different issue than one reached in an empirical study of evaluating student speaking skills.

In the *Snapshot Similarities Test*, students were graded on a zero to four point scale in two areas: amount of communication and comprehensibility. In other tests, they were graded on fluency and effort to communicate. The following descriptions were given and modeled for students:

AMOUNT OF COMMUNICATION: The quality of information which the student is able to convey concerning each picture.

- 0 = No information was conveyed by the student.
- 1 = Very little information conveyed.
- 2 = Some relevant information was conveyed.
- 3 = A fair amount of information was conveyed. Speaks without much hesitation.
- 4 = Most or all information was conveyed. Speaks without much hesitation.

COMPREHENSIBILITY:

- 0 = Could not understand anything the student said.
- 1 = Could only understand a few isolated words.
- 2 = Could understand a few phrases.
- 3 = Could comprehend some short, simple sentences.
- 4 = Could comprehend all or most of what the student said.

FLUENCY:

- 0 = No student response.
- 1 = Very halting, fragmented speech. Several "starts and restarts."
- 2 = Occasional halting speech. Some smoothness is use of short phrases or word clusters.

3 = Hardly any unnatural pauses, fairly effortless delivery.

4 = Almost effortless and smooth, but still perceptibly non-native.

EFFORT TO COMMUNICATE:

0 = No student response.

1 = Resorts to one-word responses to get his message across.

2 = Uses a very generic phrase to communicate.

3 = Incorporates appropriate phrases and vocabulary to get message across.

4 = Makes an almost over-zealous effort to communicate and uses almost all possible verbal resources to express himself.

"A fair amount of information" vs. "most or all information" must be defined by the classroom teacher, and will naturally change as the year progresses. Students shouldn't need to guess what the teacher expects; they should know. An excellent way to achieve this objective is frequent modeling during classroom activities using the same guidelines.

The important thing for teachers to remember is that they don't have to always use the exact same criteria as the teacher next door. Just as one woman's criteria for a "4-point kiss" are different from her neighbor's criteria, the husband only has to know the "rules" to satisfy the interested party! At a certain point in the year, adequate use of vocabulary or solid pronunciation may be emphasized by the teacher in Room 205, and comprehensibility and amount of effort is more in tune with the teacher in Room 201. There is certainly room for the personality of the teacher, as well as that of the student in this type of creative testing.

With teacher in-service training before teachers begin administering and evaluating such tests, there will be a consensus among the foreign language department concerning definitions of terms such as fluency and comprehensibility. But again, the differences in opinion concerning the quality of any student response may be as varied as the differences in opinion concerning the quality of a kiss, or the sincerity of a laugh.

In the *Look Who's Talking Test*, students were evaluated on fluency and effort to communication. Fluency is a term that needs to be explained to students. When they ask their teacher, "Are you fluent in Spanish?", they are asking whether the teacher knows every word that ever existed in the Spanish language! For the purpose of the test, fluency is defined as overall smoothness, continuity of thought, and naturalness of speech. Effort to communicate was added as a category because students will, by their very nature, try to find the loopholes in all types of grading systems. When they began to use the same generic answer over and over again, such as "There are people in the picture," or "It is nice weather," the author decided something had to be done to encourage more variety in effort put into the answers. Therefore, effort to communicate was defined as a student's willingness to express himself.

When students realize they will be rewarded for being more creative with what they have learned with the language and for putting in that little extra effort, their interest increases. Just getting by with the magical, "guess what the teacher is thinking" answer is now replaced with a "look what I can do" kind of answers. In the author's case, students who consistently made A or B on achievement tests were more challenged by this open-ended kind of testing, and those students who consistently made C or D on the achievement tests were more encouraged to try. Since accuracy of grammar and spelling were not the issues on these tests, many students saw hope for the first time in achieving a good grade. Testing had finally had a positive influence on learning!

The perceived subjectivity in grading is only one of the problems associated with this type of evaluation. Lack of time, lack of available tests, and difficulty in test administration are all deterrents to jumping into proficiency-oriented testing. As Genesee (1984) reminds us, "the viability and utility of any testing program depends on its being practical and efficient" (p. 139). There are few proficiency-oriented models to look at on the high school level. This scarcity, according to Huebner (1992), is because of "the perceived difficulty of implementing oral proficiency interview testing at this level" (p. 107). However, the one-on-one 30-minute interview is only one avenue for assessing proficiency. The problem posed for local school districts in implementing this kind of testing is in deciding how to assess oral proficiency in an accurate and economical manner. The most obvious solution to alleviate the time strain on teachers is to test more than one student at a time.

Teachers in secondary settings often opt for taped performance because they can simultaneously conduct other activities or even administer the listening test via a modern language lab. According to Elaine Phillips (1988), the university setting does not pose the same problem as in high school. "University teachers have the advantage of using their office hours and other time outside of class for oral exams, and as they seldom last more than a few minutes, students rarely object" (p. 57). In most cases, this luxury of time is not afforded the high school teacher. However, there are some exceptions! In the Campbell Union High School project (Huebner), the district released their teachers for two days to test students. Each teacher interviewed approximately twenty students per day on a one-on-one basis in a quiet room. This is highly unlikely to happen in most secondary school settings.

# Testing Speaking Skills in Various Foreign Language Program Types

If testing students in pairs, the teacher can do on-the-spot grading and evaluate a class of 30 students in one and one-half hours, according to the work done by Gonzalez Pino (1989). This could take up to three days of class time, depending on whether only half or the whole class period is taken up with testing. In another configuration, a class of thirty could be divided into fifteen numbered pairs. Using three cassette tape recorders in the class, Gonzales Pino assigned five pairs of students to each tape recorder. The pairs rotate within their groups as they complete the speaking task. Three groups of two students each would be recording simultaneously. However, without the option of on-the-spot grading, the teacher must take three 20-minute tapes home with her to grade. When grading tapes for five classes, it would require approximately five hours of grading outside class.

Another solution to the problem of large groups undertaking oral testing comes from a project in the Columbus Public Schools (Robison, 1992). In making decisions concerning the administration of speaking tests, small group testing was used. In the Columbus model, each team is called by the teacher to perform a two-to-three-minute speaking task. Results showed that 24 students can be tested and graded in 25 minutes. Each team member is scored individually rather than as part of a group.

As Bartz (1991) points out, teachers need to develop and evaluate various assessment strategies to apply to a variety of situations and purposes. What is successful for one teacher might not be appropriate at all for another. In the Indiana Project, it was concluded that four situations are generally possible in most classroom settings: evaluation in groups, single-student evaluation with whole-class involvement, evaluation in pairs, and single-student evaluation interview.

The author has found that language lab technology greatly assisted in test administration with single-student evaluation with the whole class involved in the testing process at the same time. With the assistance of a language lab, the teacher simultaneously gives a speaking, listening, and writing test to a class of 35 students. The class is divided into three groups. In the author's classes, each section of the test could be administered in twelve minutes. The speaking tests would have the questions pre-recorded with built-in pauses in which the students respond. The listening tape with true and false statements about certain visuals is started simultaneously for another group of students.

At the students' request, even when there might be a written section added, they wanted to listen to something through their headsets to isolate them from the rest of the group. This gave the author an opportunity to share her '70s environmental sound music with a whole new generation! At the end of twelve minutes, the teacher would change the student channel, and another portion of the test would be administered. With the "on-the-spot" grading employed by the author, she could monitor each student four times via the lab to listen for speaking samples. The students taking the test do not know when they are being monitored and graded, so they must answer every question. In this way, there is no "dead time" for the students waiting their turn. If they aren't being graded, they are getting more speaking practice than they would simply waiting for their turn. All students listen to all questions, and respond to each question.

Students in the Putnam City Schools in Oklahoma City, where the author first started using the speaking-test formats on a district-wide basis reported feeling more at ease while taking the speaking tests in a language lab setting. From comments in the student surveys at the end of the year, they said they had always been very nervous before about coming to the teacher's desk to take the test, and that it made them very uneasy to know that each time they opened their mouths they were being graded. They felt there was no room for error. Additionally, they complained that before the lab, they were embarrassed that others were listening and sometimes snickering while they were trying to speak for the test. As foreign language teachers, we know that this anxiety destroys any naturalness that we were trying to achieve through a one-on one interview. The chapter by Barr-Harrison and Horwitz in this volume provides further insights on the topic of anxiety. The author is not suggesting that the types of tests described in this chapter be used instead of the tests already part of the testing program, but, rather, that they become an important addition. As Terry (1986) points out, "without an appropriate and sufficient grammar base, no one can communicate effectively using only a list of vocabulary words" (p. 524).

The primary reason for change in any classroom is to enhance the learning for the students. Foreign language students are the big winners in this new approach to teaching/testing/assessment. Students are rewarded for what they know, and that is positive reinforcement!

It is important for second language teachers to respond to each student's abilities and interests. All students can get to the "top" in something, but not necessarily in the same way. A popular motto in the U.S. is "All students can learn." Bumper stickers have been plastered over cars and buttons worn to promote this positive attitude. Yes, all students can learn, but not all on the same day and not all in the same way.

Our tests must reflect diversity and allow us as educators to play different types of music to our listening audiences in the classroom. To play the same old song year after year is like the message the author saw on a poster in a colleague's classroom. It said, "Don't try to teach a pig to sing. It's a waste of time, and besides it annoys the pig." To continually use the same routines to teach, test, and assess is inadvisable. Whatever approaches we select as professionals, a match between our instruction and our evaluation strategies is essential!

# Notes

[1]The theme of teddy bears worked well and was not viewed as being juvenile by secondary students. In fact, they seemed to be less self conscious talking about bears than about themselves. However, any theme can be used in place of bears.

[2]Refer to Grant Wiggin's chapter in this volume.

# References

Alderson, J.C. Does washback exist? Paper presented at a Symposium on the Educational and Social Impacts of Language Tests, Language Testing Research Colloquium, Feb., 1992. ERIC ED 345 513, 23 p.

Barnwell, D. Proficiency and the schools. Paper presented at the Annual Meeting of the Central States Conference on the Teaching of Foreign Languages. Nashville, TN, April 1989. ERIC ED 319 743, 20p.

Bartz, W.H. Are They Learning What We're Teaching? Assessing Language Skills in the Classroom. In L.A. Strasheim, (Ed.), *Focus on the foreign language learner: Priorities and strategies*. Report of Central States Conference on the Teaching of Foreign Languages, Lincolnwood, IL: National Textbook Company, 1991.

Canale, M. The method effect in communicative testing. *Medium*, 1981, *6*, 4. ERIC ED 217 695, 7p.

Cooper, T.C. A survey of teacher concerns. *Foreign Language Annals*, 1985 *18*, 1, 21–50.

Genesee, F. Psycholinguistic foundations of language assessment. In C. Rivera, (Ed.), *Communicative competence approaches to language proficiency assessment: Research and application*. Papers presented at the Language Proficiency Assessment Symposium, March, 1984. Warrenton, VA. ERIC ED 249 793, 170 p.

Halleck, G.B. The oral proficiency interview: Discrete point test or a measure of communicative language ability? *Foreign Language Annals*, 1982, *25*, (3), 227–31.

Huebner, T. A study of foreign language proficiency-based testing in secondary schools. *Foreign Language Annals*, 1992, *25*, (2), 105–15.

Levine, M.G., and Haus, G.J. The accuracy of teacher judgment of the oral proficiency of high school foreign language students. *Foreign Language Annals*, 1987, *20*, (1), 45–50.

Liskin-Gasparro, J. *Testing and teaching for oral proficiency*. Heinle and Heinle, 1987.

Magnan, S.S. Proficiency in perspective in the foreign language classroom. ERIC ED 285 416, 9p.

Medley, F. Designing the proficiency based curriculum. In A.C. Omaggio, (Ed.), *Proficiency, curriculum, evaluation: The ties that bind.* Middlebury, VT: Northeast Conference, 1985.

Phillips, E.M. Overcoming difficulties in testing oral competency: A discussion of facilitating factors. Texas Papers in Foreign Language Education, 1988, *1*, 1, pp. 55–69, ERIC ED 345 467 16p.

Phillips, J.K. Teachers working with teachers: Becoming proficient with proficiency. ERIC ED 336 940, 12p.

Gonzalez Pino, B. Proachievement testing of speaking, *Foreign Language Annals*, 1987, *22*, (5), 487–97.

Rivers, W. Testing and student learning. Paper presented at the First International Conference of the Association of Teachers of English to Speakers of Other Languages, Dublin, Ireland, June, 1973. ERIC ED 086 003, 24p.

Robison, R.E. Developing practical speaking tests for the foreign language classroom: A small group approach. *Foreign Language Annals*, 1992, *25*, (6), 487–94.

Shohamy, E. Language testing priorities: A different perspective. *Foreign Language Annals*, 1990, *23*, (5), 385–93.

Terry, R.M. Testing the productive skills: A creative focus for hybrid achievement tests. *Foreign Language Annals*, 1986, *19*, (6), 521–30.

# Listening Skills: Acquisition and Assessment

Donna Reseigh Long

Janice Lynn Macián

*The Ohio State University*

## Introduction

A s both a medium and an objective of instruction, listening plays a unique role in the second language acquisition process. With the advent of the proficiency movement of the 1980s, there came an awareness of the complex nature of listening and its importance as a communication skill, as well as a recognition of the role listening plays in language acquistion. The 1986 Northeast Conference Reports presented a dual perspective on listening with two articles: Listening in the Native Language (Coakley and Wolvin, 1986) and Listening in the Second Language (Joiner, 1986). These articles reviewed the relevant research and highlighted similarities and differences in acquisition of listening skills in the native (L1) and second languages (L2). Listening, the cornerstone skill of language acquisition, is now securely established as an important topic within the second language research and instructional community. The present article provides readers with an update of the 1986 articles, links listening theory to instruction, and culminates with implications for authentic assessment.

# Theoretical Bases

Listening theory has been greatly influenced in recent years by the field of cognitive science. We now know that listening comprehension is not primarily receptive in nature, but rather an active process of constructing knowledge (Rost, 1990). In terms of relevance theory (Sperber and Wilson, 1986), communication is a collaborative process consisting of a speaker's production of signals and a listener's contextualization of those signals. The information itself consists of two layers: the actual speech and the speaker's intention. In order to comprehend, the listener must somehow connect the two layers of information in a meaningful way. According to relevance theory, misunderstandings, when they occur, result mainly from the listener's inability to establish this connection. Because L2 learners have less than full control of the target language, they are even more prone to such misunderstandings.

Models of L1 listening detailed by Witkin (1990) also hold promise for L2 listening research. Descriptive speech communication models[1] conceptualize the processes used by effective listeners within the total context of the communication process. Elements of such models include auditory and visual elements of reception, perception, discrimination, and response, as well as both cognitive and affective elements. Cognitive models[2] combine analyses of attention and memory processes, both of which are integral components of listening. From the field of speech science come models of auditory perception and processing that focus on the internal, perceptual processes in listening[3]. Qualitative models, though largely based on observation rather than experimentation, focus on empathy, mutual engagement of listener and speaker, feedback, attention and other humanistic aspects of listening.[4]

Finally, message processing[5] models incorporate world knowledge, speech act theory, and the sensory system.

# L2 Listening Knowledge Base

Teaching and assessment of listening skills should reflect the results of listening research. Since the 1986 Northeast Conference Reports were published, researchers have continued to make progress in their understanding of L2 learners' listening processes. Nevertheless, it is clear that there is still a great need for study in this area. In 1986, Barker and Fitch-Hauser reviewed the literature and found 315 variables related to L1 listening. Although it is probably safe to assume that many of the same variables are applicable to L2 listening comprehension, only a small fraction have been studied empirically. Table 1 summarizes the variables that have contributed to our present knowledge about L2 listening. It is followed by an overview of the pertinent studies published since 1986.

| Table 1. L2 Listening Variables | | |
|---|---|---|
| *Focus on Text* | *Focus on Listener* | *Focus on Speaker* |
| authenticity<br>background knowledge<br>  • advance organizers<br>    (verbal and visual)<br>  • cultural context<br>  • form of text<br>  • topic familiarity<br>difficulty of input<br>kinesic behavior<br>kinesic behavior<br>position of sentence<br>sentence length<br>visual contextual cues<br>word rate | acuity<br>apprehension<br>high school L2 study<br>instructional approach<br>L1 listening ability<br>L1 transfer<br>motivation<br>strategic processing | audience design<br>gender<br>perceived expertness |

## Focus on the Text

The majority of L2 listening research has focused on specific characteristics of listening texts and their effects on comprehension. For example, Glisan's 1985 study of L2 listening in adult learners of Spanish revealed that *word order* significantly affects comprehension of oral passages. The basic subject-verb-object (SVO) pattern, which occurs in both English and Spanish, was not only the easiest for L2 learners to comprehend, but results indicate that learners may also utilize strategic processing to mentally convert other patterns (e.g., VSO, OVS) to the SVO order. Glisan also found that longer sentences placed at the end of a passage were comprehended best. Hellebrandt (1990) examined the effects of *authentic* vs. *less authentic* videotapes and audiotapes on student's listening comprehension in Spanish. The term authentic text refers to materials that are produced by and for native speakers, such as radio and television broadcasts. Although the results of this study were inconclusive, data indicate that the question merits further research.

Kellerman (1992) surmises that *kinesic effects* (body movement) are an integral part of communicative competence and merit research in the L2 learning/teaching context. Although at present, it is unknown how L2 learners utilize kinesic behavior in decoding speech, and the question of transfer of kinesic behavior across cultures must be investigated. Although many learners find video texts more comprehensible than audio texts, Long (1991) found that some learners are unable to process video texts effectively. Such listeners find that the visual track distracts their attention from the audio message, or they focus so intently on the audio track that they miss important visual cues to comprehension. Further study is indicated in order to determine a more comprehensive profile for these listeners.

Rader-Ritz (1990) studied the effects of *word rate* on comprehension in college-level students of Spanish. She found a positive, but not statistically significant, relationship between slower word rates (135% and 150%) achieved through computerized speech expansion techniques and listening comprehension of authentic texts by third-quarter students. One possible explanation for the surprising lack of significance may have been the total control of background knowledge in the study. Because they lacked any prior knowledge of the text topics, subjects' potential for comprehension may have been minimized. Schmidt-Rinehart (1992) investigated the effects of *topic recognition* (one aspect of background knowledge) on subjects' comprehension of spoken Spanish. Her research showed conclusively that familiarity with the topic aids learners' comprehension of authentic audio listening texts. Long (1990) found similar results with authentic reading texts adapted for oral presentation. Markham and Latham (1987) found a strong relationship between adult ESL students' *religious background* and their comprehension of a passage associated with their particular religion. While this is the expected result, the study highlights the need for a better understanding of background information and how it can be applied to the development of L2 listening comprehension.

## Focus on the Listener

Knowing how learners process oral input is essential to the planning of effective instruction and assessment. However, learner characteristics affecting listening comprehension have been studied less than textual characteristics because of the complexities involved in eliciting research data. As listening is a covert skill, researchers must design data elicitation techniques that provide an accurate representation of their internal processes. Commonly, the techniques of simultaneous introspection (*think aloud*) and immediate retrospection (*immediate recall protocol*) are used in listening research, but as Færch and Kaspar (1987) have stressed, a combination of methods is necessary in order to achieve a more complete understanding of learners' "declarative knowledge, their communication and learning processes, and of the affective and social aspects that interact with the cognitive dimension" (p. 19).

*Apprehension* was found to have a significant negative effect on listener's comprehension in a study by Aneiro (1989). Conversely, college-level Puerto Rican EFL/ESL students also demonstrated lower apprehension rates as their linguistic proficiency increased. Aneiro's findings indicated that different types of listening environments produced differing degrees of apprehension in L2 learners. Most stressful were one-on-one conversations followed by group communication and TV watching. Using the Natural Approach as a method of instruction, White (1988) found that beginning college level students of Spanish were less anxious and better able to extract meaning from listening texts when instructed with a Natural Approach than were students instructed with a typical four-skill cognitive approach.

Bacon (1992b) studied the *strategic processing* of authentic audio listening texts by successful and less-successful L2 listeners. Using the stages model (perceptual, parsing, and utilization) outlined by O'Malley, Uhl-Chamot, and Küpper (1989) as the theoretical basis for the study, Bacon found that successful listeners moved from bottom-up (word-based) strategies in the perceptual stage to top-down (schema-based) strategies during the parsing stage. Recognizing the difficulty in studying covert listening skills, Laviosa (1991) used a combination of case-study and empirical approaches in determining the types of problems encountered by L2 learners, their strategies in coping with listening texts, and the correlation between such problems and strategies. Laviosa's research identified nine common listening problems, three planning processes, seven strategies, and demonstrated a significant relationship between problems and strategy use.

Feyton (1988) found a significant relationship between general L1 *listening ability* and overall L2 proficiency. In her study of college level students of French and Spanish, significant correlations were found between scores on the video version of the Watson-Barker Listening Test (1984) and locally developed tests of linguistic proficiency.

Stelly (1991) used authentic French stories in a *whole language approach* to study high school students' listening and reading comprehension, as well as their attitudes toward learning French. Using both qualitative and quantitative techniques, Stelly's study revealed that learners following a whole language approach showed statistically significant results for listening and reading recall protocols, objective reading tests, increased vocabulary recognition, and ability to handle L2 structures. In addition, they expressed feelings of pride and satisfaction from their linguistic skills and from the interactive classroom activities.

In one of the first studies involving the ACTFL proficiency guidelines, Wagnild (1988) found significant positive correlations between years of *high school French study* and performance on locally-designed tests of listening, reading, speaking, and writing based on the ACTFL proficiency guidelines. Furthermore, Wagnild's results indicate that listening proficiency improves consistently over a four to five year period of French language study, in effect converting itself from the weakest to the strongest skill.

## Focus on the Speaker

Understanding native speakers is a primary goal of second language instruction, but only a few studies have centered on characteristics of the speaker of a given listening text. Lynch (1988) explored the possibility of recording spoken texts according to the modifications of discourse that native speakers make naturally when communicating directly with non-natives. Lynch's results indicated that videotaped recordings of such *modified discourse* are significantly more comprehensible for L2 learners than are the unmodified authentic speech that native speakers used with other native speakers.

Markham's (1988) study of the effects of *gender* and *perceived expertness* of the speaker revealed that intermediate-level ESL learners listened more attentively to male speakers than female, thus increasing their ability to recall the passage. However, the gender issue was neutralized when a female speaker was provided with an introduction concerning her qualifications as an expert in the subject matter.

## Future Research

Two decades of research have provided us with important insights into the L2 listening process. At the present time, it is clear that L2 learners use strategic processing and rely on life experiences in order to make sense of target language texts, just as they do in the native language. It is equally clear that there are impressive gaps in our knowledge base. For example, Coakley and Wolvin (1986) outlined the real-life purposes of listening:

- discriminative: distinguishing audio/visual stimuli
- comprehensive: understanding message
- therapeutic: serving as "sounding board" for speaker

- critical: evaluating message
- appreciative: enjoying/gaining sensory impression

L2 researchers have focused almost exclusively on academic (non-collaborative) listening, represented primarily by the discriminative and comprehensive categories. It is imperative, therefore, that conversational (collaborative) listening, become part of the research agenda and that therapeutic, critical, and appreciative types of listening be studied within L2 contexts. Other questions also remain open and have been indicated in the discussion sections of most of the articles and dissertations summarized above. Returning to Figure 1, the questions of authenticity, word rate, instructional approach, and kinesic behavior seem particularly pertinent to the teaching of foreign languages, especially with regard to the widespread popularity of authentic video materials at all levels of instruction. In spite of the sketchy present state of knowledge about L2 listening, instructors should reflect on the issues raised here in order to make educated decisions about text selection and relevant listening tasks.

# Authentic Texts

The primary goal of language teaching is to prepare learners to use the target language in real life. In order to comprehend and interact with native speakers in a wide variety of situations, learners must have ample opportunities to listen to different speech patterns in culturally appropriate contexts. Recent studies (Joiner, et al., 1989; Rogers and Medley, 1988; García et al., 1988; Herron and Seay, 1991; Bacon 1989, 1992a; Shrum and Glisan, 1994) emphasize the importance of authentic oral input at all stages of language learning. While it is generally accepted that learners at the intermediate and advanced levels benefit from exposure to authentic listening materials, Bacon (1992a) observed that even at the beginning level, learners who were exposed to authentic radio broadcasts successfully comprehended the unedited discourse. In today's classrooms, culturally authentic videotapes and direct satellite transmissions offer optimal learning experiences and prepare L2 learners to interact with native speakers. Although Bacon observed successful processing of authentic audio texts, Weissenrieder (1987) found televised news in Spanish to be fraught with comprehension difficulties for L2 learners. "We have seen that in performance, organization, and structures, the language of newscasting is motivated economically. Its condensed, telescoped form concentrates a higher information load in a reduced linguistic space" (p. 25).

Given this problem, Weissenrieder recommends a pedagogical approach that incorporates repeated sweeps of the text with narrowly-focused objectives for each sweep.

*Simulated authentic discourse* "refers to language produced for pedagogical purposes, but which exhibits features that have a high probability of occurrence in genuine acts of communication" (Omaggio, 1986, p. 128). Simulated discourse, typically used in taped instructional materials, may be unscripted or semiscripted. In unscripted conversations, native speakers are provided a scenario or context and are allowed to converse without restrictions or control of vocabulary, grammar structures, time, etc. In semiscripted conversations, speakers are given instructions to include specific vocabulary or structures in their conversations that relate to particular chapter themes or topics. Both types of texts, however, "reflect a naturalness of form, and an appropriateness of cultural and situational context that would be found in the language as used by native speakers" (Rogers and Medley, 1988, p. 268).

# Collaborative and Noncollaborative Listening

Structured activities using unmodified and simulated authentic discourse may be grouped into two major categories of discourse: collaborative and non-collaborative. *Collaborative discourse* involves communication between two or more people in which the speakers interact with each other based on each person's interpretations of the other speakers' verbal and nonverbal messages. "It is not preplanned, but is produced in ongoing time through mutual cooperation of a speaker and hearer who exchange a variety of verbal and nonverbal signals (Richards, 1983 p. 226)." Conversations that involve routines considered necessary for everyday kinds of communication such as telephone calls, greetings, or encouraging the speaker to continue talking are examples of collaborative discourse. *Noncollaborative discourse*, however, needs no interaction with another "live" speaker. It is simply an auditory message that requires some type of response by the listener. For example, listening to a speaker and taking notes, or listening to a telephone message from a toll-free information service and inputting the correct sequence of numbers to reach the appropriate department, require a physical or written response to an oral stimulus. Instructional materials frequently provide learners with practice in non-collaborative listening, leaving development of real-life collaborative skills to the instructor's discretion. Chart 1 outlines a variety of typical collaborative discourse skills that may be incorporated into the curriculum along with a sample listening activity.

Chart 1. Collaborative Discourse Skills

| | |
|---|---|
| identifying transition points | taking turns |
| providing obligatory responses | prompting |
| shifting the topic | reformulating |
| recognizing speaker's intent | querying |
| timing one's response | developing the discourse |
| aligning oneself with the speaker | setting rules for interpretation |
| coordinating purposes | checking understanding |

Example

| | |
|---|---|
| Objective: | Identifying transition points. |
| Level: | Intermediate to advanced. |
| Text: | A recorded conversation (audio or video) about a topic with which learners are familiar. Learners have a script of the conversation to follow as they listen. |
| Pre-listening: | Have learners generate L1 phrases that they would use to make transitions during a conversation. |
| Task: | As they listen to the conversation, learners mark the phrases that indicate transition points. |
| Post-listening: | Learners converse in pairs and practice the phrases that were used in the recorded conversation. |

# Listening Strategies

Recent work in learner strategies by O'Malley, Uhl-Chamot, and Küpper (1989, 1990) has revealed that L2 learners utilize three classes of listening strategies: *metacognitive* (planning, monitoring, evaluating), *cognitive* (manipulation of information), and *social/affective* (interaction with others). Table 2 shows a breakdown of the specific learner strategies self-reported by effective listeners in three studies (O'Malley, et al (1989); Long, 1991; Bacon 1992b). In the O'Malley, et al. study, subjects were Hispanic high school students of ESL, while Long and Bacon found similar strategic processing in adult learners of Spanish as a foreign language.

| Table 2. Effective L2 Listening Strategies | | |
|---|---|---|
| *Metacognitive* | *Cognitive* | *Social/Affective* |
| (re) direct attention to task<br>motivate self<br>apply advance organizer<br>devise plan<br>manage self<br>evaluate self<br>monitor comprehension<br>express interest (loss of interest)<br>preview text | listen for intonation/pauses<br>listen for phrases or sentences<br>infer meaning from context<br>elaborate<br>transfer L1<br>use resources<br>take notes<br>use world knowledge<br>use personal knowledge<br>focus on redundancy | avoid ridicule<br>appeal for help<br>ask for confirmation<br>reassure self |

Effective listeners make frequent use of top-down processing, with occasional, appropriate application of bottom-up strategies; ineffective listeners rely almost exclusively on the latter. *Top-down strategies* incorporate knowledge of the world in general and topic familiarity in particular, while *bottom-up strategies* typically focus on word recognition. Focusing and processing at the word level renders many L2 learners unable to take advantage of the more global (top-down) strategies and negatively affects their comprehension of the text. Chart 2 shows the interaction of top-down processing and bottom-up processing (Rost, 1990).

Chart 2. Interaction of Top-Down/Bottom-Up Processing

Schema (underlying linking structure)
Script (sequence of events or parts of text)
Concept (mental representation of current segment of text)
Formula (paragraph or other visual unit)
Phrase/sentence
Word/lexical item
Morpheme (unit of meaning)
Phoneme (sound)

# Listening Activities in the Native Language

Studies reviewed by Joiner (1986) recommended a training period in native language listening to prepare learners for the types of activities that they will encounter later in the target language. Training techniques are especially useful at the middle and secondary school levels, and can be incorporated into courses on study skills that are now often part of the curriculum (Gall et al., 1990). Many of the strategy applications developed by Omaggio (1986), Oxford (1990), and Shrum and Glisan (1994) can be used in the native language at the beginning level of instruction in order to sensitize learners about the strategies they will need when they encounter authentic L2 speech. Chart 3 provides examples of L1 training activities at the beginning and intermediate/advanced levels.

---

### Chart 3. L1 Training Activities

| | |
|---|---|
| Objective: | Recognition of key vocabulary. |
| Level: | Beginning. |
| Text: | Selection from L1 radio broadcast. |
| Pre-listening: | Learners skim a script with key words deleted. |
| Task: | Learners listen to broadcast for main idea. They listen a second time and fill in the words missing from the script. |
| Post-listening: | Learners retell the report to a partner, incorporating key words. |

| | |
|---|---|
| Objective: | Note taking. |
| Level: | Intermediate-advanced (involves not only recognition of key vocabulary but also topic recognition, recognizing referents, selecting main ideas). |
| Text: | Brief lecture on culture. |
| Pre-listening: | Review note taking strategies (recognizing main idea, paraphrasing drawing diagrams or charts, writing examples, etc.). |
| Task: | Learners take notes on the main points of the lecture as they listen. |
| Post-listening: | Compare and contrast what the learners perceived to be the main points. |

# Listening Activities in the Target Language

Frequently, beginning language learners erroneously believe that they must understand every word in order to comprehend a listening text. While this is certainly not the case, it is necessary for learners to engage in tasks that require an active mode of listening. Instructional activities for active listening are designed in three stages: *pre-listening activities* that familiarize learners with the overall theme or topic; *guidance activities* that provide cues for general information getting; and *post-listening activities* that require learners to synthesize collected facts and extend them to reading, writing, and speaking skills.

## Pre-Listening/-Viewing Activities

An area of second language instruction that has generated much interest is the use of *advance organizers* (Omaggio, 1979; Mueller, 1980; Adams, 1982). Advance organizers preview concepts that will be presented in listening texts and function as bridges to form a link between the learners' background knowledge and the new concepts that they are about to experience. Subjects who were given appropriate contextual information before listening to passages were better able to comprehend and recall the content than were subjects who were not supplied with a context. Unless learners are provided with some initial guidance by way of structured tasks, many are overwhelmed by a torrent of speech that washes over them because they do not know how to focus their attention. The use of advance organizers as guides to listening and viewing provide learners with the information needed to cope with linguistic, paralinguistic (gestures and other nonverbal elements), and cultural material.[6] Advance organizers may be presented *visually* by means of an illustration, photograph, or video segment without audio; *orally* by brainstorming about the topic in the native or target language; or *in writing* with a descriptive title, a short statement, or an excerpt from the text.

Advance organizers are particularly well suited for introducing cultural concepts. When L1 and L2 cultural contexts are similar (such as the type of information included in a weather reports) instructors can draw upon the students' common background knowledge and have them predict what types of information they would expect to hear. When L1 and L2 cultural contexts are different, however, (such as situations involving etiquette) the advance organizer can highlight the cultural differences and introduce related vocabulary. Chart 4 provides examples of advance organizers. The reader is also encouraged to read Zena Moore's chapter on assessing cultural knowledge via *portfolio assessment* in this volume.

---

Chart 4. Advance Organizers

**Similar L1/L2 contexts**

| | |
|---|---|
| Objective: | Understanding airport announcements |
| Level: | Beginning, intermediate |
| Text: | Airport announcements from public address system |
| Advance organizer: | Brainstorm information typically included in airport announcements; write words and phrases on the chalkboard or on an overhead transparency |
| Task: | Learners listen and identify the announcements |
| Post-listening: | Learners work in pairs and make up original announcements |

**Different L1/L2 contexts**

| | |
|---|---|
| Objective: | Comparing soccer and U.S. football |
| Level: | Intermediate, advanced |
| Text: | Video of soccer highlights |
| Advance organizer: | Learners share background knowledge about soccer; working in pairs, learners generate words and phrases used to describe soccer and football (including the locale, players, spectators, etc.) |
| Task: | Learners watch video of soccer highlights, focusing on similarities and differences with U.S. football |
| Post-listening: | Learners discuss the similarities and differences between the two sports |

---

## Guidance Activities

Effective *guidance activities* present listeners with a two-stage approach to listening. First-stage activities focus on the main idea of the listening text, while the second stage focuses on specific details. Guidance activities for the first listening should not be so complex that they distract learners from attending to the general meaning of the oral text. Typical stage-one guidance activities for beginners include multiple choice and matching, where the learners select a visual, a phrase, or a title that corresponds with the main idea of the text. Younger learners often enjoy drawing a picture of the main idea. More advanced learners can identify the main idea by writing a title or a summarizing phrase.

In stage two, when the text is played a second time, learners listen for details or for answers to specific questions. For beginning language learners, understanding the main idea and a few supporting details would be a sufficient goal. Stage-two guidance activities for beginners include answering true/false questions, filling in forms or charts, using check lists, ordering and sequencing, and tracing directions on a map. For intermediate level learners, guidance activities can incorporate writing and speaking skills, such as listing important details, answering content questions, completing sentences, and taking dictation. At the advanced level, listening tasks can require analysis of information from the text. Chart 5 provides examples of guidance activities for the beginning and intermediate levels.

---

### Chart 5. Guidance Activity Examples

**Beginning level**

| | |
|---|---|
| Stage 1: | Listen to the text. |
| Task: | Identify the product being advertised. |
| | (a) soap     (b) soft drink     (c) car |
| Stage 2: | Rewind and listen again. |
| Task: | Write down some of the product's superior qualities. |

**Intermediate level**

| | |
|---|---|
| Stage 1: | Listen to the text. |
| Task: | Write a phrase summarizing the text. |
| Stage 2: | Rewind and listen again. |
| Task: | Write instructions for using the product. |

---

## Post-Listening/-Viewing Activities

Post-listening activities may be divided into two types: comprehension checks and extension activities. *Comprehension checks* assess whether learners have understood the listening passage and are able to recall the information. Although comprehension checks may be either oral or written, the tasks must match the level of learner ability and follow a logical progression from the pre-listening and guidance listening stages. Easy comprehension checks for beginners include multiple-choice, true/false, and questions requiring single-word or short answers. At the intermediate level, learners can show comprehension of the text by describing, retelling, or summarizing. Advanced learners should be able to analyze and interpret the significance of the text.

*Extension activities* are integrative tasks that require listeners to react to what they have heard by examining the content of the text and relating it in new and innovative ways. Such activities require learners to extend the information beyond the text and use higher order skills such as creating an original alternative, condensing information, or predicting causes, relationships, and outcomes. Because listening is a social process, and both listening and speaking are integral parts of oral communication, post-listening tasks incorporate interaction among learners and practice of real world skills. For beginning and intermediate learners, extension activities could include writing memos and short letters, role-play, learner-to-learner questions, and show-and-tell. At the advanced level, learners can exchange observations and opinions, debate, and interview. Lund (1990) has developed a particularly elegant taxonomy of real-world listening tasks with sample activities. See Chart 6 for sample post-listening/-viewing activities.

---

Chart 6. Post-Listening Activities

Text: radio commercial

**Beginning level**

| | |
|---|---|
| Stage 1: | Comprehension |
| Function: | Describing |
| Task: | Speaking/Give three reasons why you would buy this product. |

| | |
|---|---|
| Stage 2: | Extension |
| Function: | Persuading |
| Task: | Writing—Working in pairs, select a product and write a commercial. |

**Intermediate level**

| | |
|---|---|
| Stage 1: | Comprehension |
| Function: | Giving directions |
| Task: | Speaking—Tell why your partner should buy the product. |

| | |
|---|---|
| Stage 2: | Extension |
| Purpose: | Protesting |
| Task: | Writing/Write a letter to the company, explaining why you do not like this product. |

---

# Listening Materials

Because of today's interest in authentic listening texts, *audiotaped materials* are experiencing a renewed emphasis in the foreign language learning process. Many textbook publishers have enriched the listening component of elementary and intermediate language programs by adding authentic listening materials, often on student cassettes. With the ever present Walkman, learners can now hear the foreign language anytime and anywhere, provided that they are motivated to do so and have access to high interest materials (Joiner, 1984).

*Songs* are also a valuable source of auditory input. According to Morgan (1988, 1993), "not only do songs provide tremendous appeal to L2 learners, but (they) are an authentic expression of the living language and culture. Music provides a slower medium than speech, and in so doing is easier for the learners to follow. The sung text is often not as artificial and full of 'reading pronunciations' as a slowly delivered spoken text" (p. 14). By using carefully selected pieces of music, teachers are able to provide learners with moderately paced speech that is more easily comprehensible without resorting to artificially slowed conversations that frequently occur in published materials. A selection of songs from various target language countries can also provide a singularly effective medium for the illustration of dialect variation in foreign languages.[7]

Of all the technological innovations in recent years, *video* is one of the most easily accessible and appealing. Videos provide learners with skills that are easily transferable to real-life situations and provide experiences that cannot be duplicated in traditional classrooms limited by instructor-student interaction (Noda, 1993; Secules et al., 1992). This medium provides learners with a context, an auditory message, and also offers nonverbal cues such as gestures, facial expressions, and body language. Video permits teachers to present learners with up-to-date, culturally authentic information. Video also provides an excellent opportunity for learners to observe the outcomes (turn-taking, pauses, encouragement) of collaborative listening strategies in context. Learners can be guided to observe not only the language that natives use but also become more aware of the nonverbal cues. These phrases can then be practiced as post-viewing extension activities and incorporated into classroom activities on a daily basis.

## Technological Innovations

Language laboratories have been transformed into sophisticated learning environments that enable students to interact not only with taped listening materials, but also with videos, satellite transmissions, digitized speech on computer, and other forms of educational technology. According to Shrum and Glisan "educational technology refers to the uses teachers and learners make of machines to systematize practical knowledge" (1994, p. 247). In 1987 and 1989 the American Council on the Teaching of Foreign Languages (ACTFL) published two volumes devoted exclusively to media and technology in the second language classroom. These volumes, *Modern Media in Foreign Language Education: Theory and Implementations* and *Modern Technology in Foreign Language Education: Applications and Projects*, offer readers chapter-length descriptions and research on topics ranging from language laboratories to interactive video and provide an excellent point of departure for those who seek information about interactive video, computer-assisted language learning (CALL), technology-enhanced distance learning, and communication-based software. Recent research[8] reveals that by using these devices to complement live instruction the foreign language teaching profession is striving to better prepare students to interact with native speakers on a much more realistic and meaningful level. The information reported from instructors using technology in the classroom can also be used to prepare students to communicate efficiently with technology in the target language.

Designing and implementing classroom activities that provide learners with opportunities to interact with technology and to practice collaborative and non-collaborative listening via machines adds another practical dimension to language learning. One common technological interaction that many learners will encounter is a conversation on the telephone. Studies in distance learning (teleconferencing via satellite with or without video support)[9] revealed several problems observed during telephone conversations between learners and native speakers. For example, when learners could not answer in a normal response time, the native speaker sometimes switched to English. Learners experienced difficulty in comprehending colloquial expressions used by native speakers and free communication was often difficult because of the lack of language skills by the nonnative speaker. Use of speaker phones for conversations with multiple participants sometimes resulted in long awkward silences and confusion about the speaker's identity. Finally, learners spent much time conveying information in a descriptive rather than a conversational manner.

When structuring authentic or simulated telephone communication tasks, many of the above problems can be solved by pre- and post-conferencing activities: reviewing discourse features and interactional problems (such as opening gambits and turn-taking), reviewing main ideas to be discussed during the conversation, reviewing useful words and expressions related to the topic, discussing the information that has been exchanged, taping conversations for later analysis, discussing grammar errors, and analyzing conversations at the level of discourse (taking turns, paraphrasing, using repairs, etc.). Chart 7 shows applications that have been structured to invite realistic exchanges between learners and native speakers using a variety of technological devices.

---

Chart 7. Activities for Practicing Collaborative
and Noncollaborative Strategies

**Collaborative discourse**
- Call native speaker and carry on brief conversation.
- Role-play telephone conversation with instructor.
- Respond to telephone survey (computerized).

**Noncollaborative discourse in language lab or
in class with audiocassette**
- Listen to messages left on voice mail and copy information (name of caller, number, message).
- Leave message on answering machine and gives information (namer, number, message).
- Listen to recordings on 800 or 900 numbers and select appropriate message or take notes.
- Eavesdrop on staged telephone conversations and take notes.

---

# Assessing Listening Skills

As Dunkel et al. (1993) have pointed out, assessment of L2 listening comprehension is problematic for two reasons: first, there is the lack of consensus on the components of listening and factors affecting comprehension and, second, there are the difficulties in designing appropriate assessment techniques. In an attempt to address these concerns, this research group has proposed a tentative model, upon which tests of listening comprehension may be constructed. A complex framework incorporates the person, components, purpose, tasks, response category, scoring method, leveling variables, competence category, sample characteristics, cognitive operation, and sociocultural context of listening comprehension. Although this framework is still tentative, it demonstrates clearly the complexity of the listening construct and offers researchers and test developers a point of departure for further investigation.

Most tests of L2 listening are developed by classroom teachers to fit the specific needs and goals of their own programs. It is recognized that "pure" listening comprehension is probably not being measured by locally-produced instruments, but rather a hybrid variable consisting of multiple listening skills. Enmeshed in those skills are the academic purposes of listening assessment: recognizing the message, checking comprehension, delivering information, diagnosing listening problems, determining proficiency level, ascertaining general listening capability, and identifying listening strategies.

As Wiggins (1990) maintains, the key to authentic assessment is to design tasks that simulate real world tests of ability. In some instances, academic listening purposes do conform directly with real life (recognizing the message, delivering information, checking comprehension), but in other instances the challenge is to identify real-life tasks that will elicit the skills and performances implicit in the academic objectives. It becomes the task of the test designer to align such academic assessment purposes with real world listening tasks and to design valid and reliable tests that conform to Wiggin's criteria of authenticity: effective performance with acquired knowledge, a full array of instructional tasks, and polished, thorough, and justifiable answers, performances, or products. Given these assumptions, a tripartite approach is recommended for the design of authentic listening assessments, as shown in Chart 8.

While discrete-point exercises may encourage guessing on the part of the student, the other response formats are more global in nature and require the use of integrative skills. Clearly, many assessment techniques work equally well as tests and as instructional activities, but in either case it is important to match the purpose for the activity with the optimal stimulus and an appropriate response format. For example, if the assessment purpose is identifying listening strategies, then a response format that allows listeners to reflect on and identify their strategic processing must be elected. In addition, a medium that allows for such reflection must also be identified. Thus, a think aloud response format might be paired with an audiotape stimulus that allows listeners to stop the input and reflect on how they are processing the text. A second tape recorder could be used to capture the listener's introspective comments or an assessor could simply take notes as the listener thinks out loud.

---

### Chart 8. Listening Assessment Procedures

Determine the purpose of the assessment:
    ☐ academic       ☐ real life

Select a stimulus:
    ☐ authentic text     ☐ monologue     ☐ audio only
    ☐ video            ☐ realistic text    ☐ dialogue
    ☐ audio + static visual ☐ video + computer

Determine a compatible response format:
*Academic responses*
☐ discrete-point exercises (multiple choice, true/false, matching,
      checklist, visual identification)
☐ complete open-ended statements
☐ dictation
☐ immediate recall protocol (writing main idea and details)
☐ information grid (fill-in)
☐ cloze (fill in words missing from text)
☐ content question/answer
☐ think aloud, written introspection

*Realistic responses*
☐ respond orally
☐ gist (state main idea)
☐ paraphrase
☐ summarize/condense
☐ act out response
☐ transfer to another skill (e.g., take a message, fill in a form)
☐ converse

# Conclusion

In his call for a commitment to authentic assessment in education, Wiggins (1990) emphasized incorporation of real-world tasks into the instructional process. In order to accomplish such a mandate within the context of second language teaching and learning, educators need to take a realistic look at the skills and concepts that comprise the objectives of instruction, as well as the techniques being used to carry out that instruction. The reader is encouraged to read Wiggins' chapter in this volume.

In the case of listening skills, L2 learners and educators are in position to take advantage of recent theoretical and technological advances. As a result of a rapidly-expanding knowledge base, our understanding of L2 listening processes has improved dramatically. Technology is playing a steadily increasing role in listening assessment, as well as instruction. Many schools and universities are equipped today with high-quality cassette decks, compact disc players, and videocassette recorders to deliver input. Various sources offer authentic audio and video materials that may be used for both instructional and assessment purposes, and most textbook packages today feature activities and materials for teaching and testing listening skills. Prototype microcomputer-based listening comprehension proficiency tests that incorporate digitized speech have been developed for French and ESL (Dunkel, 1988), and standardized tests like the Watson-Barker (1984) evaluate overall listening abilities of learners in different age groups.

Given the present context of second language listening research and teaching, we can no longer declare that listening is the forgotten skill nor assume that listening skills will develop on their own. As Evans (1984) has pointed out, listening still seems somewhat undervalued in society, for although most people strive to be both good talkers and good listeners, good talkers are often reinforced and rewarded more than are good listeners. As a result, when instruction mirrors society, listening instruction can also become undervalued. Joiner's 1986 challenge, therefore, is still pertinent today: "the complexity of listening, its primacy in language learning, and its centrality in language use in the real world all argue for the combined efforts of researchers and teachers in many related disciplines" (p. 68). Let us shoulder the challenge as professionals and provide meaningful listening opportunities for foreign language learners.

# Notes

[1]See Coakley and Wolvin (1986).
[2]See Miller's 1956 article, now a classic, cited in Witkin.
[3]See Sanders (1977) cited in Witkin.
[4]See Purdy (1986a, 1986b) cited in Witkin.
[5] See van Dijk and Kintsch (1983), cited in Witkin.
[6]Suggestions for development of activities and use of video in the classroom are given by Altman (1989); Darst (1991); Liontas (1991, 1992); Joiner (1990); and Narváez (1992).

[7]For suggestions on music selection, preparation, teaching techniques, evaluation, and bibliography see Purcell (1992), Abrate (1992), Anton (1990), and Trapp (1991).

[8]For research in interactive video, see Fletcher (1990); for distance learning, see Gallego (1992); for computer assisted language learning, see Schrier and Fast (1992).

[9] Reports on distance learning by Wohlert (1989), Eddy (1989), Gallego (1992), Warriner-Burke (1990), Sussex (1991), and Yi, et al. 1993) provide a wealth of information that classroom instructors can use when designing activities for telephone communication. The chapter in this volume by Boyles has practical suggestions for telephone conversations, particularly using message machines. She also links speaking and listening activities.

# References

Abrate, J. The popular song: An authentic tool for enriching the foreign language classroom. In W. Hatfield (Ed.), *Creative approaches in foreign language teaching.* Lincolnwood. IL: National Textbook Company, 1992.

Adams, S.J. Scripts and recognition of unfamiliar vocabulary: enhancing second language reading skills. *The Modern Language Journal,* 1982, *66,* 155–59.

Altman, R. *The video connection.* Boston: Houghton Mifflin, 1989.

Aneiro, S.M. The influence of receiver apprehension in foreign language learners on listening comprehension among Puerto Rican college students. Unpublished Ph.D. dissertation, New York University, 1989.

Anton, R.J. Combining singing and psychology. *Hispania,* 1990, *73,* 1166–70.

Bacon, S.M. Authentic listening in Spanish: how learners adjust their strategies to the difficulty of the input. *Hispania,* 1992, *75,* 398–412.

Bacon, S.M. Listening for real in the foreign language classroom. *Foreign Language Annals,* 1989, *22,* 543–50.

Bacon, S.M. Phases of listening to authentic input in Spanish: A descriptive study. *Foreign Language Annals,* 1992, *25,* 317–34.

Barker, D.R., and Fitch-Hauser, M. *Variables related to the reception and processing of information as published in ten selected psychology journals 1976–1986.* (Working paper presented to the Research Task Force of the International Listening Association, New Orleans, 1986.)

Byrnes, H. The role of listening comprehension: A theoretical base. *Foreign Language Annals,* 1984, *17,* 317–29.

Coakley, C.G., and Wolvin, A.D. Listening in the native language. In B.H. Wing (Ed.) *Listening, reading, and writing: analysis and application.* Middlebury, VT: Northeast Conference, 1986.

Darst, D.H. Spanish video materials in the classroom. *Hispania ,*1991, *74,* 1087–90.

Dunkel, P., Henning, G., and Chaudron, C. The assessment of an L2 listening comprehension construct: A tentative model for test specification and development. *The Modern Language Journal*, 1993, *77*, 180–91.

Dunkel, P.A. *Computer-assisted testing (CAT) of listening comprehension proficiency in English as a second language: The development of a prototype.* Columbus, OH: Research perspectives in adult language learning and language acquisition, 1988.

Eddy, B.D. Interactive tele-classes from Germany. In W.F. Smith (Ed.), *Modern technology in foreign language edition: Applications and projects.* Lincolnwood, IL: National Textbook Company, 1986.

Evans, C. On comprehension. *British Journal of Language Teaching*, 1984, *22*, 23–27.

Færch, K., and Kasper, G. From product to process: Introspective methods in second language research. In Færch, K., and Kasper, G. (Eds.) *Introspection in second language research.* Philadelphia: Multilingual Matters, 1987.

Feyton, C.M. Towards establishing the relationship between listening ability and foreign language acquisition: Defining a new area of inquiry. Unpublished Ph.D. dissertation, University of South Florida, 1988.

Fletcher, W.H. Authentic interactive video for lower-level Spanish at the United States Naval Academy. *Hispania*, 1990, *73*, 859–65.

Gall, M.D., Gall J., Jacobsen D., and, Bullock, T. *Tools for learning: A guide to teaching study skills.* Alexandria, Virginia: Association for Supervision and Curriculum Development Press, 1990.

Gallego, J.C. Tele-classes: the way of the future: A report on a language exchange via satellite. *Foreign Language Annals*, 1992, *25*, 51–58.

García, C., Scott, C., and Bruhn, W. Activities for building students' proficiency in Spanish classes. In J.F. Lalande II (Ed.), *Shaping the future of foreign language education: FLES, articulation, and proficiency.* Lincolnwood. IL: National Textbook Company, 1988.

Geddes, M., and White, R. The use of semi-scripted simulated authentic speech in listening comprehension. *Audiovisual Language Journal*, 1978, *16*, 137–45.

Glisan, E.W. The effect of word order on listening comprehension and pattern retention: An experiment in Spanish as a foreign language. *Language Learning*, 1985, *35*, 443–72.

Hellebrandt, J. The effects of authentic Spanish video and audio on measures of listening comprehension of learners of Spanish. Unpublished Ph.D. dissertation, Purdue University, 1990.

Herron, C., and Seay, I. The effect of authentic oral texts on student listening comprehension in the foreign language classroom. *Foreign Language Annals*, 1991, *24*, 487–95.

Joiner, E. Choosing and using videotexts. *Foreign Language Annals*, 1990, *23*, 53–64.

Joiner, E.G. Listening from the inside out. *Foreign Language Annals*, 1984, *17*, 335–38.

Joiner, E.G. Listening in the foreign language. In B.H. Wing (Ed.), *Listening, reading, and writing: Analysis and application.* Middlebury, VT: Northeast Conference, 1986.

Joiner, E., Adkins, P., and Eyken, L. Skimming and scanning with Champs-Elysées: Using authentic materials to improve foreign language listening. *French Review*, 1989, *62*, 427–35.

Kellerman, S. 'I see what you mean': the role of kinesic behaviour in listening and implications for foreign and second language learning. *Applied Linguistics*, 1992, *13*, 239–58.

Laviosa, F. A preliminary investigation of the listening problem-solving processes and strategies of five advanced learners of Italian as a second language. Unpublished Ph.D. dissertation, State University of New York at Buffalo, 1991.

Liontas, J. Authentic videos in the foreign language classroom. In L.A. Strasheim (Ed.), *Focus on the foreign language learner: Priorities and strategies.* Lincolnwood. IL:

National Textbook Company, 1991.

Liontas, J.I. From the living room to the classroom: Working with authentic Spanish language videos. *Hispania,* 1992, *75,* 1315–20.

Long, D.R. Listening processes and authentic texts. In R.M. Terry (Ed.) *Acting on priorities: A commitment to excellence.* Southern Conference on Language Teaching, 1991.

Long, D.R. What you don't know can't help you. *Studies in Second Language Acquisition,* 1990, *12,* 65–80.

Lund, R.J. A taxonomy for teaching second language listening. *Foreign Language Annals,* 1990, *23,* 105–14

Lynch, A.J. Grading foreign language listening comprehension materials: The use of naturally modified interaction. Unpublished Ph.D. dissertation, University of Edinburgh (United Kingdom), 1988.

Markham, P.L. Gender and the perceived expertness of the speaker as factors in ESL recall. *TESOL Quarterly,* 1988, *22,* 397–406.

Markham, P.L., and Latham, M. The influence of religion-specific background knowledge on the listening comprehension of adult second-language students. *Language Learning,* 1987, *37,* 157–70.

Miller, G.A. The magical number seven plus or minus two: Some limits on our capacity for processing information. *Psychological Review,* 1956, *63,* 81–97.

Morgan, T.A. A musical Spanish dialectology. In R. Linkhorn (Ed.), *Perspectives on foreign language teaching.* Youngstown, OH: Youngstown Conference on Foreign Language Teaching, 1988.

Morgan, T.A. [Personal communication, 1993]

Mueller, G.A. Visual contextual cues and listening comprehension: An experiment. *The Modern Language Journal,* 1980, *64,* 335–40.

Narváez, L. Authentic cultural materials: the case of television programs received via satellite. *Hispania,* 1992, *75,* 74–75.

Noda, M. [Personal communication, 1993]

Omaggio, A.C. Pictures and second language comprehension: Do they help? *Foreign Language Annals,* 1979, *12,* 107–16

Omaggio, A.C. *Teaching language in context: Proficiency oriented instruction.* Boston: Heinle and Heinle, 1986.

O'Malley, J.M., Uhl Chamot, A., and Küpper, L. Listening comprehension strategies in second language acquisition. *Applied Linguistics,* 1989, *10,* 418–37.

O'Malley, J.M. and Uhl Chamot, A. *Learning strategies in second language acquisition.* Cambridge: Cambridge University Press, 1990.

Oxford, R. Language learning strategies: What every teacher should know. New York: Newbury House, 1990.

Purcell, J. Using songs to enrich the secondary class. *Hispania,* 1991, *75,* 192–96.

Purdy, M. Contributions of philosophical hermeneutics to listening research. Paper presented at annual meeting of International Listening Association, San Diego, 1986a.

Purdy, M. Research areas related to listening and concepts used in "qualitative studies." Working paper presented to Research Task Force, International Listening Association, San Diego, 1986b.

Rader-Ritz, K.E. The effects of three different levels of word rate on the listening comprehension of third-quarter university Spanish students. Unpublished Ph.D. dissertation, The Ohio State University, 1990.

Richards, J.C. Listening comprehension: Approach, design, procedure. *TESOL Quarterly,* 1983, *17,* 219–40.

Ringbom, H. On L1 transfer in L2 comprehenion and L2 production. *Language Learning,* 1992, *42,* 85–112.

Rost, M. *Listening in second language learning.* London: Longman, 1990.

Rogers, C.V., and Medley, F.W., Jr. Language with a purpose: Using authentic materials in the foreign language classroom. *Foreign Language Annals,* 1988, *21,* 467–78.

Sanders, D.A. *Auditory perception of speech: An introduction to principles and problems.* Englewood Cliffs, NJ: Prentice-Hall, 1977.

Schrier, L.L., and Fast, M. Foreign language in the elementary schools and computer-assisted language learning. *Hispania,* 1992, *75,* 1304–12.

Secules, T., Herron, C., and Tomasello, H. The effect of video context on foreign language learning. *The Modern Language Journal,* 1992, *76,* 480–89.

Shen, C.W.D. The effects of captioning on listening comprehension of English as a second language in a computer-based interactive videodisc system. Unpublished Ph.D. dissertation, University of Northern Colorado, 1991.

Shrum, J.L., and Glisan, E. *Teacher's handbook: Contextualized language instruction.* Boston: Heinle and Heinle, 1994.

Sperber, D., and Wilson, D. *Relevance.* London: Blackwell, 1986.

Schmidt-Rinehart, B.C. The effects of topic familiarity on the listening comprhension of university students of Spanish. Unpublished Ph.D. dissertation, The Ohio State University, 1992.

Stelly, C.H. Effects of a whole language approach using authentic French texts on student comprehension and attitude. Unpublished Ph.D. dissertation, Louisiana State University, 1991.

Sussex, R. Current issues in distance language education and open learning: An overview and an Australian perspective. In G.L. Ervin (Ed.), *International perspectives on foreign language teaching.* Lincolnwood. IL: National Textbook Company, 1991.

Trapp, E.A. Break down inhibitions and build up understanding with music, music, music. *Hispania,* 1991, *74,* 427–28.

van Dijk, T.A., and Kintsch, W. *Strategies of discourse comprehension.* New York: Academic Press, 1983.

Wagnild, J.V. The relationship between years of high school French study and performance on proficiency test in listening reading speaking and writing for entering freshmen at the University of Minnesota. Unpublished Ph.D. dissertation, University of Minnesota, 1988.

Warriner-Burke, H.P. Distance learning: What we don't know can hurt us. *Foreign Language Annals,* 1990, *23,* 129–33.

Watson, K.W., and Barker, L.L. Watson-Barker listening test. Auburn, AL: Spectra Communications, 1984.

Weissenrieder, M. Listening to the news in Spanish. *The Modern Language Journal,* 1987, *71,* 18–27.

White, A.S. Listening comprehension and affect in natural approach students of Spanish. Unpublished Ph.D. dissertation, University of Pittsburgh, 1988.

Wiggins, G. *The case for authentic assessment.* Washington, DC: ERIC Clearinghouse on Tests, Measurement, and Evaluation, 1990.

Witkin, B.R. Listening theory and research: The state of the art. *Journal of the International Listening Association,* 1990, *4,* 7–32.

Wohlert, H.S. German by satellite: Technology-enhanced distance learning. In W.F. Smith (Ed.), *Modern technology in foreign language education: applications and projects.* Lincolnwood. IL: National Textbook Company, 1989.

Yi, H., and Majim, J. The teacher-learner relationship and classroom interaction in distance learning: a case study of the Japanese language classes at an American high school. *Foreign Language Annals,* 1993, *26,* 21–30.

# Appendix A. Selected Listening Resources

### Arabic

Alosh, M. *Ahlan wa Sahlan.* Textbook series for first- and second-year Arabic accompanied by listening drills and comprehension exercises. Columbus, OH: Ohio State University Foreign Language Publications.

*Harvest of the Month.* Series of short passages originally broadcast on radio. British Broadcasting Corporation (the Arabic Service).

*Al-Mukhtarat.* Educational review of the Arab press accompanied by an audio cassette. Paris: Institut du Monde Arabe.

### French

*Caméra,* volumes I and II. Video with instructor's manual. Fort Worth: Holt, Rinehart, and Winston.

*French 1992 TV Commercials.* Teacher's Discovery. 1130 E. Big Beaver Rd., P.O. Box 7048, Troy, MI 48007-7048. (800) 521-3897.

Petit, B. *French Way.* Video for beginners and intermediate learners. Boston: Heinle and Heinle. 20 Park Plaza, Boston, MA 02116. (800) 354-9706.

Rey, J.N. *Video France: Panorama de la France, Profils de Français,* and *Optiques: La vie quotidienne.* Video series with instructor's manuals; for advanced beginners through upper intermediate level. Lincolnwood, IL: National Textbook Company.

### German

*Deutsche Welle.* Offers a full program of short-wave radio and satellite TV programming. The TV magazine, *Schauplatz Deutschland,* has been available on many cable and public television stations. Each segment centers around a geographic region or city; within each segment are reports and interviews on a number of topics. Videotapes of *Schauplatz Deutschland* (with or without subtitles) can be ordered from EuroTel, Inc., P.O. Box 2031, Corvallis, OR 97339, or call (505) 758-5029.

*Deutsche Welle* has recently expanded its satellite television offerings to several hours each day. The varied programming can be received in English, German, and Spanish. Write to *Deutsche Welle,* 50588 Köln, Germany, for schedules and satellite coordinate information. Tel. (0221) 389-0; FAX (0221) 389-4155.

*Goethe-Institutes* have many materials for loan. Write or call your nearest Goethe-Institute for a catalog.

*Inter Nationes* has an extensive catalog of inexpensive materials, many of them authentic. Write to Inter Nationes, Audiovisuelle Medien, Kennedyallee 91-103, D-53175 Bonn 2, Germany, for a catalog.

*Lernexpress,* a production of the BBC, is designed for beginning learners. Offers simple interviews with young people on a variety of topics, such as school, home, food, sports. Best suited for high school students, it can also be used with beginning college students. Available through Films Incorporated, Education Division, 5547 Ravenswood Ave., Chicago, IL 60640-1199; (800) 343-4312.

### Japanese

Jorden, E.H., and Noda, M. *Japanese: The spoken language.* Core conversation video 1, 2, and 3 accompanies textbooks Parts 1, 2 and 3. New York: Sony America. Order from Cheng and Tsui Company (617) 426-6074.

Jorden, E.H., and Noda, M. *Japanese: The spoken language.* Audiotapes, "eavesdropping" section, accompanies textbooks Parts 1, 2, and 3. Ithaca, NY: Cornell University

Phonetics Lab. Order from Cheng and Tsui Company (617) 426-6074.

Hori, U., et al. *Nyûsu de manabu nihongo.* Listening comprehension for intermediate students. Tokyo: Bonjinsya.

Hori, U., et al. *Nyûsu de manabu nihongo.* Interviews for listening comprehension. Tokyo: Bonjinsya.

*Yan and the Japanese people.* Video skits from Let's learn Japanese, Basic 1 and Basic 2. Santa Monica, CA: The Japan Foundation Language Center. Not for public sale and distribution; may be borrowed.

### Russian

*KONTAKT.* Video series for advanced students. Albany: New York Network. P.O. Box 7012, Albany, NY 12225. (518) 443-5333.

### Spanish

*America Video Library,* I and II. Authentic video from U.S. television broadcasts; activity manual available. Boston: Heinle and Heinle. 20 Park Plaza, Boston, MA 02116. (800) 354-9706

*Mosaico cultural.* Video based on typical cultural themes; activity manual available. Boston: Heinle and Heinle. 20 Park Plaza, Boston, MA 02116. (800) 354-9706.

Project for International Communication Studies (PICS). Large selection of authentic videos from Spain and Latin America. PICS, 266 International Center, University of Iowa, Iowa City, IA 52242. (800) 335-2335.

### Various languages

The American Council on the Teaching of Foreign Languages (ACTFL) SLOM bibliography of instructional materials for the teaching of foreign languages in grades K-12. Includes titles, authors, publishers, instructional/proficiency level, descriptions, and criticial revies and evaluation information. The following languages are included: Arabic, Chinese, French, German, Classical Greek, Modern Hebrew, Italian, Japanese, Latin, Portuguese, Russian and Spanish. Audio cassettes, computer software, dictionaries, word lists, filmstrips and slides, grammars, periodicals, readers, textbooks, teacher resources, video cassettes and more are represented. Write to ACTFL, 6 Executive Plaza, Yonkers, NY 10701-67801.

# Appendix B. Checklist for Selection of Listening Materials

Program
- At what level will the auditory materials will be used?
- Will they be used in language laboratories, in-class, or out-of-class?
- Is the material appealing?
- Are ancillaries included in the program?
- What topics are covered?
- What is the total cost of the program?
- Are the materials to be used by more than one instructor?
- Could inexperienced instructors use the materials effectively?
- Where are the materials currently being used and what are some positive and/or negative comments from current users?

- What statements about listening instruction and assessment are made by the author(s) and/or publisher of the program?
- Does the program offer alternatives that allow instructors to choose the pace and structure that will be most beneficial for the class?

Learners
- Are the materials motivating; do they capture the learners' interests?
- Are they "on-target" with ability levels?
- Do the situations and vocabulary on the tape match student interests?
- Do students have cognitive maturity to understand the cultural concepts?
- Will learners be able to transfer their real-world knowledge to the listening materials?
- Will the material hold students' attention for a 5–10 minute period?
- Are the accompanying activities (if included) innovative and interesting?
- How might students compare these materials to those that are currently being used?

Language
- Is the quality of the tape very clear?
- Are a variety of subjects represented (males, females, children, adults)?
- Is the language authentic (redundance, pauses, hesitations, etc.)?
- Does the language occur within a context?
- Is most of the emphasis on production (listen-repeat, listen-respond) or comprehension?
- Does the response that the student would give resemble natural discourse?
- Does the language accurately reflect the culture of which the language is a part?
- Is it free from stereotypes and sexist language and references?
- Does the language contain vocabulary and structures just slightly beyond what the learner is actually able to produce?

Language activities and ancillary materials
- Is the vocabulary integrated with the theme or topic of the class?
- Can the tape be divided into logical segments for easy adaptability to the in-class text and lesson plan?
- Do the activities make use of skills that are part of listening in the real world?
- Are skill-getting and evaluation activities included?
- Do pre-listening guides provide a variety of formats?
- Do the activities invite real communication or are most of them designed for receptive/recognition responses?
- Do tasks that are designed for production also include interactive practices that stress comprehension or communication?
- Is there a balance of collaborative and noncollaborative tasks?
- Do activities encourage learners to become active listeners, guessers, and risk-takers as they listen?
- Do the guidance and post-listening activities follow a logical progression?
- Are there a variety of activities at each level?
- Does the ancillary workbook or activity book contain materials that are of equal quality to the basic program?
- Do the themes, structures, vocabulary in ancillaries correlate with the language program?
- Are tapescripts provided?
- Are activities and tests packaged with the program?
- Can supplementary activities and exams be duplicated from black line masters?

# Authentic Assessment: Reading and Writing

James J. Davis

*Howard University*

## Introduction

This Report offers a brief historical overview of reading and writing in the second or foreign language classroom. The overview will be followed by a limited review of the research literature on teaching and testing reading and writing. Specific attention will be given to the constructivist model of foreign language reading and writing as a process rather than a product. The last section of the report will be dedicated exclusively to authentic strategies for assessing reading and writing skills in the foreign language classroom.

In this Report, the main focus is on reading and writing in the beginning stages of foreign language learning. References will made to the advanced levels of reading and writing to emphasize the required careful pedagogical attention that needs to be given to producing proficient readers and writers in a foreign language. Also, no distinction is made between second and foreign language, except for cases in which English as a second language (ESL) is contrasted with foreign language (FL) research or language teaching activities. Rather than defining "reading" and "writing," I shall clarify how these terms will be used in this Report. Reading refers to reading for comprehension (silent), not oral reading. This distinction is made because, as Chastain (1988) put it:

Language teachers often use the word "reading" to refer to two entirely different processes. In one case, they have in mind an activity in which students read aloud from the printed paged in the other case, they mean an activity in which students read a passage for comprehension (p. 216).

Chastain (1988) and Dvorak (1986) divide writing into two categories: (1) *transcription* (a means of learning language forms) and(2) *composition* (a way to communicate a message). Omaggio (1993) however, offered that "perhaps *writing* might be best viewed as a continuum of activities that range from the mechanical or formal aspects of 'writing down' on the one end to the more complex act of composing on the other" (p. 291). In this report, I refer to the act of composing, i.e., writing as communication.

A definition of assessment is offered elsewhere in this volume. It is therefore not necessary to dwell on its descriptions and characteristics here. However, the reader should keep in mind that assessment is not simply testing, although testing can be and is usually a part of an assessment program. One of the central ideas of the so-cal led assessment movement is that it is a "quality enhancement" effort that should provide an opportunity to reflect on the overall goals of a particular program of instruction and the curriculum (Terenzini, 1993). The use of teacher-made (and standardized) tests as the major instrument for program assessment has been deemed ineffective if they do not truly assess the overall objectives of the instructional program. All testing must be related to the curricular goals of a program. Henning (1990) warned about the danger of not integrating teaching and testing with the curriculum:

There is continuing need to integrate tests with the curriculum. If there is no concerted effort to subordinate testing to explicit curricular goals, there is an ever-present potential danger that the tests themselves with all their inherent limitations will become the purposes of the educational encounter by default (p. 380).

In this Report, the discussion will center on the use of assessment strategies of reading and writing skills which incorporate authentic or authentic-like materials. Authentic materials refer to those which were produced for native speakers of a language, and authentic-like refers to those teacher-made assessments which model as closely as possible "real world" language activities.

# Historical Perspective on Reading and Writing in the Foreign Language Classroom

One might argue that reading has not received adequate attention in the foreign language classroom. Perhaps a more accurate statement is that adequate attention has been given to the *teaching* of reading in the foreign language classroom. Historically, reading has enjoyed much attention in the foreign language classroom. One should be reminded that in the United States, during the early decades of this century, modern language instruction was very similar to traditional instruction of classical languages. Consequently, modern language instruction followed the traditional pattern of requiring a prescribed, often enormous, amount of memorization and translation. The approach was referred in the language teaching profession as "grammar-translation method" and later as the "reading method." In the reading method, students learned grammar rules, did translation exercises, read materials of increasing difficulty and responded to questions mainly in writing. In fact, a "Committee of Twelve," formed by the Modern Language Association (MLA) in 1897 to investigate the study of modern languages in the nation's schools and to make recommendations regarding language teaching methodologies, underlined that one of the principal values and goals of foreign language instruction should be "to prepare for intellectual pursuits that require *reading* the foreign language for information" (p. 6). With the advent of the audiolingual approach in the fifties, however, the emphasis on reading dwindled.

Historically, writing as a communicative skill has not been given much attention in the foreign language classroom. During the grammar-translation era, "writing," like "reading," held a rather prominent place as it was used to translate into or out of English. Regarding this point, Donald Walsh (1969) amusingly described the grammar-translation era as

> those years when our students ploughed dutifully through the classics of French or German or Spanish literature, converting great foreign prose into juvenile English at a steady rate of five pages a day.
>
> The translation days were periodically interrupted by grammar days, when we attempted to communicate to our students our love for syntactical irregularities and then test them with artfully contrived sentences such as, 'If Professor Martin had known that Doctor Brown intended to leave for Southern France the next morning, he would have asked him to take little Peter with him.' (p. 62)

He went on to describe what he termed "a strange inversion or perversion of pedagogical thinking" (p. 62) when teachers marvelled at how many grammar tricks they could play on students. This practice, in this writer's opinion, is not totally absent from foreign language teaching and testing in the 1990s, especially on the translation sections of in-class examinations.

Currently, the common order of the four skills (speaking, listening, reading, and writing) seems to indicate indeed the priority rating of the skills in the foreign language classroom. There is a tendency to view writing as the least useful skill in language learning (Chastain, 1988). Offering a possible reason for that view, Terry (1989) stated that "writing is perhaps the most poorly understood and the skill that is given, in fact, the most cursory attention" (p. 43). Because writing is so poorly understood may explain why so little attention is given to it. That does not mean that foreign language teachers are not concerned with developing composition skills in the beginning language classes. It is interesting, however, that when Cooper and others (1985) prepared a very helpful book on research-guided responses to the concerns of foreign language teachers, writing was not discussed anywhere in the text. Writing, then. continues to be "the forgotten skill," and that may very well be because "writing is . . . the most difficult of all the language skills to master" (Larson and Jones, 1984, p. 132).

# The Reading and Writing Connection

Historically, there has been a persistent link between reading and writing. The following statement may seem overly simplistic, but the purpose is to make the connection between reading and writing even more evident. When people read, they read something that has been written by someone. The notion that reading great works of prose and poetry will lead to the development of good writing skills dates back to ancient Greece (Dvorak, 1986, p. 146). Today, leading foreign language methodologists (Omaggio, 1993; Rivers, 1968, 1988; Chastain, 1988) suggest that "real writing" be introduced after students are able to read. The idea is that one of the most effective ways to learn to write well is to learn to read well first.

There is an increasing interest and research focusing on the relationship between reading and writing instruction. For example, Tierney and others (1989), in a study investigating the effects of reading and writing on critical thinking, reported that the subjects who read a topic-related passage before writing engaged in more critical thinking when writing. Some teaching materials have been developed along those lines.

One Spanish as a foreign language text, *De lector a escritor* (From Reader to Writer) (Finneman and Carbin Gorell, 1991), serves as an excellent example. In the introductory section of the text, the authors state that "the activities . . . encourage students to act as readers in the writing process in order to verify both that they have accurately and effectively communicated their intended meanings and that they experience the intended responses on the part of their readers" (p. 3). Greenia (1992) summarized the genuine connection between reading and writing when he asserted that

> real competence in writing must stem at least in part from the learner's reading a large volume of texts that model the types of prose they will eventually create.

Reading allows an individual to acquire a sense of how a given text is forged and presented to a reader (p. 33).

# Current Research and Views: Foreign Language Reading

During the past twenty years (especially in the 1980s), there was a boom in the literature regarding foreign and second language reading. Numerous books dealing specifically with reading in a second or foreign language were published; these included: Alderson et al., 1984; Bernhardt, 1991; Grellet, 1981; Mackay et al, 1979, Swaffar et al, 1991; Ulijn and Pugh, 1984. Major foreign language journals issued complete volumes focusing on the research and pedagogical implications and practice in teaching reading skills. For example, the September 1984 volume of the *Foreign Language Annals* and the 1986 *Northeast Conference Reports* devoted much content to reading in a foreign language.

In 1988, *The Modern Language Journal* devoted issue number 2 of volume 72 to the topic. MacLean (1985) compiled a bibliography of journal articles and books on reading in second/foreign language over the period 1974–1984. She discovered well over 200 entries.

A review of the research literature on foreign language reading is not appropriate for the purpose of this Report. Several excellent review articles are already available. What I propose to do is to briefly summarize the theories and models that have informed current research efforts that have influenced, to some extent, the current directions in the teaching of foreign language reading.

Based on first-language reading research, the two major models that have emerged as the theoretical framework for current foreign/second reading research are Coady's (1979) psycholinguistic model and Bernhardt's (1986) constructivist model. The psycholinguistic model of first language reading, advanced by Goodman (1970), defines reading as an interaction among three factors: conceptual abilities, background knowledge, and process strategies. With regard to conceptual abilities. Coady indicated that second language readers simply may not be intellectually equipped to understand the concepts presented in a particular text. Of course, level of difficulty is closely related to experiential background.

The second component, background knowledge or *schemata*, considers the importance of meaningfulness and organization of background knowledge in the learning process. That is, learning must involve active mental processes and be relatable to existing knowledge the learner already possesses (Ausubel, 1968).

The third interactive component is processing strategies. These involve a knowledge of the linguistic features of a language. Simply stated, a reader must know the alphabet, sound system, word order, and word meaning to read a given text. The mental processing of information is based on the not.ion that humans inherently strive to make sense of the world. This process is complex with regard to reading, and its complexity is enhanced when related to foreign language reading. Process strategies refer to what Phillips (1984) called "mental subroutines" that a reader uses in order to comprehend what is read.

The constructivist model by Bernhardt (1986) is influenced greatly by and includes the major elements of Coady's psycholinguistic model. In the constructivist's model, the following elements are included: prior knowledge, word recognition, phonemic/graphemic features, metacognition, syntactic feature recognition, and intratextual perceptions. Metacognition is defined by Bernhardt (1986) as "the extent to which a reader is thinking about what he/she is reading" (p. 105). The result of the successful interaction of these factors is comprehension. As Bernhardt (1986) noted, an important contribution of this approach is that it underlines the notion that reading involves readers and not just the reading text. In short, the constructivist model centers around the reader in the reading process and the interaction of reader and text.

The constructivist model evolved from data involving recall protocols (Bernhardt, 1983a). That is, readers are allowed to read a text as many times as they want to, then they are asked to recall, in their native language, orally or in writing as much as they can. Through an analysis of the data generated, the teacher/researcher can pinpoint grammar problems and other information on how the reader is processing the text for comprehension. It should be pointed out that another important feature of this view of reading comprehension is that it takes into consideration that the comprehension of a reading passage may be impeded when that passage contains unfamiliar cultural referents. This notion, while seemingly trivial, however, is not always recognized and addressed by foreign teaching professionals.

We must accept as a premise that while there are some similarities in the process of learning to read for comprehension in the first and second language, there are some very important differences. Phillips (1984) noted that good native language reading strategies, while helpful to the foreign language reader, do not necessarily "automatically transfer" (p. 385) to foreign language reading. Similarly, Yorio (1971) and Clarke (1980) pointed out that the differences Between good and poor readers were minimal when they were confronted with a foreign language text.

Current research on foreign language reading urges teachers to take into account many factors that have received little attention heretofore. Zvetina (1987) summarized three major directions in which foreign language reading research should lead in the teaching of reading skills. They are: (1) the organization of the L2 learners' prior knowledge of the content of the text, during the pre-reading phase, (2) the explicit teaching of metacognitive skills during the reading act, and (3) the careful selection of L2 texts, with attention given to their content, rhetorical structure, and authenticity (p. 234).

## Current Views and Research: Foreign Language Writing

Dvorak (1986) and Omaggio (1993) indicated that research on the development of second language writing is currently not abundant. In the relatively small number of studies, however, there are two major directions: (1) the documentation of processes writers engage in as they compose and (2) the effects of feedback strategies on writing, that is, approaches to and patterns of evaluating student writing. The process approach has been used largely in studies involving more advanced students of English as a Second Language while the feedback approach has been more frequent in studies in foreign languages.

Citing Hairston (1982), Hudelson (1989) indicated that there is a revolution going on in the teaching of composition. That statement was prompted by a basic shift in the thoughts regarding the act of composing. The traditional view was that writing was a linear process in which the writers knew what they were going to say before beginning to write. They wrote and made cosmetic changes later. The traditional focus was on the final written product, not on the writer and the processes involved in the act of writing. The new view, however, is that writing is not linear; it is recursive. That is to say that writing involves "a process or set of processes, through which writers, as they write, discover what they want to say" (Hudelson, p. 210). Proponents of writing as process argue that effective writing is rarely achieved in a single draft. The process requires the stages of idea development, the reevaluation of ideas, and the re-writing of the text.

Regarding feedback strategies, there are varying ideas on how and when to measure writing proficiency. There is conflicting data reported in empirical research conclusions regarding the use of corrective feedback in which the teacher underlines or circles grammatical mistakes using the proverbial "red pen." Two major studies (Semke, 1984; Lalande, 1982) using foreign language samples serve to illustrate the conflicting conclusions. In Semke's study, she concluded that students who were given feedback only on the content and amount of information successfully communicated developed higher levels of proficiency in writing than did the students who were evaluated only on the form, i.e., grammaticality, of their written work. Lalande used a control group in which students were asked to rewrite their compositions based on the traditional "red pen" evaluative method by their instructors and an experimental group in which instructors, in addition to the "red" underlining, pinpointed the general category of each error and asked students to rewrite. He found that students in the experimental group corrected more grammatical mistakes in their rewrite than those in the control group.

When foreign language teachers exclaim that their students have an abundance of writing exercises, they more than likely mean that their students complete in-class or homework assignments which require writing down responses to a list of questions or filling in blanks with vocabulary or verb forms. Such activities, however, do not involve critical thinking or creativity on the part of the language learner. Greenia (1992) suggested that foreign language teachers should not be so surprised that their students can not write (compose) when he revealed that "Johnny can't *escribir* because we have not *trained* (emphasis is mine) him to do so" (p 30.).

Teachers of foreign languages often complain that students can not write a simple sentence after they have covered the grammar to equip them for the tasks assigned. We should be aware constantly that the mastering of one's native language grammar does not necessarily lead to efficient writing abilities. Knowing the grammar of a language is certainly a prerequisite for writing well, but it does not insure it (Greenia, 1992). Dvorak (1986) very aptly summarized two important research conclusions related to the above discussion: "(1) writing improvements are unrelated to grammar study, whether of traditional or transformational variety, and (2) intensive correction of student writing, which has negative effect on writing in terms of student attitudes and motivation, has little positive effect at all.

The extent to which research has influenced approaches to the teaching and testing of writing in the foreign language classroom cannot easily be determined. In many ways, we are still in the developmental stage of systematically focusing on writing as a communicative skill and activity. Dvorak (1986) noted that views on the teaching of writing have changed over the years, but there have not been many changes in classroom practice in the teaching and testing procedures. Dvorak (1986), Chastain (1988), and Terry (1981) suggest that the prevalent current method of teaching writing is to teach grammar, assign writing tasks, collect papers, and then to correct student writing samples. The approach to the teaching of writing is to correct it (Dvorak).

Citing Magnan, Terry (1989) pointed out that are two purposes for second language writing in the foreign language classroom: (1) as a support skill (class and homework exercises to practice grammatical forms and structures, vocabulary and spelling) and (2) as a communicative skill (to inform, relate, question, persuade, etc). The point here is that students should be carefully guided through the writing process, starting with the word, then the sentence, and finally the paragraph.

Several writers (Huebener, 1965; Rosengrant, 198S; Terry, 1989; Steele Marechal-Ross, 1993) have urged and petitioned teachers to take a different view of writing and not abandon the teaching of writing skills. Rosengrant (1985) summed up that sentiment when she wrote that:

> Writing is for many students less stressful than speaking. It gives them the opportunity to formulate their ideas at leisure, to use reference works, to experiment with more elaborate structures than we would normally use in speaking, and to reflect on their mistakes, or even to correct themselves, in private (p. 487).

Regarding the teaching of writing, a review of foreign language methodology textbooks (Huebener, 1965; Rivers, 1968, 1988; Allen and Valette, 1977; Chastain, 1980; Omaggio, 1993) revealed that in the last thirty years methodologists have given noteworthy attention to the teaching of writing. They all outlined a prescribed sequence of writing activities moving along the continuum from copying down to the writing of free compositions. It was not until the 1980's that methodologists were able to cite research in foreign languages that supported this sequence.

# Toward Integrating the Teaching, Testing, and Assessing of Reading and Writing Skills

One of major goals of teaching reading and writing is to provide students ultimately with the ability to communicate through these modes. We are now aware that these skills should be taught as separate skills and in a systematic manner. There is a call to use as many authentic materials as possible and be as realistic in our goals and objectives as possible. In the foreign language context, authentic assessment does not mean assessing skills levels in the same way as it would be done with native speakers of a language. Using authentic (real-life) activities is as important as using authentic materials. When authentic materials are not available, the teacher has the option of authenticating the experience while teaching and testing.

In order to underline the importance of setting and maintaining realistic goals and objectives in the foreign language classroom, the concept of inter-language will be explored. Briefly defined and broadened to include language acquisition in general, interlanguage is that phase through which all language learners go before "comprehensible" language emerges. This concept is applicable to all the skills involved in second language learning, but it is easily observed in the productive skills: speaking and writing. We might liken interlanguage in the second/foreign language context to the stage when a baby is beginning to develop speech. During this period, only the child seems to know and understand what he is saying.

## Teaching and Assessment of Second Language Writing

The student's native language must be taken into account at all stages of teaching and testing. Regarding foreign/second language writing skills, learners will go through the interlanguage stage and model their writing on first language habits. To illustrate this point, it seems necessary to pursue a bit further a point that may seem trivial. Teachers are often disappointed that students omit diacritical markings on words when they begin to write. The reality is that students will not gain automatic control of the written accent (and of spelling) in the target language just because they have consistently seen them in the models offered by their teachers or in their texts. This mastery comes later after much practice with writing (Paulson, 1993). In fact, teaching the rules of accentuation, unfortunately, does not seem to make a significant difference when learners are given "free" writing assignments. Paying more attention to meaning rather than form, beginning language learners often do not apply the accentuation rules. What is even more vexing to teachers is when students copy materials from a text and fail to copy the accents. It should be pointed that many native writers never gain a mastery of the diacritical marks in the native language during a life time. When teaching the demonstrative adjectives and pronouns in Spanish, for example, the teacher painstakingly drills students on the difference between *este* (this, masculine) and *iste* (this one, masculine), noting that the written accent makes an immense difference in meaning. This writer does not argue that accents and spelling mistakes should be overlooked in the beginning foreign language class, but must be carefully weighed in the evaluation of a writing sample. This thinking follows that of Paulson (1993) who stated that teachers/evaluators must "make sure that assessment of writing reflects the goals of the course; errors in accentuation, spelling, and syntax must be kept in perspective with the overall communicative purpose of the test" (p. 13). One cannot dismiss the fact that the speaker of English is not accustomed to making or recognizing marks on words other that the frequent dots on i's and crossings on t's.

Rosengrant (1985), Terry (1989), and Paulson (1993) suggested a hierarchy of writing assignments which follow as closely as possible the ACTFL guidelines. Rosengrant argued that "what is needed, therefore, is a more conscious structuring of writing assignments so that students are indeed guided through a hierarchy of functions on their way to relative proficiency" (p. 489). In the teaching and presentation of writing techniques in the foreign language class, practitioners must look carefully at what the learners should be able to do and how well they should be able to function at specific levels of instruction. While the aforementioned notion is not new, it is not commonly practiced by second language teachers.

Teachers are accustomed to giving more "creative" writing assignments in advanced classes. However, writing activities and assignments given in advanced composition classes may be adapted and used in beginning classes. Larson and Jones (1984) classified the basic writing tasks of second language learners into five categories:

1. correspondence
2. providing essential information
3. completing forms
4. taking notes and
5. formal papers

Each of these classifications is indeed "real" writing tasks in which students will engage during their academic careers.

Preparation for writing tasks is as important as the act of writing. Lee and Paulson (1992) prescribed specific steps # which should be taken in the teaching of writing as process, asserting that students should first be required to think about the topic on which they will write. They then must organize their thoughts and information, write a draft, and revise any section that need it. The final stage is to edit the draft for submission to the teacher. The teacher must monitor each of these steps carefully to insure that students understand not only what the tasks are, but also to insure that they understand that writing is a powerful tool of communication. If the message is made clear that through writing one can empower, convince, and persuade, then students will take writing more seriously.

Before offering several examples of writing assignments, it should be made clear that students, before approaching a writing activity, need to know who their audience is and the purpose of their communication. The teacher must authenticate a context in which a piece of writing is to be consumed. Terry (1989) offered the following example of practical and realistic writing task in the classification of correspondence:

> You have just arrived in France for a semester study abroad. Your French teacher has asked you to send a telegram when you arrive. Fill out the following telegram form, telling your teacher that you are in Paris, that there are 15 students in your group, that you like them, and any other pertinent information. Don't forget . . . you pay per word (p. 45).

Note that the context and intended audience are clearly defined. Also, students are given the specific information to include. They are allowed, however, to add more if they wish to. There is a warning that they should not try to write too much because it could become to costly. It may become too costly for teachers too if they allow students to write open-ended essays in the beginning level. They will spend an enormous amount of: time rewriting students compositions. The activity given above can be particularly effective in beginning classes because the telegraphic style of writing is, after all, the type of language that beginning students produce. Writing a telegram message does not require paragraph development or extended discourse. This type of activity also gives the teacher control on length, content, and specific points of grammar. A similar activity, using authentic materials like post cards, telephone message forms, facsimile cover sheets and the like, can be used at all levels of instruction.

Davis (1986) described an authentic writing activity used in Business Spanish course which could be applied to all levels of instruction. Students were provided a sheet of official letterhead from the university president's office and told that they were to assist the instructor in responding in Spanish for the president. They were provided with a copy of real letter in Spanish received by the president's office. The letter was used to teach the conventions of letter writing in Spanish. This led to a discussion of formal and informal letter-writing in Spanish. The use of authentic official university letterhead and an authentic letter from a Spanish-speaking native prompted a more serious approach to their assignment. One caveat, however, is that students may become so consumed in the content and message to be communicated that they lose sight of the native culture letter-writing conventions.

Mathews and Jacquet (1992) reported that in a study conducted with second year students of Spanish, the subjects were asked to respond to a personal ad in a newsletter (written by other students) and request information on a personal problem. They discovered that an overwhelming number of letters were ingenious and interesting, but the students followed English letter-writing conventions. They further observed that if the assignment had been "to write proper target-language letter with emphasis on form rather than on content, the letters would have been superior grammatically, but less creative and spontaneous" (p. 174). The pedagogical implication is that teachers should promote creativity and spontaneity in writing assignments so that students will build up their confidence and realize that the purpose of writing is for the communication of a message in the second language as it is in their native language. While teaching appropriate cultural conventions is imperative, beginning language students should be not overly penalized for failing to follow them. The process of learning to communicate and create in the foreign language will involve trial and error.

As stated above, placing writing activities in the appropriate cultural context is important. Teachers should note any outstanding cultural similarities and differences when giving an assignment or conducting a classroom activity. In a textbook, *Amicalement: For Basic Functional Writing Proficiency in French* (Steele, Marechal and Ross, 1993), for example, offered the following strategy for introducing students to writing a postcard in French. In their introduction, they stated that:

> "French people, like people of many countries, often send a postcard (une carte postale) to other members of their family or to friends when they are on vacation (en vacances)" (p.1).

Not only does the above give an example of how to approach authentic writing, it also points out two important cultural similarities between Americans and the French by focusing on two vocabulary items: the postcard and vacation. To add to the authentic and cultural aspect, the model post card bears the actual penmanship of a native speaker of French from France. This feature is maintained throughout the text. That the text includes sample handwriting sample is a lesson in and of itself. Students learn that there are some distinguishing features of penmanship that are typical of a particular culture. Pointing this out can facilitate students' ability in reading natively handwritten texts.

Rosengrant (1985), focusing on the development of descriptive language in the beginning language class, suggested that students begin creative writing practice by describing pictures in which no action is occurring. This requires identifying objects in the picture—a novice level task. The ultimate goal is to get students to be able to narrate and describe in a variety of tenses—an advanced-level task. This training must begin at the beginning level of instruction through the use of carefully arranged and selected writing activities. Below are sample instructions of one of Rosengrant's writing activities:

> Describing a Static Scene: Students are given an illustration from a popular Russian cookbook and asked to describe it. In addition to the instructions they receive a brief vocabulary list that contains the proper words to describe the container in the picture (bottle, can) and certain adverbs of place (on the left, on the right). (Rosengrant, 1985, p. 489)

Providing students with that type of detailed instructions informs them that they are not expected to know all the vocabulary needed to produce the description. This follows the pattern of building student confidence as demonstrated with the "Situation Cards" produced by Educational Testing Service (1984) and used in the Oral Proficiency Interview developed by ACTFL. Students read the following statement at the bottom of novice level cards: "We realize that you may not have the vocabulary for this situation, but do the best you can to make yourself understood."

Focusing specifically on the process approach to teaching writing, Steers (1992), offered a diagram of natural communicative needs of second language learners. To illustrate her point, she suggested that teachers imagine a circle in the middle of a sheet of paper with "I" in the center. Around that centers circle is a series of concentric circles which would include other topics about which students should write as they gain increasing knowledge and confidence. The student writer moves away from "I" to the more detailed and more detailed description and analysis of family, friends, classroom, daily activities, physical needs, fears and hopes, interests, and experiences. The diagram suggests careful selection of grammatical items that students should be expected to use. For example, to express fears and hopes could require the use of the subjunctive in Spanish. Inherent in Steers' diagram is that careful attention should be given to moving from directed to free writing assignments in the beginning language class.

Regarding writing prompts in the beginning second language class, it seems that the overwhelming majority of writers suggest that they be given in the native language in the beginning phases of second/foreign language instruction. This is to insure that students understand exactly they being asked to do. As a case in point, many universities have courses which that focus on "reading and writing." At this writer's institution, the course is called "Reading and Writing Workshop." The purpose of the course is provide students with intensive practice in reading materials which reflect the natural language usage used and cultural issues. Efforts are made to insure that writing assignments are closely linked to what the students read and discuss in class. One important feature of this course is that students are allowed to read on occasion materials in their native language and asked to respond in essay form in the target language. As an aside, students are generally quite pleased with this. In the case of using articles from magazines or newspapers, the written response may take the form of a letter to the editor or rebuttal letter. In beginning classes, the student's response may be limited to: "Your article is very interesting, but I do not agree with you." As students gain greater ability to support opinions, teacher can insist that they put in "because" statements. Using the language of the proficiency guidelines, teachers can create a "situation with a complication" to elicit higher levels of performance.

If we agree that writing is a "communicative act," then it should be taught and assessed as such. The traditional assessment of the writing skills has been to assign a composition of some sort and assign a letter grade to it. Perhaps, our greatest failure in the assessment of foreign language writing skills has been our procedures for grading. Too often, language teachers get too consumed by the content of a composition that they lose sight of the fact that they are assessing writing skills (Bernhardt and Deville, 1991). A major question that teachers must ask when grading written compositions is: Am I assessing content, quantity, writing ability, or all of the above? This question must be answered honestly prior to grading.

Communicative abilities must be assessed through instruments which allow the examinees to use communicative abilities. Students be allowed to demonstrate what they can communicate. If, for example, in a Spanish composition, the erroneous "Yo gusto la casa" instead of the correct "Me gusta la casa" appeared, what should be the penalty? The answer can only be determined after the purpose of the assessment has been determined. Is it strictly to test grammar rules or it is to test communication? Certainly, a mistake like "Yo gusto el caso" or "Me gusta el caso" would cause failed communication because of the error in gender which changes the meaning of the intended message.

Regarding the evaluation of writing, holistic scoring is more effective than discrete-point scoring. Discrete-point scoring involves deducting points for specific erroneous grammatical and other linguistic features. Simply stated, an evaluator using holistic grading procedures bases the overall grade on the degree to which communication is achieved. In holistic scoring, the most pristine English teacher would have to award some credit for a statement like "He ain't got no mo' money."

Because the beginning second language learner experiences a faulty and incomplete linguistic pattern in the language learned, it is imperative that teachers/evaluators be as fair as possible in assessing their language skills. Assessment protocols in second language learning have addressed the issue of whether or not a native speaker, who is accustomed to dealing with second language on the level, is able to comprehend the message to be communicated. School districts and college and universities should use native speakers in their assessment program. If they do not have native speakers employed in the foreign language departments, they could seek them #n other departments or in the community. This would require training of the native speaker evaluators, but if teachers and administrators are dedicated to authentic assessment in their second language programs, they must spend the money as well as commit the time and effort to carry it out appropriately.

Teachers often assume that students' writing should be better than their speaking because they can use a dictionary and have greater opportunities for self-correction than when speaking. It should be reiterated that second language learners must be trained to "create" in the language, mixing and matching the limited foreign language that they know in beginning stages. We cannot assume that learners will use the appropriate vocabulary in the appropriate cultural context because of the mere exposure to textbooks and dictionaries.

If the required attention is to be given the notion that creative writing should be developed from the beginning of the writing instruction, then we must also believe and practice a hierarchical procedure in the assessment of writing skills. The assessment of writing skills should follow the same general guidelines for speaking. Embedded in this notion is that writing is a developmental process.

Paulson (1993) offered an evaluation criteria for writing in the beginning foreign language courses. The evaluation grid is designed to measure four areas: comprehensibility, cohesiveness, information conveyed, and vocabulary. Each category is fully explained with the accompanying points. The weights assigned to each area may vary according to the course objective and teacher preference.

# Teaching and Assessing
# Second Language Reading

As stated, reading is as an interactive process between reader and text. Thus, students must be taught to interact with the main idea of the reading selection in carefully prepared consecutive activities. Regarding this, Phillips' (1984) five-phase model has been perhaps the most influential and often cited during the past ten years. Phillips proposed the following five stages:

1. Preteaching / Preparation
2. Skimming / Scanning Stages
3. Decoding / Intensive Reading Stage
4. Comprehension Stage, and
5. Transferable / Integrating Skills

Using Phillips' model as a basis, many textbook writers have incorporated similar or a modified model in the preparation of reading texts. One book, for example, *¿Sabias que...?* by VanPatten, Lee, Ballman, and Dvorak (1992), offers a three-stage model: (1) *Anticipación* (pre-reading), (2) Exploración (reading), and (3) *Síntesis* (post-reading).

The above-mentioned book will serve as the major source for the development of this section of the teaching of reading. It provides, in this writer's view, one of the most comprehensive reading programs found in a generic four-skills textbook for beginners. The authors cautiously guide themselves by research in the area of second language reading comprehension. One important notion from the research literature is that students' background knowledge must be tapped and activated prior to the act of reading in a second language. Carrell (1983), further advancing the reality that a given text does not carry meaning in and of itself, wrote that the "text only provides directions for listeners and readers as to how they should retrieve or construct meaning from their own, previously acquired knowledge (p. 556).

The pre-reading activities (in English translation) i presented below are based on a reading entitled "El cidigo oculto de los elefantes" (The Secret Code of Elephants) which appears in chapter 15 of the text. As a point of clarification, the pre-reading activities are presented in English at the beginning of the text, but the authors progressively move into the target language as students gain greater command of the grammar and a more extensive vocabulary. The pre-reading activities will be fully described to demonstrate the full range and variety of exercises characteristic of all the chapters and what the authors call the "instructional support sections" of the reading program. For the other stages, only one sample will be given here. The following is taken from pages 408–409 of *¿Sabias que...?*

> Step 1. The title of the article on pages 410–412 is "El cidigo oculto de los elefantes." Do you know what 'oculto' means? Read what it says to the right of the title and look for a synonym of 'oculto.' Write that word here.
>
> Step 2. What do you think is the general idea of the article? (Students are given four choices from which to choose).
>
> Step 3. Now, read the first two paragraphs. According to what is said in the two paragraphs, what do you think is theme of the article? (Students are given four choices from which to choose.)
>
> Step 4. Look at the pictures and read what it says at the bottom of each one. Indicate if the following sentences are true or false. (Four statements with areas to check whether the statement is true or false follow.)
>
> Step 5. Look for the following words and phrases in the subtitle. What do they mean? Quickly read the section of the article pertinent to the word or phrase to clarify its meaning. Write the meaning here. (Several words appear along a blank in which the meaning.)
>
> Step 6. It is not possible to deduce the meaning of all the words that appear in the article. Below are some definitions. (A list of nine words with definitions in Spanish is given.)

Note that the above activities center around previewing key vocabulary items and making predictions about the content of the reading. In many ways, these strategies are similar to those that we use in "real world" reading tasks in our native language. Take, for example, reading the newspaper or a magazine. We often look at pictures and titles to guess or determine the possible content of an article. The foregoing observations are especially relevant to second language learning, and particularly significant with regards to teaching the receptive skills— reading and listening. In the foreign language comprehension process, researchers agree that at least three types of background knowledge are potentially activated: (1) linguistic information, or one's knowledge of the codes; (2) knowledge of the world; and (3) knowledge of discourse structures (such as conversations, radio broadcast, literary texts, newspaper accounts, fables, political speeches, etc.) (Omaggio, 1986).

In the second phase, reading activities, students deal directly with the reading selection. In the previous stage, students were guided through activities which made them about the topic to be read about. Here, they read and reread, skimming for main ideas, scanning for specific information, reading paragraph by paragraph or section by section, guess word meaning, and verify predictions made in the pre-reading activities. During this stage, students are encouraged to skip words that are hard to guess. They are also told to skip detail and read only for what is required in the specifically assigned task. Significant in this approach to developing reading skills is that students are required to think and do something at each level.

A sample reading activity taken from page 409 of *¿Sabias que...?* is:

Step 3. Complete the following sentences based on you remember from the reading. (A series of sentences with the choices for sentence completion follow.)

The third stage, "Síntesis," allows the students to reflect globally on the content. To make second language learning teaching and learning relevant and meaningful, we must never lose sight of the fact the our students on the secondary or postsecondary level have thoughts and opinions about moral, societal, and other world issues that directly affect the lives of students. The next example from page 413 of *¿Sabias que...?* demonstrates this point.

Step 1. An important theme in the article is the social organization of a herd of elephants. Use the table below to compile the data relevant to the theme. First, synthesize your ideas in a sentence. Then write some key words to help you record the information. (A chart entitled "The Social Organization of Elephants" is provided).

Following "Exploración" is an additional section entitled ¡Sigamos! (Let's Continue) designed to allow students to apply reading content to the meaningful personal experiences. After all, all learning must be meaningful to be effective and permanent. The mind, when involved in meaningful learning, will organize the materials into meaningful chunks and relate them to existing cognitive structure in a way that they will be become "implanted" (Ausubel, 1968, p. 6). What follows is a sample activity from ¡Sigamos! found on page 414 of *¿Sabias que...?*.

Step 4. Make a list of the actions, attitudes, and qualities that characterize the traditional role of the woman in the family. Then, make a list of those that characterize the behavior of the female in the elephant family.

Regarding the use of authentic materials in the teaching and assessment of reading, a survey of recent textbook will reveal a claim that reading materials are taken from authentic sources that carefully reflect the culture of the language taught. However, Shulz (1981) warned that "we cannot advocate that foreign language learners should be exposed to so-called 'authentic' texts in unedited form, indiscriminately chosen without regard to linguistic difficulty" (p. 44). She noted that non-native readers must be approaching the same level of "linguistic and emotional maturity of the group of native speakers for whom the original prose was written (p.44). Specialists in reading have noted that editing or rewriting authentic texts will distort the meaning of the original text and can obscure the true 'cultural' meaning of the text. Avoiding the common practice of using or perhaps overusing concocted reading passages in assessing reading proficiency, several writers that suggest that appropriate authentic texts be edited for length, but not for language (Van-Patten, et al., 1992) for low-level proficient students.

It is nonetheless important to choose reading materials from a variety of culturally authentic sources that are appropriate for lower level proficient speakers. Hadley (1993) on pages 201-221 included lucid examples of several sample formats for using

authentic materials for reading comprehension. Samples include samples for the novice through the advanced levels. As an sample activity for the novice level at the scanning-for-detail stage, she used duplications of four real French tickets for parking and admission. In this activity, students are required to match the function of the ticket with an English description. As a means of assessing true comprehension, five descriptions are given to lower the level of lucky guessing.

The Pre-CPT (Preliminary Chinese Proficiency Test), developed by the Center for Applied Linguistics, offers an example of basing instructional and/or test items on "real-world [authentic] language use rather than on textbook language" (Stansfield et al., 1992. The reading comprehension section, for example, contains three types of reading groupings. The first two groupings are referred to as "nonlinear texts", i.e., non-prose forms. In the first grouping, test items were book titles, stamps, schedules, identification cards, labels and so forth. The second grouping included authentic "signs" that would be seen in China or Taiwan. The third grouping included reading passages that follow conventional norms of sentence and paragraph structure.

Again, activating prior knowledge is important. A study of the importance of cultural background in reading such as the one done by Steffenson, Joag-Dev, and Anderson (1979) serves to reiterate the point. The results will seem obvious, but they further illustrate the importance of comparing and contrasting cultures for beginning level foreign language students. In their study, they concluded that those reading a foreign language text that include elements of their own cultural background will read and comprehend more easily than those readers who lack the same cultural heritage.

Regarding the traditional assessment of reading comprehension, Larson and Jones (1984) offered a thorough review of the methods of measuring reading comprehension: translation, reading aloud, true-false questions, multiple choice questions, question-answer, and clove testing. Perhaps the most commonly used procedure has been the question-answer format readily seen in textbook as well as on many class room examinations. Usually the reading selection is one by non-native textbook or teachers. If they were prepared by native-speakers, they are usually contrived to include certain grammar structures or other linguistic features. Bernhardt (1991) argued that an effective mechanism for assessing reading must be integrative in that it should examine the extent: to which a text actually communicates a coherent message to the reader. She further stated that most conventional measures of reading comprehension have failed because they have not taken into account that reading is a "constructive construct, not one that is a sum of a number of discrete points" (p. 50). It is not easy to measure reading comprehension directly, because reading occurs in the mind (Larson and Jones, 1984).

A valid assessment of reading must attempt to measure comprehension as globally as possible. Bernhardt as well as Larson and Jones called to our attention to the inadequacy of multiple-choice questions for directly measuring reading comprehension. Bernhardt that the multiple-choice format for assessing reading skills is nothing more than a grammar test. Similar attacks have been made cloze testing, which has been widely used for assess reading skills. Shulz (1981), for example, argued that a Cloze test is not strictly an assessment of reading comprehension because of its limited ability to measure comprehension beyond specific clauses within a reading text.

Research results lead to us to conclude that the more effective way to measure second language reading comprehension is to permit students to write summaries of what was read in the native language. For example, Lee (1986) found that students recalled significantly more of the reading passage when they wrote their recalls in their native language. It is believed that this procedure will yield a global assessment of the students' reading skills. Immediate recall is currently considered a practical and sound assessment strategy (Bernhardt, 1991) for measuring reading comprehension. Described elsewhere in this Report, the immediate-recall procedures involve allowing reading to recall orally or in writing as many propositions (main ideas) in the reading passage. The grading is based on the total number of propositions in the reading minus the total number that readers can recall. Major idea units identified and recorded are given more weight than other details and insignificant information.

Final comments in this Report on the teaching, testing, and authentic assessment of the reading and writing must include some general and specific observations on the topic. It is disturbing that many teachers continually fail to use truly communicative activities for the global assessment of communicative abilities. The belief that there are no "creative" ways, in beginning second language classes, to test language skills (usually reduced to discrete-point grammar items) is still in the minds of many foreign language teachers. Teachers are more willing to employ creative and innovative approaches in instructional activities than they are to use them in testing and program assessment. Bernhardt and Deville (1991) admonished, however, that "any testing mechanism must conform to the real objectives of any program." This implies that a program frankly admit to its real intentions. If the implementors of a program want explicit grammatical competence, they should teach and test for it" (p. 45). This further suggests that the formats used in presentation of instructional materials should appear on the examination in a format similar. If, for example, students are provided the practice filling out a job application in the target language in class, then it follows that this activity should included on a major assessment item. As Henning (1990) indicated, we must go beyond asking whether a test is valid to asking *for what* is the test valid. One of the major problems of teacher-made tests, he noted, is that many teachers at all levels of instruction have not been adequately trained in test preparation. Teachers often base both their teaching and testing/assessing on their own experiences as students. We must, therefore, ensure that various positive new experiences are provided for our students, for they are the next generation of language teachers!

Hence, we must continually ask ourselves if we are teaching, testing and assessing in a connected way. In conclusion, we should be emphasizing *function* and *content* in reading tasks, as well as *accuracy* for meaningful purposes of importance to our students.

# References

Alderson, J.C., and Urquhart, C., (Eds). *Reading in a foreign language*. London: Longman, 1994.

Allen, E. and Valette, R. *Classroom techniques: Foreign languages and English a second language*. New York: Harcourt, Brace and Jovanovich, 1977.

Arcuri, G. Pre-reading and pre-writing activities to prepare and motivate foreign language students to read short stories. *Hispania*, 1990, *73*, 262–56.

Ausubel, D. *Educational psychology: A cognitive view*. New York: Holt, Rinehart and Winston, 1978.

Barnett, M.A. Writing as process. *French Review*, 1989, *63*, 31-44.

Bernhardt, E.B. Proficient texts or proficient readers? *ADFL Bulletin*, 1991, *21*, 25–28.

Bernhardt, E.B., and Deville, C. Testing in foreign language programs and testing programs in foreign language departments: Reflections and recommendations. In R.V. Teschner (Ed.), *Assessing foreign language proficiency of undergraduates*. Boston: Heinle and Heinle, 1991.

Bernhardt, E. Reading in a foreign language. In B. Wing (Ed.), *Listening, Reading and Writing: Analysis and Application.* Middlebury, VT: Northeast Conference, 1986.

Bernhardt, E. Towards an information processing perspective in foreign language reading. *The Modern Language Journal,* 1984, *68,* 332–31.

Bernhardt, E. Three approaches to reading comprehension in German. *The Modern Language Journal,* 1983, *67,* (2), 111–15.

Bernhardt, E. Testing foreign language reading comprehension: The immediate recall protocol. *Die Unterrichtspraxis,* 1983, *16,* (1), 27–33.

Carrell, P. and Eisterhold, J. (1983). Schema Theory and ESL Reading Pedagogy. *TESOL Quarterly,* 1983, *17,* 553–73.

Chastain, K. *Developing second-language skills: Theory and Practice.* Orlando: Harcourt, Brace, and Jovanovich, 1988.

Clarke, M. The short-circuit hypothesis of ESL—reading—or when language competence interferes with reading performance. *The Modern Language Journal,* 1980, *64,* 203–09.

Coady, J. A psycholinguistic model of the ESL reader. In Mackay, Barkman and Jordan (Eds.), *Reading in a second language,* Rowley, MA: Newbury House, 1979, 5–18.

Cooper, T.C. (Ed.). *Research within reach: Research-guided response to the concerns of foreign language teachers.* Athens, GA: Agee Publishers, 1985.

Davis, J. A working syllabus for a commercial Spanish course. *Newsletter: Northeast conference on the teaching of foreign languages,* Fall 1986, *20,* 38–40.

Dvorak, T.R. Writing in the foreign language. In B. Wing, (Ed.). *Listening, reading, and writing: Analysis and application.* Middlebury, VT: Northeast Conference, 1986.

Finneman, M. and Carbon Gorell, L. *De lector a escritor: El desarollo de la comunicacion.* Boston: Heinle and Heinle Publishers, 1991.

Goodman, K.S. Reading: A psycholinguistic guessing game. In D.V. Gunderson (Ed.), *Language and Reading, An Interdisciplinary Approach.* Washington, DC: Center for Applied Linguistics, 1970.

Greenia, F. Why Johnny can't escribir: Composition and the foreign language curriculum. *ADFL Bulletin,* 1992, *24,* 30–37.

Grellet, F. *Developing reading skills: A practical quide to reading comprehension exercises.* New York: Cambridge University Press, 1981.

Henning, G. Priority issues in the assessment of communicative language abilities. *Foreign Language Annals,* 1990, *5,* 379–84.

Hudelson, S. Writing in a second language. *Annual Review of Applied Linguistics.* 1988, *9,* 210–22.

Huebener, T. *How to teach foreign languages effectively.* New York: New York University Press, 1965.

Lalande, J. Reducing composition errors: An experiment. *The Modern Language Journal,* 1982, *66,* 140–49.

Krapels, A. R. An overview of second language writing process research. In B. Kroll (Ed.), *Second language writing: Research insights for the classroom.* Cambridge, U.K.: Cambridge University Press, 1990.

Larson, J., and Jones, R. Proficiency testing in the other language modalities. In T.V. Higgs (Ed.), *Teaching for proficiency: The organizing principle.* Lincolnwood, IL: National Textbook Company, 1984.

Leel, J., and Paulson, D. Writing and compositions. In B. VanPatten et al (Eds.), Instructors' Manual: *¿Sabia que ...? Beginning Spanish.* New York: McGraw-Hill, 1992.

Leel J.F. Background Knowledge and L2 Reading. *The Modern Language Journal,* 1986, *70,* 350–54.

MacLean, M. Reading in a second/foreign languages: A bibliography 1974–1984. *Canadian Modern Language Review,* 1985, *42,* 56–66.

Mackay, R., Barkman, B., and Jordan, R. (Eds.), *Reading in a second language*. Boston: Newbury, 1979.

Mathews, T.J., and Jacquet, R.C. Using strategic interaction in L2 writing. *Hispania*, 1992, *75*, 171–76.

Omaggio Hadley, A. *Teaching foreign language in context: Proficiency-oriented instruction*. Boston: Heinle and Heinle, 1993.

Paulson, D. Evaluation of FL learners' writing ability. *Newsletter: Northeast conference on the teaching of foreign languages*, Fall 1993, *43*, 12–15.

Phillips, J. Practical implications of recent research in reading. *Foreign Language Annals*, 1984, *17*, 285–96.

Rivers, W. *Teaching foreign language skills*. Chicago: University of Chicago Press, 1968.

Rivers, W. *Teaching French: A practical guide*. Lincolnwood, IL: National Textbook Company, 1988.

Rosengrant, S. A hierarchy of Russian writing assignments: *Foreign Language Annals*, 1985, *18*, 195-202.

Schulz, R. Literature and readability: Bridging the gap in foreign language reading. *The Modern Language Journal*, 1981, *65*, 43–53.

Semke, H.D. Effects of the red pen. *Foreign Language Annals*, 1984, *17*, 195–202.

Shohamy, E. Language Testing Priorities: A different perspective. *Foreign Language Annals*, 1990, *23*, 385–94.

Stansfield, C., Kenyon, D.M., and Jiang, X. *The Preliminary Chinese Proficiency Test (Pre-CPT): Developmental Scaling and Equating to the Chinese Proficiency Test (CPT)*. Washington, DC: Center for Applied Linguistics, 1992.

Steele, R. and Marechal-Ross,P. *Amicalement: For Basic Functional Writing Proficiency in French*. Lincolnwood, IL: National Textbook Company, 1993.

Steers, K.Z. Starting with self-awareness: Basic experiences in foreign language writing. *Hispania*, 1992, *75*, 420–23.

Steffensen, M., Joag-Dev, C., and Anderson, R. Perspective on reading comprehension. *Reading Research Quarterly*, 1979, *15*, 10–29.

Swaffar, J., Arens, K., Byrnes, H. *Reading for meaning: An integrated approach to language learning*. Englewood Cliffs, NJ: Prentice Hall, 1991.

Terenzini, P.T. Assessment: What it is and what it isn't. *ADE Bulletin*, 1993, *No. 104*, 14–17.

Terry, R. Teaching and evaluation writing as communicative skill. *Foreign Language Annals*, 1989, *22*, 43–54.

Ulijn, J., and Pugh, A. *Reading for professional purposes. Methods and materials in teaching languages*. Leuven, Belgium: ACCO, 1984.

VanPatten, B., Lee, J., Ballman, T., and Dvorak, T. *¿Sabias que . . .? Beginning Spanish*. New York: McGraw-Hill, 1992.

Walsh, D. The four fundamental skills. In S. Newell (Ed.), *Dimension: Languages 67*, Spartanburg, SC: Southern Conference on Language Teaching, 1967.

Yorio, C.A. Some sources of reading problems for foreign language learners, *Language Learning*, 1971, *21*, 107–15.

Zvetina, M. From research to pedagogy: What do reading L2 suggest? *Foreign Language Annals*, 1987, *20*, 233–37.

# The Portfolio and Testing Culture

Zena T. Moore

*University of Texas, Austin*

## A Brief Overview

The last three decades have witnessed major debates on the issue of teaching culture within the foreign language profession. Some language experts are convinced that language cannot be separated from culture (Brooks, 1969; Crawford-Lange and Lange, 1984; Lafayette, 1976; Kramsch, 1983; Nostrand, 1974; Seelye, 1991; Moore, 1993). National strifes and persistent global inter-racial tensions have underscored this conviction and national leaders in the profession have begun to invest more in foreign language education programs, summer intensive institutes and language resource centers which prepare teachers to help students develop skills in interacting (communicating) with speakers of different languages and cultures (Simon, 1980; U.S. Department of Education, 1991).

As an indication of the profession's own effort to integrate language and culture studies in foreign languages, an array of theories and strategies has been proposed. Culture capsules (Taylor and Sorenson, 1961), culture clusters (Meade and Morain, 1973), culture assimilators (Fiedler et al., 1971), mini-dramas (Gorden, 1968), the micrologue (Mydlarski, 1979), and the cultoon (Morain, 1979) are some of the more widely recognized techniques recommended for teaching culture. More recent research in the area of cross-cultural studies has renewed debates and identified new strategies to teaching culture (Breslin, 1993).

Clearly, there has been no lack of recommended approaches on how to teach culture. Yet, there still persist some unresolved questions. What aspects of culture can we teach? Whose culture should we teach; (mainstream cultures, subcultures or pop cultures) ? And, if we do succeed in teaching some cultural skills, how can we measure what we have taught?

This paper focuses on two areas. First it deals with the issue of teaching and assessing culture in general, and secondly it specifically recommends the use of portfolio assessment which is shown to be more in keeping with the teaching of culture as a process, "as a constellation in a continual process of change brought about by participants in the culture as they live, play and work" (Crawford-Lange and Lange, 1984).

## Testing Culture: Three Decades of Research

In spite of the many calls for further research into new strategies and innovations for evaluating the students' cultural skills (Lafayette and Schulz, 1975), the development of valid and reliable tests for assessing cultural skills in the language classroom still remains elusive and difficult. In fact there are very few documented studies on the topic of testing culture learning. For example Morain (1983) listed over twenty-five articles on the subject of teaching culture, and only three works on the testing or evaluation of culture, that of the Nostrands (1970), that of Lafayette and Schulz (1975) and that of Born (1975).

Part of the difficulty in testing culture learning arises from the fact that many believe that the validity of a test must be referenced against the skill, performance, ability or whatever the instructional program purports to instill (Oller, 1979). In other words, unless we know what we are testing or assessing, we cannot develop adequately appropriate measurement tools. Culture has been taught as bits and pieces of information included in areas of cultural studies, in multicultural programs, in social studies programs and in foreign language programs. Testing culture has traditionally measured the knowledge of bits and pieces of information, rather than insights or awareness of the essence of a culture or society.

In spite of many brave efforts over the last three decades, the language teaching profession has not succeeded in developing a valid standardized measuring process for cultural learning. Some believe that testing culture is "even more difficult than testing language" (Damen, 1987). Others point to the lack of clear statements and selections of categories for teaching culture and consequently for testing and assessing it. Born (1975) believed that unless we have clear goals, not only will teaching be difficult but testing and assessing learning outcomes are likely to be unsystematic and inconsistent.

The need for clearly defined goals and objectives is emphasized by Seelye (1991) who recommended that teaching culture should begin with teaching for attitude changes. He argued that before students can begin to understand another culture, they must first understand their own cultural values, beliefs and attitudes. Instructional goals that specify cultural understanding and behavior can then serve as guidelines for devising more practical ways of assessing attitude changes.

While he presented some very useful criticism on the "endemic weaknesses" of tests and assessment procedures as well as the "confusion of literary knowledge with behavior patterns," Seelye did express faith in objective tests and recommended that we "test the test" before it is administered. He suggested using native informants. In this way, he argued, greater content validity is assured. The examples of culture tests which Seelye presented, however, use traditional testing formats (e.g., multiple-choice items). Examples of some of Seelye's objective test items are presented below in Chart 1.

One of the problems with these test items is that they are examples of the type of tests which Seelye urges teachers to avoid because they create and perpetuate stereotypes and over-generalizations. Presumably, Seelye recognized the problems inherent in testing culture using these formats, because he did urge teachers to "explore the possibilities of tactile tests," (p. 188), and although he offered no substantial guidance for the construction nor scoring of such tests, he did stress the importance of validating "the most discrete items" (p. 188).

Lafayette (1976) believed that culture can be learned as active cultural knowledge, or passive cultural knowledge, and that there are only three culturally oriented goals that can be tested in most schools in the U.S.A, knowledge, understanding and behavior. Therefore, he suggested formulating tests for evaluating cultural understanding and behavior. While Lafayette's tests were designed to test material that was different from the more traditional cultural content of most school syllabi, the sample formats presented are multiple-choice questions which test the students' reading and listening skills more than their cultural knowledge. Chart 2 shows an example of testing "active cultural knowledge and passive cultural knowledge." It also reveals problems endemic to multiple-choice items construction.

---

Chart 1
Examples of Seelye's Culture Testing

1. When a Guatemalan gets up from the table after eating, he
   *a. says thank you, or some other pleasantry.
   b. just smiles.
   c. says nothing.
   d. says nothing, but taps his chest lightly.
   * The correct answer is a.

2. Sometimes a store displays a red flag (about 1' square) outside its door. This indicates
   a. the employees are striking
   b. the store is closed for repairs or inventory
   *c. they are selling fresh meat
   d. none of the above
   * The correct answer is c.

3. Which of the following times would a Guatemalan traditionally eat tamales?
   a. Sunday noon
   *b. Saturday evening
   c. For breakfast
   d. There is no preferable custom
   * The correct answer is b.

---

Nostrand (1974), on the other hand, recognized that objective tests cannot measure the ability to "put together one's experience and knowledge." He cautioned against the use of those tests based on true/false statements and multiple-choice questions which are meant to evoke the "correct" answer, the "truth." While it is true that these objective tests certainly can test some geographical and historical facts, tests like these reduce cultural, historical and geographic studies to the learning of fragmented, incomplete and some-times inaccurate information, promoting the teaching of culture that lead to over-generalizations and stereotypes (Arizpe and Aquirre 1987).

---

Chart 2
Examples of Lafayette's Culture Testing

1. (Understanding) Which of the leisure-time activities listed below would the "average" French teenager engage in less frequently than his American counterpart?
   a. Walking around town or in parks.
   *b. Driving around town or around the countryside.
   c. Watching television or listening to the radio.
   d. Going to a café or to a movie theater.
   * b is correct
2. (Understanding) Give two plausible reasons for the answer you chose above. (Note: This item is not an independent test item, as it is based on Item#1. Students should check their answers to item #1 with the teacher before going on. Evaluation: Regardless of length or form of student response, count only relevant information for points given, for example, minimum age for driver's license is 18; exorbitant cost of cars, gasoline, maintenance of cars, etc.)

---

In her text on testing, Valette (1977) devotes the shortest section to the "Testing of Culture." This brevity might reflect the difficulty of testing culture as well as the paucity of work in the area in the mid '70s. Valette's definition of culture included the testing of (1) civilization questions; (2) testing cultural differences between people; and (3) testing literature. The bulk of her suggested tests focused on testing literature (14 of the 19 pages), and although she suggested many useful ways of testing culture in a later edition of the book, the formats suggested are the traditional multiple-choice questions, true/false statements, oral or written responses. An example of an early item is presented in Chart 3.

---

Chart 3
An Early Example of Valette's Culture Test

Question: Is this a typical action or not?
   Use A = true; B = false
1. For breakfast Herr Braun had orange juice, ham and scrambled eggs.
   Answer: A

---

As one indication of the progress in this area of testing and assessing culture in our profession, the reader is asked to compare the latest views of Professor Valette in Chapter 1 of this volume. The perspective presented here, in 1994, is much more holistic and shows testing of culture in the context of meaningful situations heavily influenced by authentic cultural referents.

A recent survey of foreign language teachers (Moore, 1993), shows that true/false statements, and multiple-choice questions continue to be the most frequently used formats for testing culture. This unchanged pattern has led some foreign language educators to express gloomy pessimism in the area of testing culture suggesting that because of the absence of "a well-defined assessment model for culture" teachers should concentrate their attention on developing and organizing cultural activities based on clear instructional goal statements (Omaggio, 1986). Others believe that the solution to the problem is best handled in a top-down way, presumably by the leaders in the field:

> Until teachers have been shown a way to work towards the goal of increasing students' cognitive abilities to process and understand cultural phenomena in an active, analytical way, assessment will remain impossible. (Galloway, 1985, p. 11)

One way to resist an overly pessimistic perspective is to look beyond the boundaries of foreign language education and examine what has been recommended by colleagues in the field of cultural studies. Renwick (1979) advocated the importance of the formats or methods used for evaluating culture to be compatible with "the values, preferences, and customary modes of response of the students" (p. 219). He recommended that self-reports, role-play, simulation, production, and observation be included by those who test the effects of any instruction based on knowledge, attitudes, perceptions, skills, and patterns of behavior.

Renwick's recommendation forces us to reexamine the apparent contradiction between our pedagogical perceptions and our popular approaches to foreign language instruction and assessment. On the one hand we are concerned with developing communicative competence, linguistic proficiency and cultural literacy. On the other hand, we suffer the restrictions of a narrowly goal-driven curriculum, one based on setting instructional goals and testing the attainment of these goals (Langer, 1987).

The problems with testing culture, therefore, seem to derive from both a failure to set instructional objectives that are more closely related to real life competencies, defined as cultural literacy, and the failure to be innovative in the use of testing procedures. Since the teaching and learning of culture, cannot be done in bits and pieces, more creative and imaginative teaching, testing and assessing must be designed.

Furthermore, traditional testing formats have been developed on what

Cizko (1992) criticized as an imperfect basis for measuring human learning and cognitive development (i.e., the quantitative research paradigm which has long dominated the field of measurement of student behavior) and testers may have placed undue credulity in its ability to provide accurate descriptors of learning. Many of the objective testing formats used in testing culture have been the product of quantitative statistical principles, multiple-choice formats and true-false statements, items that test the knowledge of cultural facts and are therefore easy to prepare and score, that is, easy to quantify, and subject to rigid item analysis. Seelye's twelve general questions to assess the strength of items, for example, include the ability of the items to be objectively scored and their reliability as determined through item analysis.

Dissatisfaction with these procedures has led many educators/researchers to discontinue the use of such testing formats based on the belief that they perpetuate pedagogically unsound principles on the part of the teachers and retard pupils' intellectual growth. The examples given by Lafayette (1976) and Seelye (1991) show quite clearly how objective tests can encourage faulty generalizations and incorrect assumptions. Again, the goal is to identify valid ways of teaching, assessing, and testing culture within the field of foreign language education.

## The Movement toward Portfolio Assessment

The country's oldest example of portfolio assessment dates back to 1972. The College Board Advanced Placement Studio Art Portfolio Evaluation is designed, administered, and scored by Educational Testing Service. The panel of scorers/judges is selected from college and high-school art faculty and has been trained in standardized testing procedures. An art portfolio consists of subportfolios each containing items for several established categories, for example creative, still life, and oil and canvas. Each category is assessed by three trained raters to ensure reliability. The worth and effectiveness of this type of assessment is illustrated through the widespread use of the procedure: the evaluation board now assesses portfolios from students whose Advanced Placement credits are accepted by over 2,500 colleges.

Over the last decade increased attempts have been made to adopt similar qualitative-based procedures in assessing students' behavior. For example, ethnographic procedures and other forms of "authentic assessment" and "performance assessment" have been recommended as procedures that can reveal data which are more accurate in describing student behavior, by observation of students, as they perform both in and outside the classroom. These forms of assessment encourage the production of what best describes the students' performance, particularly within meaningful contexts. For a more comprehensive treatment of authentic assessment, the reader is directed to Stansfield's chapter in this volume.

The increased awareness of the need for more authentic forms of assessment is seen in the number of states, which to date have declared a policy of moving their evaluation systems toward performance assessment. Arizona, California, Connecticut, Kentucky, Maryland, New York, and Vermont have all adopted various forms of assessment more in keeping with measuring students' learning as process rather than product. Vermont, for example, has implemented a portfolio process in writing and mathematics and the New York Education Task Force for foreign language instruction has already begun to examine the possibility of using portfolio assessment in areas of foreign language learning (NYSAFLT, 1993).

Portfolio assessment is presently being used in assessing students' reading (Tibbetts et al., 1992; Johns, 1990): in assessing students' skills in language arts and literature (Purves et al., 1992; Roe, 1991): in students' writing (Gentile, 1992; Partridge, 1990; Valencia et al., 1990); in science education (Collins, 1992), in teacher education (Collins, 1991), in art education (Gitomer et al., 1992), and in higher education (Boe, 1992).

# What Are Portfolios?

In the absence of a tradition of using portfolios in many disciplines, discussions on objectives, structure, contents, scoring, and purpose are still debated. The essential characteristics of portfolios, however, have been summarized by Roettger and Szymczuk (1990) as collections of students' works over a period of time. Tierney et al. (1991) describe them as

> systematic collections by both students and teachers that can serve as the basis to examine effort, improvement, processes, and achievement as well as to meet the accountability demands usually achieved by more formal testing procedures. (p. 41)

According to these writers, a portfolio is a collection of evidence used by the teacher and student to monitor the growth of the student' s knowledge of content, use of strategies, and attitudes toward the accomplishment of goals in an organized and systematic way.

*Portfolios*
- are goal based
- show reflection between what a student wants to accomplish and what is being

accomplished
- contain samplings of students' work, projects, anecdotal comments and tests
- contain evidence of students' growth
- span a period of instruction
- allow for reflection, feedback and improvement
- are flexible and versatile.

In addition, those who use and advocate portfolios attest to their ability to capture the richness, depth and breadth of a student's learning, and to show evidence of growth not measured by standardized tests. The students themselves are involved in setting their goals and striving to accomplish them themselves. Moreover, portfolios have the additional value of empowering teachers, for

> When teachers are given autonomy and respect, they can create classrooms with positive, supportive environments that can foster excellence among students. (Tierney et al., 1991, p. vii)

# Portfolio Assessment and Culture Learning: Items and Implementation

The types of portfolio best suited for assessing culture learning are similar to those used for assessing writing, as outlined by Gentile (1992), who identified three types of portfolios, classroom portfolios, which are a collaborative effort of teacher and student; combination portfolios which can contain works selected by students alone and works selected by teacher and student, and assessment portfolios which can contain various files reflecting various areas within one discipline or the students' work in all discipline areas.

How can the classroom teacher begin to create a portfolio for culture learning? What will the items look like? Who decides on the items to be included in the portfolio? How are the items assessed? These and more are questions which have to be addressed in implementing a portfolio on culture learning. Readers are referred to Roettger and Szymczuk's draft version of a checklist for developing student portfolios (1990). A twelve-step procedure for implementing the portfolio for culture learning at the classroom level will be presented here with the clear understanding that there is no one "right way to implement a portfolio" (Tierney et al., 1991, p. vii). These suggestions are based on findings from two pilot studies conducted over two semesters in two rural high schools in upstate New York.

12 Steps in Implementing a Class Portfolio

1.  Discuss with the students what is portfolio assessment.
2.  Decide on the number of items. These will vary according to the grade level. For example, in the first year students may submit one item per semester from the topics that make up the syllabus. Second year students may submit two items per semester.
3.  Discuss the format of the items. Items can be school-based research studies, case-studies, group projects, which can be either descriptive, experimental, exploratory, or longitudinal. Formats can include video and audio productions, pictorial displays, clay models and collages.
4.  Once the number of items is decided, let students select their first topic. Create a period of activity where students brain storm aspects of the first topic. This period, like a pre-reading or pre-writing activity, allows for discussion of students preconceived ideas on the topics, of discussion of their own cultural patterns, of how culture is constructed, etc. Reports of these discussions, which in the pilot studies took three class sessions, can be the first items in the portfolio.
5.  Decide on a time frame. This may be negotiated by teacher and student and depends on the level and testing schedules of the school.
6.  Decide on the mode/s of inquiry/ research. Students collaborate with the teacher to select the procedures best suited to achieve their objectives. Will they use interviews? If so, how many? Will they use secondary sources? If so, what will be the minimum?
7.  Develop a plan of activity for the successful accomplishment of the objectives. The pilot studies showed that creating a plan was very useful not only in keeping students focused on the task, but also in keeping track of their progress. This plan or outline was the second item in the portfolio. See Appendix A for the plan used in the pilot studies.
8.  Identify the resources needed. Where can the resources be found? What support can the school and community provide? Will parents be involved?
9.  Decide on the physical nature of the portfolio. Will it be a manila folder? A three-hole binder? A simple box? Or a combination of these?
10. Working in collaboration with students, establish the criteria for grading. This allows students to be true partners in setting standards for themselves.
11. Organize a schedule of conferences with students.
12. Create a form for the students to do their own evaluation. The purpose of this self-evaluation is to help students work through the process in a *reflective* manner. The evaluation form used in the pilot studies is presented in Appendix B.

# Examples of Items in a Culture Portfolio

*Example 1.*

Cindy and Lauren, 8th grade Spanish students, undertook a study of Mexican food. They selected what they thought was typical Mexican dish, "arroz con pollo." They prepared an oral presentation of the sources of the ingredients, how the dish was prepared, and they prepared the dish for their classmates to sample. They were not sure if they wanted this item placed in their portfolio as originally presented or whether they could work on improving it. After three conferences with the teacher they opted for improving the item and identified three areas to work on. These included the source/s of the raw material used in the dish, the region from which the dish originated and the routine associated with the meal itself.

The preliminary presentation of Cindy and Lauren showed behavior in and knowledge of an aspect of the Mexican culture, by preparing and sampling an authentic Mexican dish, and by presenting information on the ingredients and directions for preparing the dish.. Their primary interest, like most teenagers was in sampling the food. It was left to the teacher working with the students to build on this first experience, to help the students delve deeper into questions of class, status, and income which are at the base of all cultural activities.

*Example 2.*

Chaz, a 7th grade student originally from Quebec, undertook a study on "Greetings and Leave-Takings" in French. He and his teacher worked together to identify eight French speakers, of both sexes, different ages and economic status, in the community. Armed with amateur enthusiasm and experience and a school-owned camcorder, Chaz interviewed these eight French speakers. Two were students from Haiti, two were native-speaking French teachers from France, two were students from Quebec, and two were neighbors who came from the Ivory Coast. He prepared five questions with the help of his teacher: (1) How do people in their French community greet each other? (2) How do they take leave of each other? (3) Do these forms vary among age groups? (4) Do they vary by sex? and (5) What gestures accompany these acts?

Chaz spent over twenty hours on this project. The result was a collection of speech samples in French of greetings and leave takings in real life situations. During the learning experience, Chaz developed more positive feelings about himself as a Quebecois, and learned more about French cultural patterns of greetings and leave takings. But Chaz learned more than this. The video production developed his ability to use a camcorder as an instrument to gather data, gave him practice in speaking, gave him the opportunity to combine artistic taste and content, as well as to plan and execute a project.

## Assessing the Items

How does Chaz's work compare to Cindy and Lauren's? Can they be assessed using the same criteria? These were some of the questions which puzzled the teachers who expressed uncertainty about doing the assessment. They were concerned that the grading of the portfolio items, as with other forms of assessment, may suffer from subjective bias. They decided to use a holistic approach in assessing the individual items in the portfolio. They also decided to create a list of criteria to include subject matter, presentation, method of collecting data, organization of material, accuracy of facts, and documentation of sources. Moreover, they believed that the criteria they created were in keeping with the New York State Regents Examination criteria. Table 1 presents the grading criteria used in the pilot studies. Again, this is a suggestion and may need to be improved.

| Table 1. Grading Criteria | | |
|---|---|---|
| Letter Grades | Criteria | Descriptors |
| Superior A+ , A, or A- | Outstanding in presentation Outstanding in content Outstanding in creativity; Appropriate format Accurateinformation Several errors but faults or weaknesses are not grave | There is coherence in presentation Sources are well-documented Information is well gathered Validity is ensured by using multiple sources; Citations well documented Manifests excellent skill in organizing information |
| Satisfactory B+ , B, B- | Very good but not as creative Errors in content Several weaknesses in presentation Similar in meeting criteria for superior but not as outstanding, nor creative and contain more weaknesses | Topic not thoroughly researched Sources documented but with several errors Insufficient sources |

| Table 1 (cont'd). | | |
|---|---|---|
| Unsatisfactory C+ , C, C- | Many weaknesses Insufficient content Inadequate length Presentation sloppy Inaccurate information | Topic not well researched Insufficient evidence of work done Few resources used Incomplete citations |

# Portfolio Assessment of Culture and the Language Test

The teachers, who were all new to this type of assessment, felt the need for collaboration in creating the criteria and in assessing the items. The teacher involved in the first pilot study said "I felt that it would have been better to have another opinion, even when I thought I did a good job with grading." Greater inter-rater reliability was ensured by having more than one teacher grade the students' work. The teachers further pointed out that the assessment of culture is only one part of the foreign language test. How can they use a portfolio assessment in only one area of the language test? In order to do this they decided to view the language test as a composite test. The portfolio grade for culture can then be converted to a percentage of the total language test. The use of a 100% point scale worked well since students were familiar with this system. Table 2 gives a suggested overall distribution of percentages in a composite language test.

| Table 2. The Foreign Language Test, Distribution and Weighting | | | | | |
|---|---|---|---|---|---|
| Culture | Listening | Speaking | Reading | Writing | Total |
| 20 | 25 | 25 | 20 | 10 | 100 |

The teachers also thought it pedagogically sound to use authentic material for developing tests in the other skill areas, speaking, listening, reading and writing, a recommendation made by Valette in the first chapter of this volume.

# In Defense of Portfolios

Portfolio assessment has been used in other countries as more effective ways of measuring students' learning in areas such as in Social Studies and in History, because it is believed that such evaluation procedures avoid regurgitation of facts, minimizes the memorization of totally unrelated bits and pieces of information, and encourages more realistic achievement of educational goals and objectives. Portfolio assessment and other authentic assessment procedures allow for self-directed work, self-correction, greater autonomy and greater time frames. Students can work outside the time constraints of the school timetable. Students are free to select topics in which they have personal interests, thus portfolios have the potential for encouraging greater motivation. They also have greater appeal in that they are self-directed forms of learning.

It is a well established fact that teachers teach to the test (Madaus, 1988). It has also been demonstrated that the use of tests that encourage higher level thinking and higher level writing skills (essay types) encourage instruction in higher level skills. This is another reason why tests that attempt to measure student's performance, should encourage performance in intellectually challenging ways. Moreover, the introduction and implementation of portfolios as a new method of assessment is in keeping with the new reform movement in internal assessment called for by the *Holmes Group Forum* (Spring 1993), a reform movement that is aimed at drastically improving "tomorrow's teacher educators," many of whom are students of the present system. If reform is to be successful, it must take place at all areas of education. Schnyer and Hammadou have described the Holmes effort more fully in their chapter on teacher education in this volume.

In 1979 the National Conference on Achievement Testing and Basic Skills agreed that the essential means to improve quality in public schools is helping teachers and principals to do a better job (Department of Health, 1979). If we hope to help our students develop competence in understanding and appreciating their own culture and other cultures, we need to encourage the development of instructional and testing material that encourages students to perform in ways that demand more than just learning bits and pieces of information. While research must continue in the areas of testing, teaching and assessment of culture, we may find it beneficial to use portfolio assessment as it provides opportunities for students to learn about the cultures of peoples in "more varied and reasoned ways" (Langer, 1987). If in fact the students today will be the teachers of tomorrow, then it is highly possible that they will teach as they have been taught. The research skills demanded and developed in portfolios at the high-school level will no doubt have tremendous effects on the quality of foreign language teachers of the 21st century.

There is the likelihood that foreign language testing, like all the other subjects that are nationally tested, may need to emphasize standardized and norm-referenced procedures. The use of portfolio assessment at this stage is one way of ensuring that foreign language teachers continue to assess what is taught in the classroom. In this respect, portfolios can be useful in creating a greater balance within the overall testing program, both in internal testing (what is done in the schools) and external testing (what is done at both the state and national levels).

Arguments for introducing the portfolio assessment are guided by the qualitative paradigm that employs ethnographic approaches and naturalistic inquiry to allow for more accurate assessment and evaluation of the students' performance and not simply of his/her knowledge. The use of portfolios is also based on several pedagogical principles: involving students in decision-making about what they learn and how they learn it.

Portfolio assessment upholds the Dewey principle that learning is self-directed, and also is not compartmentalized. It also assumes that there is a difference between instruction (what the teacher does), and learning (what the student does). Testing formats have traditionally measured what has been taught. The portfolio is recommended as a method of assessment of what and how students learn. Furthermore, they are more "authentic" in that they encourage an integrative approach to learning by fostering development of multiple skills across content areas. Other chapters in this volume have addressed aspects of this topic. Most of all, portfolio assessment has the advantage of producing students who become independent of the teacher, people who are taught to accept the responsibility for their own learning, a major goal of education.

Portfolio assessment also supports the Piagetian model for learning, since it allows students' work to be assessed in a cumulative way, at all levels and stages of learning. Students are not expected to be at the same levels of intellectual growth at the same time, and so assessment is not synchronic. As Romer puts it: "What is fixed is what you need to know and be able to do. What is variable is how long it takes you to learn that" (cited in *Holmes Group Forum*, p. 2). With the portfolio, students at the beginning levels of classroom instruction may undertake several projects on cultural topics, at very simple levels, from which they can select and submit *one* which *they* judge to be their best work. This one selected project is assessed at the end of each testing period depending on school requirements. At the intermediate level they can be given the option of submitting *two* of their best pieces of work for each testing period. At the advanced level, they can submit several projects on different topics, or on different aspects of the same topic, completing a portfolio of works which they judge to represent their finest efforts. At the various stages of learning the criteria for scoring/grading the portfolio item may carry different weightings, gradually progressing from lower level cognitive skills to higher-level analytic ones.

Creating a portfolio is in itself a type of formative evaluation. Students go through the steps of *selecting, planning, organizing,* and *producing.* The portfolio is also a type of summative evaluation (Purves, 1993) because it enables the teacher and student to see the final products of the learning experiences.

Portfolios encourage "consciousness-raising and critical thinking" in keeping with the Freirean philosophy that encourages students to go beyond textbook information, into understanding their communities, by immersion into the "culture" of those communities, thereby having the opportunity to understand their own values and attitudes. Students, according to Freirean principles, will have the opportunity to arrive at the understanding that culture is not static, that culture is defined by forces in society, and that these forces may vary from group to group, neighborhood to neighborhood, community to community, and society to society. Since culture is learned, negative values and attitudes can also be unlearned, and positive attitudes can be inculcated, which is one of the general goals of most education. The student working on a portfolio may be exposed to far more influences in his/her learning than if he/she were to be the passive recipient of "knowledge" handed down by the teachers. As Freire asserts, "education must begin with the solution of the teacher-student contradiction, by reconciling both poles of contradiction so that both are simultaneously teachers and students" (Freire, p. 59), learning from each other. In this way, knowledge is interactive, and learning is empowering to both students and teachers. Education becomes a joint responsibility.

# References

American Council for the Teaching of Foreign Languages, *ACTFL proficiency guidelines: Culture.* Yonkers, New York, 1988.

American Council for the Teaching of Foreign Languages, *ACTFL Newsletter.* Yonkers, New York. 1992, 5 (1), 1–3.

Arizpe, V., and Aquirre, B. Mexican, Puerto-Rican and Cuban ethnic groups in first-year-college-level Spanish textbooks. *The Modern Language Journal*, 1987, *71* (2), 125–37.

Boe, D. Integrating prior learning assessment into a traditional 4-year institution. In S. Reithlingshoefer (Ed.), The future of nontraditional/interdisciplinary programs: Margin or mainstream? Selected papers from the Annual Conference on Nontraditional and Interdisciplinary Programs. Fairfax, VA: George Mason University, 1992, 3–12.

Born, W. Goals clarification: Implementation. In W. Born (Ed.), *Goals clarification: Curriculum, teaching, education*. Middlebury, VT: Northeast Conference, 1975.

Breslin, R. *Understanding culture's influence on behavior.* New York: Harcourt, Brace and Jovanovich, 1993.

Brooks, N. Teaching culture in the foreign language classroom. *Foreign Language Annals*, 1969, *1*, 204–17.

Brooks, N. Culture the new frontier. *Foreign Language Annals*, 1971, *5*, 54–56.

Caribbean Examination Council. *The SBA. social studies syllabus.* Mona, Jamaica, 1979.

Collins, A. Portfolios for science education: Issues in purpose, structure, and authenticity. *Science Education*, 1992, *76* (40), 451–63.

Crawford-Lange, L., and D. Lange. Doing the unthinkable thing in the classroom. In T. Higgs (Ed.), *Teaching for proficiency: The organizing principle*. The ACTFL foreign language education series, 15. Lincolnwood, IL.:National Textbook, 1985.

Cziko, G. Purposeful behavior as the control of perception: Implications for educational research. *Educational Researcher*, 1992, *21* (9), 10–26.

Damen, L. *Culture learning: The fifth dimension in the language classroom*. Boston: Addison-Wesley Publishing Company Inc., 1987.

Department of Health, Education and Welfare. *Testing, teaching and learning. report of a conference on research on testing*. Washington, D.C., 1979.

Department of Education. *America 2000. Compact for learning*. Washington, D.C., 1991.

Dewey, J. *Lectures in the philosophy of education*. New York: Random House, 1899.

Fiedler, F., et al. The Culture assimilator: An approach to cross-cultural training. *Journal of Applied Psychology.* 1971, *55*, 95–102.

Freire, P. *Pedagogy of the oppressed*. New York: Herder and Herder, 1970.

Galloway, V. Communicating in a cultural context: The global perspective. *Proceedings of the 1981 Summer Cross-Cultural Workshop for Foreign Language Teachers*. Columbia, S.C., South Carolina State Department of Education, 1985.

Gentile, C. Exploring new methods for collecting school-based writing: UNAEP's 1990 portfolio study. *National assessment of educational progress*. Princeton, N.J., 1992.

Gotomer, D., et al. Portfolio: Culture in art education. *Art Education*, 1992, *5*, 7–15.

Gorden, R.L. *Initial immersion in the foreign culture*. Yellow Springs, Ohio: Antioch College, 1968.

Higgs, T. *Teaching for proficiency: The organizing principle*. ACTFL Foreign Language Series 15. Lincolnwood, IL: National Textbook, 1985.

The Holmes Group. *The Holmes Group Forum*. East Lansing: MI, 1993, *7*, No. 3, 1–2.

Johns, T. *Literary portfolios*. Northern Illinois University Reading Clinic, 1990.

Kramsch, C. Culture and Constructs: Communicating Attitudes and values in the Foreign Language Classroom. *Foreign Language Annals*, 1983, *16*, 437–48.

Lafayette, R., ed. *The culture revolution in foreign language teaching*. Skokie: National Textbook Co., 1976, 91–103.

Lafayette, R., and R. Schultz. "Evaluating cultural learnings." In R. Lafayette, (Ed.), *The culture revolution in foreign languages: A guide for building the modern curriculum*. Skokie, IL.: National Textbook Co., 1975.

Langer, J. Literacy and schooling: A sociocognitive perspective. In J. Langer, (Ed.), *Language, literacy and culture: Issues of society and schooling*. Norwood, New Jersey: Ablex Publishing Corporation, 1987.

Madaus, G. The influence of testing on the curriculum. In L. Tanner, (Ed.), *Critical issues in curriculum, 87th yearbook of the national society for the study of education*. University of Chicago Press, 1988.

Meade, B., and Morain, G. The culture cluster. *The Modern Language Journal*, 1973, *6*, 331–38.

Moore, Z.T. Teaching and testing culture: A way and ways. Workshop conducted at NYSAFLT Annual Conference N.Y., 1992.

Moore, Z. Teachers teaching culture: continuing the debate. Paper submitted to *Foreign Language Annals*, 1993.

Morain, G. Commitment to the teaching of foreign cultures. *The Modern Language Journal*, 1983, *67* (4), 402–12.

Mydlarski, D. Using the micrologue in the language classroom. *Canadian Modern Language Review*, 1979, *35*, 625–28.

New York State Association of Foreign Language Teachers, *NYSAFLT Bulletin*, Fall 1993.

Nostrand, F. and H. Testing understanding of the foreign culture. In H.N. Seelye, (Ed.), *Perspectives for teachers of Latin-American culture*, Springfield, IL.: Superintendent of Public Instruction, 1970.

Nostrand, H. Empathy for a second culture: Motivations and techniques. In G. Jarvis, (Ed.), *Responding to new realities*. ACTFL review of foreign language education. Lincolnwood, IL.: National Textbook Co., 1974, 5.

Oller, J., Jr. *Language tests at school*. New York: Longman Inc., 1979.

Omaggio, A. *Teaching language in context: Proficiency-oriented instruction*. Boston: Heinle and Heinle Publishing Inc., 1986.

Purves, Alan. Gathering standards, responses, cultures, plays, and classrooms into a portfolio of literature learning. Paper presented at Connecticut Conference, Old Saybrook, 1993.

Renwick, G. Evaluation: Some Practical Guidelines. In M. Pusch, (Ed.), *Multicultural education: A cross-cultural training approach*. Chicago: Intercultural Press, 1979, 205–30.

Roe, M. Portfolio:From mandate to implementation. Paper presented at the Annual Meeting of the National Reading Conference, California, 1991.

Roettger, D., and Szymczuk, M., (Eds.). *Guide for developing student portfolios*. Draft Version. Heartland Area Education Agency, IA, 1990.

Seelye, N. *Teaching culture: Strategies for intercultural communication*. Skokie, IL: National Textbook Co., 1991.

Simon, P. *The tongue-tied american: Confronting the foreign language crisis*. New York: Continuum Publishing Corp., 1980.

Shohamy, E. Beyond proficiency testing: A diagnostic feedback testing model for assessing foreign language learning. *The Modern Language Journal*, 1992, *76*, 513–19.

Taylor, D., and Sorenson, J. The culture capsule. *The Modern Language Journal*, 1961, *45*, 350–54.

Tibbetts, K., et al. Development of a criterion-referenced, performance-Based Assessment of Reading Comprehension in a Whole Literacy Program." Paper presented at AERA Conference, San Francisco, 1992.

Tierney, R., et al. *Portfolio Assessment in the Reading-Writing Classroom*. Norwood, MA: Christopher Gordon Publishers Inc., 1991.

Valette, R.M. *Modern language testing: A handbook*. 2nd Ed. New York: Harcourt, Brace and Jovanovitch, 1977.

Valencia, S., et al. Assessing reading and writing: Building a more complete picture for Middle School Assessment. Technical Report. Urbana, Illinois: Center for the Study of Reading, 1990.

# Appendix A. Culture Project Outline

Name:　　　　　　　Class:
Grade:

1. TOPIC:

2. CONTENT:
   a. What is/are my objectives?

   b. What do I hope to learn?

3. FORMAT:
   What is the design of the study? Interviews, creating a clay model, a
   video production, an oral presentation with visuals?

4. STRUCTURE:
   a. How am I going to do the study?

   b. What steps are involved?

   c. What materials and resources will I need?

5. EVALUATION:
   a. How did the study come out?

   b. What improvements can I make?

# Appendix B. Evaluation Form

Rank your performance by circling a number from 1 to 5. (5= highest)

| | | | | | | |
|---|---|---|---|---|---|---|
| 1. CONTENT | (self) | 1 | 2 | 3 | 4 | 5 |
| a. use of at least 2 sources and | | | | | | |
| documented with bibliography | (group) | 1 | 2 | 3 | 4 | 5 |
| b. ability to communicate ideas clearly | | | | | | |
| c. accurate information | | | | | | |

| | | | | | | |
|---|---|---|---|---|---|---|
| 2. PREPARATION | (self) | 1 | 2 | 3 | 4 | 5 |
| a. completed outline of project | (group) | 1 | 2 | 3 | 4 | 5 |
| b. completed tasks weekly | | | | | | |
| c. held conferences with teacher | | | | | | |
| d. was always on task | | | | | | |
| e. made group decisions and assigned individual tasks | | | | | | |

| | | | | | | |
|---|---|---|---|---|---|---|
| 3. CREATIVITY | | | | | | |
| a. used information in a unique way | (self) | 1 | 2 | 3 | 4 | 5 |
| | (group) | 1 | 2 | 3 | 4 | 5 |

| | | | | | | |
|---|---|---|---|---|---|---|
| 4. ORGANIZATION | | | | | | |
| a. ideas were presented clearly | (self) | 1 | 2 | 3 | 4 | 5 |
| | (group) | 1 | 2 | 3 | 4 | 5 |

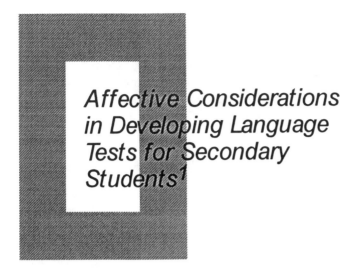

# Affective Considerations in Developing Language Tests for Secondary Students[1]

Pat Barr-Harrison

*Prince George's County (MD) Public Schools*

Elaine K. Horwitz[2]

*University of Texas, Austin*

William James once wrote that "the art of being wise is the art of knowing what to overlook" (James, 1950). In testing, teachers cannot test all the content they teach nor all the knowledge their students gain. When preparing tests, teachers often ask themselves, "What did students overlook in their learning of the second language?" At the same time, students are often puzzled by what teachers seem to overlook in creating a test and wonder why some of what they have studied is not on the test. Of course, any test is of necessity, a compromise between all that makes up the learner's developing target language competence and what the teacher can realistically elicit in a classroom test. Thus, any language test is likely "to feel" incomplete to both students and teacher. The goals of this Report are three-fold. In the first section, we discuss secondary-age language learners and how language assessment procedures need to be adapted to their special needs, concerns, and cognitive abilities. Secondly, we report on the recent development of a battery of proficiency-oriented tests for secondary students of Spanish in the Prince George's County (Maryland) Public Schools. We conclude with an overview of student affective reactions to the reading portion of the test battery and make suggestions for other educators who recognize the importance of considering students' feelings about tests and taking them into account when designing assessment procedures.

# Considerations in Developing Language Tests for Secondary Students

*Characteristics of Adolescent Learners*

When devising language assessment procedures for secondary students, it is essential to keep in mind several important features of adolescents' cognitive and social development.[3] Any teacher who has worked with adolescents knows that they are active, concrete, and often self-conscious. Wiseman, Hunt, and Bedwell's (1986) research on the cognitive development and mental growth of eleven- to fourteen-year-old learners found that students in this age group preferred concrete items over abstract descriptions on listening comprehension activities. Students responded well to instructional activities when the teacher used objects, pictures, and realia to illustrate vocabulary and grammatical concepts. This preference for the concrete over the abstract also manifested itself in the students' desire to know clearly what their teachers expected them to learn. We will return to this point when we discuss student reactions to the new Prince George's County reading test in a later section.

Physical appearance was also an important issue for these learners. Wiseman et al. (1986) note that their subjects experienced some amount of difficulty adjusting to changes in their appearance associated with adolescence. These physical changes caused many students to view themselves as unattractive. Consequently, these changes resulted in substantial mood swings that had a strong impact on their classroom performance. Many middle school teachers have observed that an adolescent who is cooperative and positive one day can become uncooperative and sullen the next. It is not surprising then, that adolescents, in their search to be viewed as attractive and "normal," place great emphasis on the reactions and opinions of their peers. Lipsitz (1980) found that adolescents were more concerned with their peers' rather than their own parents' perceptions of them. Peer reaction also influenced subjects' participation in classroom activities; if their peers were involved in a classroom activity, then other students would want to participate. Lipsitz suggests that adolescents are more responsive to their peers than adults because they feel connected through age and shared concerns. We return to the issues of level of abstraction/concreteness and group identification several times in this Report as they are related to our testing formats.

### Secondary Language Learners

In addition to being adolescents, many secondary language students are also language learners and several characteristics of successful and less-successful language learners, particularly motivation, beliefs about language learning, and foreign language anxiety, are relevant to a discussion of secondary school language learners and their reactions to language tests. We also discuss the appropriateness of small group activities for language testing from the perspective of adolescents' needs for social connections with their peers.

### Motivation.

From Gardner and Lambert's original formulations in 1972 to the present, foreign language teachers have recognized that motivated students will likely achieve higher levels of language competence than unmotivated language learners. Gardner and Lambert distinguish a pragmatic purpose for language learning (instrumental motivation) from a personal desire to get to know the target language people (integrative motivation) (Gardner and Lambert, 1972; Gardner, 1985).[4] Graham (1984) distinguishes a third motivational category, the learner's desire to assimilate into the new culture (assimilative motivation). The impact of motivation on language learning has been discussed from the perspective of the type of motivation as well as from a consideration of the extent of the student's motivation. On both counts, American secondary students would seem to be at a disadvantage. In order to have a "type" of motivation, learners must be able to identify specific reasons why they want to learn the language. While many secondary students may have generalized positive feelings about learning a particular language, a much smaller number tends to associate language learning with a specific career- or life-goal such as using Spanish as a health care provider or wanting to speak Arabic to get to know and understand the people of the Middle East. For many English-speaking Americans knowing a second language is, unfortunately, not seen as an essential life skill. At the present time, few career paths require foreign language proficiency. The American situation can be contrasted with the situation in one of Gardner and Lambert's early studies (1972), which was conducted in the Philippines. In the study, Gardner and Lambert found that students who were more instrumentally motivated generally had higher levels of achievement in English. Ultimately, Gardner and Lambert attribute the greater success of the instrumentally motivated learners in this study to the intensity of their motivation, rather than to instrumental orientation. At the time of the study, university entrance in the Philippines was based primarily on English achievement. As the university functioned as a gateway to middle class status, poor achievement in English had serious consequences. Few if any American secondary students, on the other hand, undertake language study with as clear a societal emphasis.

*Beliefs about Language Learning*

Many students undertake language study with unrealistic expectations and misinformed ideas about how to learn a language (Horwitz, 1988). In a study of beginning language classes at a major university, more than 30 percent of the students thought that you could become fluent in a foreign language in less than two years of casual language study (one hour a day), and more than 30 percent felt that learning a new language was mainly a matter of learning to translate from English or memorizing a large number of new vocabulary words. Although we have not studied secondary students' beliefs about language learning or language testing systematically, we have also encountered some disconcerting examples. Horwitz (1985) reported several occasions where secondary students offered a belief which she called the "English is the base language of the world belief." Students who embrace this idea think that all people across the world first think in English and then have to translate their ideas into their particular native tongue. Although Horwitz originally dismissed this belief as idiosyncratic, she has consistently found at least a small number of learners who express this belief in many secondary school settings.

Students' beliefs about the nature of language learning are important when designing evaluation procedures. Adolescents want to know what is expected of them and how to go about achieving their teachers' expectations. If their own misconceptions about how to go about learning a foreign language go unchallenged, they will likely spend their test preparation efforts in unproductive ways leading ultimately to frustration and possibly the development of a negative self-image as a language learner.

*Foreign Language Anxiety*

Significant numbers of high school and college-age foreign language students report feeling anxious about some aspects of language learning and their language classes (Horwitz and Young, 1991). Testing situations would seem to be particularly difficult for anxious language learners because they have the potential to evoke foreign language anxiety, test anxiety, and fear of negative evaluation simultaneously (Horwitz, Horwitz, and Cope, 1986). Since much foreign language anxiety is associated with understanding and speaking the foreign language, oral tests can be especially traumatic for some learners. Horwitz, Horwitz, and Cope (1986) report that some anxious language learners experienced an indecipherable buzz whenever they were asked to listen to the foreign language, and Horwitz (1989) found that many language learners believed that they were supposed to understand every word when their teacher spoke in the target language and that they became anxious whenever their teacher spoke to them. Even larger numbers of students report feeling anxious when they are asked to speak in the target language. In fact, speaking publicly in the target language was found to be extremely anxiety-provoking for many students, even those who felt no stress in all other aspects of language learning (Horwitz, Horwitz, and Cope, 1986).

While all the components and causes of foreign language anxiety are not completely understood (Horwitz and Young, 1991), some teaching and testing approaches have been found to be less anxiety-producing for many students. Young (1992) found that secondary language students preferred and felt more comfortable participating in oral activities in small groups rather than in front of the whole class. Interestingly, Koch and Terrell found that even within Natural Approach classes, a teaching method designed to reduce learners' affective filters, learners were more comfortable participating in some activities, such as pair-work and personalized discussions, than other activities. At the same time, teachers should recognize that activities that are not stressful for the majority of learners may still be anxiety-provoking for some students (Koch and Terrell, 1991; Price, 1991). In such situations, the teacher and most students may not perceive any kind of threat, while other students feel very uncomfortable. Discussions of foreign language anxiety have focused primarily on classroom learning and activities, but language testing situations would seem to be particularly conducive to anxiety reactions.

*Language Learner Preferences for Group Work*

For many reasons including increased opportunity for social contact with peers and reduced feelings of conspicuousness, adolescents prefer group tasks over other types of instructional organization. Consistent with Young's (1992) findings reported above, a number of studies have found that adolescent language learners perform better when instruction is organized around social considerations and small group tasks, including testing situations. Robeson (1992) draws similar conclusions based on results from "An Oral Assessment Project." The project emphasizes a small-group approach in administering speaking tests.

The North Carolina Department of Public Instruction (1991) describes middle school-age students as preoccupied with a concern about how adults view them. They feel more at ease working with their peers and perceive the small group as safe, protective, and accepting. The Maryland State Department of Education (MSDE, 1990) also recognizes the value of small group activities with this age-group: "Cooperative learning is a highly effective instructional strategy. . . (which) aids students in the socialization process so important at the middle school level" (p. 25). With respect to foreign language classes, MSDE also advocates small group and cooperative learning instructional strategies. Small group and paired activities allow students to practice the language among their peers before having to respond in front of an entire class. In this way, it is argued, students have a safe forum in which they can develop confidence in speaking the foreign language.

Some researchers argue for the use of small groups and cooperative group structures with young adolescent language learners. In a study of two junior high French classes, Gunderson and Johnson (1980) found that teachers were able to increase student participation and the amount of target language talk while at the same time decreasing learner anxiety by using games and group activities. In addition, students seemed to take more risks and were less inhibited in helping each other when participating in the group activities than when they participated in more traditional language exercises. As the traditional exercises also contributed to higher levels of frustration in the students, Gunderson and Johnson concluded that cooperative activities may also promote more positive attitudes toward the target language. We anticipate that these more positive attitudinal outcomes would also be associated with the testing aspects of a language program.

Gunderson and Johnson's findings are consistent with Nerenz' (1990) analysis of middle school language learners. According to Nerenz, early adolescent students highly value belonging to a group of peers. Although middle school students are often shy about expanding their responses to open-ended questions in front of the whole class, they can be highly motivated to speak in paired or small-group activities. Consistently, these learners appear to hold more positive attitudes toward group work than toward individual tasks. Nerenz speculates that middle school students tend to emphasize their individuality with parents and adults while valuing conformity and solidarity with peers. As testing approaches—in foreign languages as well as in most content specialties—have typically emphasized individual performance, correctness, and competition with peers, it would seem that alternative testing strategies are necessary if teachers want to decrease negative affective reactions of language learners. In the next section, we describe one school district's recent testing initiatives to foster positive aspects of testing.

# The Development of the Prince George's County Tests

*Underlying Philosophy of the Prince George's County Tests*

In general, assessment allows for the testing of knowledge, performance, and skills associated with a particular subject matter. In many ways, assessment procedures which have been thoughtfully designed provide the teacher as much feedback about the quality of instruction as they do about the performance of individual learners. Wiggins (1989) argues that good testing procedures—as contrasted with poorly designed ones—retain the essential element of human interactions and judgments. Several scholars (Fredriksen and Collins, 1989; Wiggins, 1989; Shohamy, 1991) maintain that the primary purpose of testing students should be the improvement of instruction. Wiggins' chapter in this volume emphasizes this connection strongly. Shohamy (1991) cites a study, conducted in Israel, of the impact of new oral testing procedures on a language program. Unfortunately, the implementation of the oral testing procedures produced some unintended results: teachers began teaching directly to the test. In addition, an analysis of the test protocols found that the students primarily produced "test language," rather than spontaneous "real-life language." Thus, any changes in testing format should be monitored carefully to identify undesirable side-effects. Moreover, the evaluation of specific instructional objectives should not be the only purpose of classroom assessment. Surveys, classroom observation protocols, student portfolios, learner interviews, peer and self-assessments, classroom interactions—among others—can all contribute to a broader picture of student learning and performance. As foreign language classes employ a wide variety of teaching strategies and approaches, similar assessment approaches are needed.

There is also some evidence that students feel more comfortable with certain types of foreign language tests than others. Madsen, Brown, and Jones (1991) studied the reactions of university German students to varying testing formats including—among others—dictation, translation (both English to German and German to English), oral questions, sentence formation, grammatical fill-ins, listening comprehension, and culture matching and true/false items and found significant differences in student reactions to the varying test types. Student reactions were not entirely consistent, however; reactions varied to some extent based on student achievement and instructional level. Thus, although it appears that students may feel more comfortable with one testing format than another, we should not expect that student reactions will be uniform. However, it is recommended that whatever testing approach is used, it should not differ from that used in instruction.

## A Criterion-Referenced Model

In many high schools, the semester and end of year tests consist of both teacher-made and textbook-published instruments. In some cases, final exams may be based entirely on the textbook learning objectives while in others, the exam may reflect both the textbook unit tests and additional instruments related to the teachers' and/or school district's curricular objectives. While Valette (1977) reminds us that there are several possible types of language tests including progress tests, achievement tests, and proficiency tests, secondary schools have traditionally employed achievement tests to evaluate student learning in foreign language classes. In her chapter in this volume, Valette defines various types of testing formats including an interesting hybrid form called a prochievement test. The reader will find her chapter a valuable resource on this topic.

Many states have now begun to emphasize Criterion Reference Tests (CRTs) in secondary schools. As contrasted with the more traditional norm-referenced achievement tests, CRTs measure how much students have learned in a specific course based on parts of a syllabus or a curriculum. By definition, a norm-referenced test compares a student's performance to that of other students while a criterion-referenced test measures a student's performance with respect to specific content objectives.

In the state of Maryland, the Department of Education has initiated the Maryland School Performance Assessment Program (MSPAP). As part of this program to improve learning for all students, the state and twenty-four school districts are developing CRTs in mathematics, language arts, science, and social studies. In a few of the 24 districts, foreign language planners have developed drafts of proficiency or diagnostic tests as forms of CRTs. The language CRTs set a minimum standard and stress the diagnostic function of evaluation. It is hoped that the language CRTs will guide language teachers to develop strategies to help students achieve and function successfully at specific levels of language study.

The next section will describe the effort in Prince George's County Schools to incorporate CRT's into its language assessment program. The effort was made to gauge student and teacher reactions to the new testing procedures.

No matter how appealing conceptually, new testing protocols are destined to failure without support from their major users, language learners and language teachers. We describe the specific language objectives as well as the test development process. And, in order to facilitate the acceptance of the new testing formats, we describe opportunities for student and teacher input throughout the development process.

# The Prince George's County Diagnostic Level I/II Test Model[5]

*The Development Process*

The following test model was developed by the Prince George's County (Maryland) Public Schools. The testing content and format evolved over a period of two years with numerous consultations and feedback opportunities.[6] Specifically, the following steps were taken:

1. A survey was sent to ten high schools and fourteen middle schools asking teachers to describe student performance goals in speaking and writing at the end of a level one course in French, German, Italian, or Spanish.[7] These statements were reviewed and incorporated in a draft document of desired student performance outcomes. (See Appendices A and B.)
2. A small committee of foreign language teachers was convened to discuss curriculum goals, teaching objectives, student outcomes, and testing. The committee developed a set of topics and test-items based on the information collected from the survey described in step one and the county foreign language curricula.
3. The test-items were presented to a foreign language program area team representing the four target languages for discussion, criticism, and refinement.
4. New members were added to the original committee. After a workshop on assessment and the development of test-items, a preliminary draft was developed for the Spanish version of the Diagnostic Reading Test to be used at the end of level one or the beginning of level two.
5. The draft together with a survey was sent to all high school and middle school foreign language teachers. Teacher feedback was favorable, and several recommendations were offered.
6. The testing director for Prince George's County met with the foreign language testing committee and discussed development of test-items,

pilot-testing of the reading component in ten Spanish I classes, and the creation of a student survey.

As a result of this process, the following objectives were established for the listening, speaking, reading, and writing tests:

## Listening
- Listening for information about sports and appropriate equipment.
- Responding to interrogative words.
- Identifying people through a picture and giving the exact time.
- Categorizing specific information—who and where.

## Speaking
- Speaking for communication.
  - Describing sports and the use of appropriate equipment.
  - Describing likes and dislikes.
  - Identifying family members and using descriptive adjectives in context.
  - Using verbs correctly to describe activities.
  - Giving likes and dislikes.
  - Understanding vocabulary (food, colors, leisure).

## Reading
- Demonstrating understanding of vocabulary from selected topics taught in the level 1 course.
- Reading for specific purposes in the target language.
- Showing competency in the target language through the following reading tasks:
  - Identifying vocabulary related to family, food.
  - Understanding word associations.

Using appropriate language over the telephone.
Telling time.

## Writing
- Writing for communication.
  - Giving likes and dislikes.
  - Describing self to a pen pal.
  - Discussing school, classes, family, sports.

As a number of approaches are used in teaching for the above objectives, a variety of formats and item-types have been selected for inclusion in the tests. Other item-types will be considered for various forms of the test:
1. Pictures and multiple-choice questions.
2. Word associations (for testing vocabulary and thinking skills).
3. Cloze passages.
4. Comprehension questions.
5. Selecting correct information.
6. Composing a paragraph (for a post card).
7. Completion items within a context.

In general, testing topics correspond to county curricular objectives and center around information about self, the family, school (e.g., content subjects, sports activities, and other school activities), shopping, and leisure. Although the above goals, item-types, and topics allow for great flexibility in student evaluation, it is anticipated that several different student-assessment approaches will be employed; these include:

1. Reading target language magazines (and other authentic media) and completing pairing tasks.
2. Creative writing.
3. Small group interviews on selected topics (including peer-assessment).
4. Teacher-made tests in listening, speaking, reading, and writing.
5. Self-assessment.
6. Portfolios.
7. Computer assignments.

# Student Reactions to the Diagnostic Reading Test (Spanish)

The Spanish version of the Prince George's County Diagnostic Reading Test was recently pilot-tested in ten secondary schools. The test consisted of a picture of a family followed by multiple-choice questions, a vocabulary component, a telephone conversation, a restaurant scenario, and a section on reading times (from watches). (See Appendix C.) In conjunction with the pilot-testing, students at three schools were asked to complete a questionnaire eliciting their reactions to the reading test in general and the specific test components. (See Appendix B.) These results were supplemented by two high school teachers who summarized their students' comments about the test. In all, 72 level 1 Spanish students responded to the survey. Fifty (middle school) students were age 13 and 14, and an additional twenty-two (high school) students were between 15 and 18 years of age. The sample was almost equally divided between males (33) and females (39), and approximately 80% of the respondents were native speakers of English. About 40% of the students had studied Spanish in elementary school, and all of the students had studied Spanish in middle school.

The first part of the questionnaire asked students to select the part of the Diagnostic Reading Test they liked best. Approximately 40% of the students preferred the family section, 36% liked the section on telling time, and the telephone conversation and restaurant dialogue drew 8% of the respondents each.[8] We next asked why the student preferred a particular part of the exam. The overwhelming majority of the responses—especially among the younger students—was that the section was "easy" or covered material that they had understood well in their classes.

Among the high school students, few reported liking a test section because it was interesting or challenging, but again the majority opted for test sections which they felt they could respond to easily. We also note that only a very small number of the students at either level felt that they liked parts of the test because they found them "interesting" or "challenging." While the developers of the test were motivated to create a test based on authentic language and integrated language performance, most of the students thought of the test as a "test" rather than viewing it as an opportunity to show off their developing proficiency in Spanish. As has been previously noted in university students (Horwitz, 1989), these secondary students perceived themselves primarily as students in a language class rather than as language learners. Consequently, they evaluated the Diagnostic Reading Test for its consistency with their classroom experiences rather than for what it told them about their ability to read in Spanish.

For example, we asked the students what frustrated them in the test. A number (36%) indicated that they had difficulty understanding the vocabulary, and another 21% found it difficult to understand the questions. An additional 16% of the students found "just taking the test" frustrating. When asked to explain these responses, students indicated that they did not remember the material elicited by the test, that they had not been taught the relevant vocabulary, or that the material was too difficult.

We also asked the students what they would like to see on a reading test. Thirty-eight percent of the respondents selected a story with basic questions such as who, what, when, and where, and 26% of the students preferred real-life situations such as dialogs followed by questions. Another 30% of the students thought that both of these testing-types should be included in a reading test. Thus, in this case, it appeared that the students were reasonably satisfied with the types of items included on the Diagnostic Reading Test being pilot-tested. When asked if they had any additional comments for the test developers, a range of opinions was offered. Some students said that the test was too easy, while others said it was too hard. Some students said that the test should not be used while others said it should be required. And some found the test too repetitive, while others found it too short. In addition, several item-types were suggested including asking questions in English for response in Spanish and more role-play activities.[9]

What, then, do these responses tell us about the students' affective reactions to the Diagnostic Reading Test? First, it did not appear that the students were used to being asked their opinions about either tests or instruction in general. Almost all the students checked the appropriate boxes on the questionnaire, but only a few offered comments on the free-response items, even though from our experiences as teachers we know that students typically have much to say about the language curriculum and their language classes.[10] It would seem that teachers and curriculum developers who wish greater student input need to convince students that their input is valued and will be taken seriously.

From the responses we received, several important themes emerged. First, the vast majority of students wanted tests which corresponded with what had been taught and favored "easy" tests. Such responses—while probably not surprising to teachers of this age-group—are entirely consistent with the adolescent's developing cognitive systems and self-concept. Adolescents want to know what is expected of them and will likely become uneasy when experiencing tests they do not feel prepared for. The element of "fairness" enters here as well. Our students seem to be expressing a belief in an implicit contract between students and teachers: students will learn what the teachers teach, and teachers will test what the students have learned. Thus, a lack of congruity between the students' expectations and what they actually encounter on a test may cause discomfort and even resentment. If the latter affect the test results, they must be questioned in terms of being a fair representation of student learning.

The respondents also tended to prefer concrete parts of the test over more abstract components. As adolescents tend to have difficulty dealing with less structured situations, less familiar target language material tested in unfamiliar ways would be particularly difficult for them.[11] Interestingly, there was no clear agreement as to which sections of the test were "easier" than others.

It seems, rather, that students preferred the sections that were most like what they had experienced in their own Spanish classes. This finding is important because it implies that the students did not find any of the content or testing formats inherently difficult; rather, they seemed to react to the material as being more familiar or less familiar. This finding also reinforces the decision of Prince George's County Foreign Language Office to use criterion-referenced tests for diagnostic purposes. These language learners conceived of reading Spanish in terms of specific components such as telling time or reading about family situations. Thus, basing the curriculum and subsequent evaluation of students on specific criteria would seem to be consistent with student expectations about language classes as well as the current thinking of professionals.

# Suggestions to Teachers and Curriculum Developers

As language teachers adopt more authentic and more demanding language tests, language learners—particularly secondary students—are likely to have strong affective reactions. To help students and teachers adjust to current proficiency-based testing approaches, we make the following suggestions:

*Make Instruction Consistent with Testing*

Of all the messages we received from students, this one was the strongest. As expected, students felt more comfortable with the sections of the Diagnostic Reading Test which resembled what they had experienced in their own language classes. Their reactions seem to indicate that they are able to "handle" the content of the test as long as they have sufficient opportunities for using the content in class. On the other hand, authentic language tests make authentic classroom practice mandatory. If instructional practices do not match innovative testing procedures, we can anticipate frustrated and disappointed language learners. So, it is recommended that teaching, testing, and assessment be correlated, a key point of this entire NEC volume.

*Use Criterion-Referenced Tests*

Using criterion-referenced tests facilitates the match of instructional and evaluation procedures advocated above. In the case of the Prince George's County Diagnostic Reading Test, the test development process focused county teachers and curriculum developers on the specific instructional objectives they hoped to achieve. Having clearly defined objectives, it is easier to coordinate teaching and assessment.

## Use a Variety of Classroom Activities

The above discussions should not be interpreted to mean that the language classroom must provide practice-items identical to the kind of items students will encounter on tests. In fact, authentic and integrative language tests should make it less likely that students will be able to prepare for tests without actually internalizing the target language material. Using language in a variety of realistic contexts is the best way to prepare for authentic language tests. We are particularly enthusiastic about the promise of small group and cooperative learning activities for helping students develop truly integrative language skills.

## Establish Feedback Channels for Students

It would be impossible to give serious consideration to students' affective reactions to language tests without providing them with opportunities to express opinions about testing and assessment procedures. In the case of the pilot-testing of the Spanish version of the Reading Diagnostic Test, a simple questionnaire afforded a great number of useful insights. In addition, by asking students for their opinions, teachers demonstrate sincerity in the belief that language learning is based on a partnership between language learners and language teachers.

Opportunities for student feedback should not be limited to testing procedures. Recently, a forum of secondary language students, university language students, language teachers, and program directors was organized at the University of Maryland, College Park. Students offered a wide range of interesting comments concerning—among others—course content, secondary–postsecondary articulation, and effective language learning strategies. Ongoing communication between teachers and their students is essential and can prevent or lessen students' negative affective reactions. In addition, increased opportunities for student input should result in more valid assessments of student learning. Learning theory supports active student involvement.

## Give Advice about How to Prepare for Tests

In the language learner forum described above, students strongly urged teachers to help them *learn how to become better language learners*. Advice about test preparation—and language learning in general—should be a regular part of language classes. Language learners do not naturally know how to learn a language effectively, and they often adopt approaches that teachers find unproductive or even counterproductive (Horwitz, 1988). Since language learners instinctively use a number of learning strategies, it is the teacher's responsibility to make students aware of the most appropriate language-learning strategies for particular language tasks.

## Look for Especially Anxious Students

Although most students will be only mildly anxious about tests, it appears that there are some students who find language classes and particularly language tests extremely anxiety-provoking. Such students are not easily reassured by suggestions that they "just relax" or that "it is all right to make errors." Highly anxious students will need advice, encouragement, and understanding. In some cases, it would be wise to consult the school's guidance staff, as the student may require professional help.

## Use Test Results for Instructional Feedback

The results of language tests tell us as much about the effectiveness of instruction as they do about student achievement. When students are not able to cope with a language test, we must consider the possibility that their language classroom experience did not adequately prepare them for the task. In light of student comments from a number of sources, asking students to perform in ways they are unprepared for on tests is likely to lead to frustration and negative affective reactions. Therefore, testing and assessment results should be routinely discussed with students. In this way, students learn to be less anxious and uptight during the subsequent testing and assessment.

# Conclusion

During the next decade we can anticipate many changes in language testing. In developing new testing approaches, language teachers and program developers should base their practices on both the characteristics of their students and the content of their curriculum. When working with adolescent learners, it is especially important to monitor student affective reactions. Secondary learners are often self-absorbed and sensitive, and negative experiences with language tests and assessments can be damaging to their self-images as well as their motivation to continue language study. To insure that new testing procedures will ultimately contribute to positive attitudes toward language learning and the improvement of student language abilities, we must communicate with students on a routine basis and carefully observe their affective reactions. This information should guide our efforts as professionals to foster a learning, testing, and assessment environment in which students affective as well as cognitive factors are valued.

# Notes

[1]See Shohamy in 1991 NEC Reports for other considerations in developing tests for students.

[2]The authors are listed alphabetically. Elaine Horwitz has also worked as a foreign language teacher in the public schools of Maryland.

[3]See Nerenz in 1990 NEC Reports for additional information on this topic.

4There have been numerous critiques. In his 1985 book, Gardner stresses the importance of the intensity of motivation over the motivational orientation.

[5]Copyright Prince George's County (Maryland) Public Schools.

[6]There were several important background sources for the project including student assessment and CRT workshops in the state of Maryland, a foreign language testing course at the University of Maryland, Shohamy's (1991) article, and consultations with outside experts.

[7]Although this Report focuses on student affective reactions to the test, considerable effort was also extended throughout the development process to ensure that teachers felt included and comfortable with the new testing procedures.

[8]All percentages may not sum to 100 due to rounding.

[9]From the responses to this last item, it appears that the students did not limit themselves entirely to reading tasks.

[10]A small number of students—fewer than five—used the questionnaire as an opportunity to express their general discontent with their teacher or class.

[11]See *CooperativeLearning in the Foreign Language Classroom*, a publication of the New York State Foreign Language Teafchers Association.

# References

Barr-Harrison, P. Guidelines for testing students in secondary schools. Paper presented at University of Maryland, Guest Lecturer Series, 1992.

Fredriksen, J., and Collins, A. A systems approach to educational testing. *Educational Researcher, 1989, 18* (9), 27–32.

Gardner, R.C. *Social psychology and second language learning: The role of attitudes and motivations.* London: Edward Arnold, 1985.

Gardner, R.C., and Lambert, W.E. *Attitudes and motivation in second language learning.* Raleigh, MA: Newbury House, 1972.

Georgia Department of Education. *Middle school foreign languages: A planning guide.* Atlanta, GA: Division of Instruction, 1989.

Graham, C.R. Beyond integrative motivation: The development and influence of assimilative motivation. In P. Larson, E.L. Judd, and D.S. Messerscmitt (Eds.), *On TESOL '84: A brave new world for TESOL.* Washington, DC: TESOL, 1984.

Gunderson, B., and Johnson, D. Building positive attitudes by using cooperative learning groups. *Foreign Language Annals,* 1980, *13* (1), 39–43.

James, W. *Principles of Psychology.* Holt and Co., (1890, 1950). 369.

Heilenman, K.L. Self-assessment and placement: A review of the issues. In R.V. Teschner, (Ed.), *Assessing foreign language proficiency of undergraduates.* Boston: Heinle and Heinle, 1991.

Horwitz, E.K. Adapting communication-centered activities to student conceptual level. *Canadian Modern Language Review / La Revue canadienne des langues vivantes.* 1986,

*42* (4), 827–40.

Horwitz, E.K. The beliefs about language learning of beginning university foreign language students. *The Modern Language Journal*, 1988, *72*, 182–93.

Horwitz, E.K. Facing the blackboard: Student perceptions of language learning and the language classroom. *ADFL Bulletin*, 1989, *20* ( 3), 61–64.

Horwitz, E.K. Using student beliefs about language learning and teaching in the foreign language methods course. *Foreign Language Annals* 1985, *18*, 333–40.

Horwitz, E.K., Horwitz, M.B., and Cope, J.A. Foreign language classroom anxiety. *The Modern Language Journal*, 1986, *70*, 125–32.

Horwitz, E.K., and Young, D.J. *Language anxiety: From theory and research to classroom implications*. Englewood Cliffs, NJ: Prentice-Hall, 1991.

Kagan, S. The structural approach to cooperative learning. *Educational leadership*, 1990, *47* (4), 12–15.

Koch, A.S., and Terrell, T.D. Affective reactions of foreign language students to natural approach activities and teaching techniques. In E. Horwitz and D. Young (eds.),*Language anxiety: From theory and research to classroom implications*. Englewood Cliffs, NJ: Prentice-Hall, 1991.

Lipsitz, J. The age group. In M. Johnson (Ed.), *Toward adolescence: The middle schools years—The age group. Seventy-ninth yearbook of the National Society for the Study of Education*. Chicago: University of Chicago Press, 1980.

Madsen, H.S., Brown, B.L., and Jones, R.L. Evaluating student attitudes to second-language tests. In E. Horwitz and D. Young (Eds.), *Language anxiety: From theory and research to classroom implications*. Englewood Cliffs, NJ: Prentice-Hall, 1991.

Maryland State Department of Education. *Maryland State Performance Assessment Program*. Baltimore, MD: MSDE, 1990.

Maryland Task Force on the Middle Learning Years. *What matters in the middle grades: Recommendation for Maryland middle grades education*. Baltimore, MD: MSDE, Bureau of Education Development, 1989.

Nerenz, A.G. The exploratory years: Foreign languages in the middle level curriculum. In Sally Sieloff Magnan (Ed.), *Shifting the Instructional Focus to the Learner*. South Burlington, VT: Northeast Conference, 1990.

North Carolina Department of Public Instruction. *Building Bridges*. Raleigh, NC: author, 1991.

Price, M.L. The subjective experience of foreign language anxiety: Interviews with highly anxious students. In E. Horwitz and D. Young (Eds.),*Language anxiety: From theory and research to classroom implications*. Englewood Cliffs, NJ: Prentice-Hall, 1991.

Robison, R.E. Developing practical speaking tests for the foreign language classroom: A small group approach. *Foreign Language Annals*, 1992, *25* (6). 487–95.

Shohamy, E. Connecting testing and learning in the classroom and on the program level. In June K. Phillips, (Ed.), *Building Bridges and Making Connections*. South Burlington, Vermont: Northeast Conference, 1991.

Shohamy, E. Beyond proficiency testing: A diagnostic feedback testing model for assessing foreign language learning. *The Modern Language Journal*, 1992, *76* (4), 513–21.

Valette, R. *Modern language testing*. New York: Harcourt Brace Jovanovich, 1977.

Wiggins, G. A true test: Toward more authentic and equitable assessment. *Phi Delta Kappan*, May 1989, 703–13.

Wiseman, D.G. , Hunt, G.H., and Bedwell, L.E. Teaching for critical thinking. Paper presented at the annual meeting of the Association of Teacher Educators. Atlanta, GA, 1986.

Wolf, D. P. Portfolio Assessment: Sampling student work. *Educational Leadership*, 1989, *46* (7), 35–39.

Young, D.J. Creating a low anxiety classroom environment: What does language anxiety research suggest? *The Modern Language Journal*, 1991, 75 (4), 426–39.

# Appendix A. Prince George's County Public Schools Foreign Language Expected Learning Outcomes

Students will communicate with predictable expressions and vocabulary in the present tense. Language is still personal and related to self, family, school, a typical day, telling time, giving information, describing a person or object. Most students will reach novice high. The outcomes below are minimal and do not represent every outcome students can obtain; rather, outcomes that are basic requirements of successful learning in Level I. Culture should be integrated through all four skill areas. Non-European cultures should be included in materials used in Level I when appropriate for specific languages.

## Level I

### Listening
Students will be able to:
- understand sounds of the language and comprehend a simple conversation with a native—who, where, when, how;
- understand simple questions about the weather;
- understand simple conversation and questions about personal likes and dislikes, such as sports, school, food;
- understand time, dates, and numbers 1–1000;
- respond to commands in classroom situations.

### Speaking
- greet someone in the target language;
- use numbers up to 1000 and tell time
- give basic information about the weather
- give personal information;
- describe family members, leisure activities, some professions, likes and dislikes
- respond to predictable questions and situations with expressions and fillers such as, of course, no way, o.k., maybe, great, never, why, etc.
- pronounce with some degree of accuracy sounds of the target language
- request information, such as items from a school store or selected foods from a vendor ask and answer questions in brief dialogue situations about sports, colors, hobbies, school, friends, clothing, family, leisure activity, and about geography of the countries where the target language is spoken
- make a phone call, and ask for someone
- invite a friend somewhere
- ask for food items

## Reading
- read and understand simple instructions using learned vocabulary
- read and understand a simple menu in the target language
- read and understand statements about the weather; information related to telling time
- read a schedule or calendar of times and activities
- read and understand simple stories, dialogs, vignettes, covering basic topics such as family, sports, food, shopping, clothing, school subjects, etc. in the present tense

## Writing
- fill in a form eliciting personal information, such as a passport
- write:
  - basic greetings
  - the day's date
- express likes, dislikes and certain needs
- write simple questions and answers related to topics listed in the curriculum guide
- create a simple dialogue in practiced situations.

## Culture
- discuss or demonstrate how the target culture views the concepts of:
  - time (duration)
  - family
  - formal vs. informal
  - food
  - celebrations

## Base Content
- vocabulary and grammar (pronouns, adj.) related to family, school, sports, leisure activities, food, travel, telephone, shopping, clothes, weather, time, etc.
- specific functions:
  - expressing likes and dislikes related to the above
  - describing family, friends, places, objects, etc.
  - requesting/giving information/following directions
  - using regular and irregular verbs in the present, especially the verbs: to be, to have, to do, to go, to be able, to bring, to speak, to show, to look at, etc.

# Appendix B. Teacher Survey

In 24 schools, teachers were asked to give at least one student outcome they thought was essential to know or do at the end of level 1.

| Teacher choices for tasks on tests | No. of teachers responding |
|---|---|
| Describing self, school, giving vital information | 13 |
| Talking about topics in the textbook: school, likes, dislikes, phone conversation | 13 |
| Asking for and giving directions | 3 |
| Using basic expressions—past & present | 2 |
| Asking questions, requesting foods, formulating sentences | 2 |
| Reading daily items such as menus | 1 |
| Composing paragraphs | 1 |
| Speaking in general conversation about weather, asking for someone over the telephone | 1 |

# Appendix C.

I. The Diagnostic Test

A. Objectives

**Listening**
- listening for information about sports and appropriate equipment
- responding to interrogative words
- identifying people through a picture and giving the exact time categorizing specific information—who and where

**Speaking**
- speaking for communication
  - describing sports and the use of appropriate equipment
  - describing likes and dislikes
  - identifying family members and using descriptive adjectives in context

- using verbs correctly to describe activities
- giving likes and dislikes
  - understanding vocabulary (food, colors, leisure)

## Reading

- Demonstrating understanding of vocabulary from selected topics taught during the level 1 course
- Reading for specific purposes in Spanish
- Showing competency in Spanish through the following reading tasks:
  - Identifying vocabulary related to family, food
  - Understanding word association
  - Using appropriate language over the telephone
  - Telling time

## Writing

- writing for communication
  - giving likes and dislikes
  - describing self to a pen pal
  - discussing school, subjects, family, sports

B. Formats—item types
  A variety of item types were used in teaching; therefore, a variety of item types were maintained in testing

- pictures and multiple choice questions
- word association (vocabulary testing and thinking)
- Cloze test
- understanding questions
- selecting correct information
- creating a paragraph (for a post card)
- completion items within context
- (Other item types are being considered in the various forms of the test)

C. Topics
  Topics on the test correspond to the student learning performance outcomes and the teaching objectives

- information about self
- family
- school (content subjects, sports activities, general activities at school, etc.)
- shopping
- leisure

II. Other components of the assessment

- reading Spanish magazines and completing pairing tasks
- using other authentic materials in the assessment process
- creative writing
- small group interviews based on selective topics with peer assessment
- teacher-made test—all four skills

- curriculum and semester self appraisal of "Do You Know"
- portfolios or computer assignments

III. Piloting the Spanish I Diagnostic Test Reading Component
The reading component was piloted in 10 schools. The item types consisted of:
- a picture of a family with multiple-choice questions
- a vocabulary component
- a dialogue with two people talking over the telephone
- a restaurant scenario
- reading times on watches, with multiple choices for selecting the correct time.

IV. Comments from the student survey form (based on the reading part of the test)
Three schools received their survey forms in time to elicit responses from their students. In addition, two high school teachers who did not receive the survey forms have summarized their students' comments.

| Level-1 Student Responses | | |
|---|---|---|
| Age | 13–14 | 50 |
| | 15–18 | 22 |
| Sex | Male | 33 |
| | Female | 39 |
| Native speaker of English? | Yes | 57 |
| | No | 15 |
| Studied Spanish in Elementary School? | Yes | 29 |
| | No | 40 |
| Studied Spanish in Middle School? | Yes | 72 |
| What part of the assessment did you like best? | family part | 28 |
| | telephone conversation | 8 |
| | restaurant dialog | 8 |
| | telling time | 25 |

| | easy | 42 |
|---|---|---|
| Why? | interesting topics | 10 |
| | had a picture | 1 |
| | understood the material | 6 |
| | did not understand | 7 |
| Which part of the test was frustrating? | understanding vocabulary | 25 |
| | just taking the test | 11 |
| | understanding the question | 15 |
| | none of the responses listed | 19 |
| Source of frustration? | did not remember material | 7 |
| | was not taught vocabulary | 16 |
| | material was difficult | 10 |
| | not clear | 3 |
| What do you prefer to have on a reading test? | a story with basic questions, who, what, when, where, etc. | 25 |
| | real-life situations such as dialogues with responses to select | 17 |
| | both of the above | 20 |
| | other choices | 4 |
| | free response | 0 |

| | | |
|---|---|---|
| | alphabets | 4 |
| | nothing else | 27 |
| | more dialog | 3 |
| What did you want to learn this year that you did not learn? | speak informally | 3 |
| | tell time | 1 |
| | speak more fluently | 12 |
| | how to order food | 1 |
| | don't know | 1 |
| If you have something else you would like to say to the developers of the test, please write your comments on the back of this form. | Test should be required.<br>Test is too hard.<br>Need to know more vocabulary.<br>Make test longer.<br>Ask questions in English and require Spanish answers.<br>Too repetitive.<br>Have more role playing.<br>Test was easy.<br>Should not use proficiency test. | |
| Total no. of respondents | | 72 |

## Sample from Reading Diagnostic Test*

I. INSTRUCTIONS: You will read a short telephone conversation in which words or phrases have been omitted. There is a space for each omitted word or phrase in the passage. For each space, choose the letter that best completes the sentence as it appears in the passage. Circle your choice. You may have to read the sentences that follow in order to choose the correct answer. Select one response. y Carlos contesta el teléfono y dice:

1. CARLOS: _____ .

   a. Hola.                b. Hasta pronto.              c. Adiós.

2. PALOMA: Carlos, _____ ¿Cómo estás?

   a. Él no está.         b. Es Paloma.                 c. ¿Quién habla?

   CARLOS: Bien. ¿Qué pasa? ¿Vas al restaurante esta noche?

3. PALOMA: No. _____

   a. Tengo mucha hambre.    b. Tengo que estudiar.    c. Es un restaurante bueno.

   CARLOS: ¡Qué lástima!

4. PALOMA: _____ el número de Juan.

   a. Bailo               b. Juego                      c. Necesito

   CARLOS: Es el 3-2-2-4-5-6-1.

5. PALOMA: ¿Tu sabes si Juan _____ en su casa ahora?

   a. está                b. compra                     c. va

   CARLOS: Creo que sí.

   PALOMA: Gracias. Hasta luego.

6. CARLOS: _____

   a. Bueno.              b. Muy bien.                  c. Hasta mañana.

*©Prince George's County (MD) Public Schools, 1993. Used by permission.

# Appendix D

| Prince George's County (MD) Public Schools Student Self Assessment of Foreign Language Performance | | | |
|---|---|---|---|
| Grade | | Male | Female |
| Read the descriptions of tasks that you can do as a result of completing level 1. Check the appropriate areas that indicate how you rate yourself. | | | |
| I can do the following: | Agree | Agree somewhat but need a lot of improve-ment | Cannot do |
| greet someone; ask the person how she/he feels | | | |
| tell someone my name, where I live, my age | | | |
| tell someone a little information about my family | | | |
| question someone if it relates to me, my family, my school | | | |
| describe my best friend | | | |
| discuss 5 countries where the foreign language is spoken and tell a few interesting points about those countries | | | |
| understand and respond to questions asked to me about my name, age, where I live, and the music I like | | | |
| read a simple short paragraph if it is about someone who is discussing him/herself, school, or friend | | | |
| write a note to a pen pal telling about myself | | | |

| | | | |
|---|---|---|---|
| write my teacher and describe a typical day from the time I get up to the time I go to bed | | | |
| write the correct endings on verbs because I understand which endings go with specific subjects | | | |
| read, write, and tell the time | | | |
| order something in a school store, a restaurant, a department store | | | |
| Describe other tasks that you can perform | | | |

List three tasks identified above that you are willing to demonstrate:
   1.
   2.
   3.

# Assessment in Foreign Language Teacher Education

Leslie L. Schrier

*The University of Iowa*

JoAnn Hammadou

*The University of Rhode Island*

## Introduction

> We must constantly remind ourselves that the ultimate purpose of evaluation is to enable students to evaluate themselves (Costa; 1989, p. 36).

The teaching of foreign languages has changed in the last decade; foreign language instruction has gone from a curricular design based on grammar translation to a more communicative or interactive approach. One early catalyst of this change was the criticism of the foreign language competence of our nation's youth expressed in a presidential commission report, *Strength through Wisdom: A Critique of U.S. Capability* (1979). This report emphasized how the nation's lack of competence in foreign language and international studies affected its economic competitiveness in an ever-expanding world marketplace. One of its many recommendations was the improvement of the professional development of foreign language teachers in the areas of their language and cultural competence. The high concentration of literary studies that forms the content area during the foreign language teacher development was criticized as well. This criticism cited the need for foreign language educators "to teach the spoken language more effectively" (p.20).

The foreign language education profession reacted to this criticism in several ways. The first criticism helped spark the reassessment of the process of evaluating foreign language achievement. This reassessment culminated in the publication of a set of guidelines for the assessment of a language learner's proficiency (American Council on the Teaching of Foreign Languages, 1986). Second, the need to particularize the foreign language knowledge base and teacher education process was proposed by Hancock (1981), Jarvis (1983), and Lange (1983). In the latter part of the 1980s, the profession addressed the need to form new models for the preparation of foreign language teachers with the publication of the American Council on the Teaching of Foreign Languages (ACTFL), *Provisional Program Guidelines for Foreign Language Teacher Education* (1988). Most recently, the early part of the 1990s finds the foreign language profession producing documents that propose standards for subject matter knowledge in specific languages (e.g., AATF, 1989; AATSP, 1990; Schulz, et al., 1993). There are, therefore, optimistic signs from the foreign language education community that an interest, and indeed commitment, to the improvement of teacher development remains strong.

Given the current amount of interest in foreign language teacher preparation within the profession, it is understandable that an interest in *measuring* the quality of that preparation would follow. At the same time, pressures from outside of the profession to "prove" effectiveness persist. A call to establish instruments or guidelines to help judge the quality of all teachers is on the lips of everyone from government officials to parents. These diverse groups generally agree on two things: that teaching is at the heart of education and that the single most important action the nation can take to improve schools is to strengthen teaching (Baratz-Snowden, 1993). However, uncertainty about the characteristics of "good teaching" plagues all stages of teaching but may be most apparent during the process of evaluating preservice and beginning teachers as they enter the profession.

The purpose of this chapter is to present to the foreign language practitioner and teacher educator an overview of the most recent assessment instruments proposed to evaluate teachers' competencies and then to explore the potential benefits of portfolio assessment for preservice foreign language teacher assessment.

# Evaluation and Assessment: Assumptions

Assessment, or measurement, is defined as the accurate, objective description of performance. In the domain of teacher education, this means measurement of the quality of teaching performance. Evaluation means placing value upon what is being measured. The attempt to separate the concept of objective measurement from subjective evaluation has been an ongoing struggle and subject of much debate within the field of educational testing. Many educators disagree on both the feasibility and the advisability of this dichotomy. In this chapter we accept the notion that no measure is completely objective—subjective judgment always plays some role in assessment—and will advocate evaluation systems that strive to acknowledge and accommodate this inherent subjectivity.

Another critical assumption that is necessarily fundamental to work in teacher evaluation is that good teaching behavior is (1) identifiable, (2) stable, and (3) reasonably consistent in its effects on students across contexts (Andrews and Barnes, 1990, p. 572). If efforts to measure and evaluate teaching are to be worthwhile, there must be aspects of teaching that can be named, agreed upon as worthwhile, identified repeatedly, and proved useful in more than one teaching/learning setting.

# Current Assessment Practices

Testing the general teaching competence of teachers is not unique to the last decade. Attempts to identify and assess important teacher attributes appeared earlier in this century (see Ellena, Stevenson, and Webb, 1961). What is new is the prominence that assessment has achieved. This prominence is evidenced, for example, by several national and regional projects to create alternative methods of teacher evaluation and by the major publications on the topic such as *The New Handbook of Teacher Evaluation: Assessing Elementary and Secondary School Teachers* (Millman and Darling-Hammond, 1990). The *Handbook* identifies the following typical circumstances in which teachers are assessed: the selection process of teacher education candidates, preservice evaluation, licensure, merit pay, development, and recognition.

Traditionally, teacher assessment is accomplished via paper-and-pencil tests and/or classroom observations. Alternative methods to teacher assessment are advocated in the *Handbook* and in other publications (e.g., Haertel; 1990, 1991). One is the Teacher Assessment Project (TAP), funded by the

Carnegie Corporation between 1986 and 1990. TAP sought to develop exercises to assess teachers' "critical understanding" of a few highly specific parts of school curricula, such as the teaching of equivalent fractions and the American Revolution. Additionally, TAP examined the feasibility of assembling and judging portfolios of teachers' everyday work done in the performance of regular duties.

In another innovative program, the National Board for Professional Teaching Standards (NBPTS), also Carnegie-supported, is sponsoring the development of alternative teacher assessment instruments and materials. These include videotapes of teaching performance and portfolios of teachers' work. Meanwhile, certain state departments of education have formed the Interstate New Teacher Assessment and Support Consortium (1992) administered by the Council of Chief State School Officers. The consortium's purpose includes the development of teacher assessment tools "compatible with the vision of NBPTS" (p. 15). Even the Educational Testing Service (ETS), has developed a performance test for first-year teachers as part of its new Praxis series (Dwyer and Villegas, 1993).

Traditional, paper-and-pencil preservice teacher tests have assessed teachers' *knowledge* of general, subject area, and/or pedagogical content. Among the most common assessment instruments are the American College Test (ACT), Scholastic Aptitude Test (SAT), Pre-Professional Skills Test (PPST), National Teacher Examination (NTE), and university grade point average. Research on the predictive validity of these paper-and-pencil teacher assessment measures suggests that they seldom are valid predictors of future teaching performance (Ayers, 1989; Ayers and Qualls, 1979; Goodison, 1985), and that these measures are tremendously redundant (Ayers, 1989; Duke and Duke, 1990; Nance and Kinnison, 1988; Silbert, 1989; Stocker and Tarrab, 1985). Furthermore, advocates of other than paper-and-pencil assessment stress that although teachers' general, subject, and pedagogical knowledge is important, ways must be found to determine whether teachers are able to *utilize* that knowledge in real or simulated teaching situations. What have been lacking traditionally are samples of their potential for performance as teachers.

Shulman (1986) outlines the historical changes over time in beliefs about the knowledge that is essential for teachers. In the late 1800s, the focus of such examinations was on the subject matter to be taught by the prospective teacher. In the 1980s the experts pressed for review and evaluation of prospective teachers' pedagogical skills, such as: "organization in preparing and presenting instructional plans, evaluation, recognition of individual differences, cultural awareness, understanding youth, management, and educational policies and procedures" (p. 5). In other words, the experts' focus has vacillated over time between teachers' knowledge of the subject that they teach and their knowledge of learners and classrooms.

Shulman suggests that neither the exclusive focus on subject matter nor the preoccupation with pedagogical knowledge constitutes adequate assessment criteria for teaching credentials. He proposes an assessment plan that balances knowledge, skills, and dispositions from both the subject matter and pedagogical domains of knowledge and proficiency.

Assessment programs will always serve multiple purposes and have multiple effects, some intended, others unintended. Obviously, assessment plans do not occur in a vacuum. When a program is created to measure the quality of preparation that beginning teachers undergo, it may also affect the public's perceptions of teachers as qualified experts or affect teachers' morale or job satisfaction either negatively or positively. During the creation and implementation of new assessment plans, foreign language educators will need to be very explicit about the plans' purposes and very careful to predict all likely effects of the new programs.

# Foreign Language Assessment Issues

The foreign language community has made an effort in the last five years to develop guidelines and standards that define what constitutes a competent foreign language teacher. This effort can be divided into three areas: first, generalized guidelines for foreign language education programs; second, language specific standards that concentrate on subject matter preparation of the teacher; and, third, specific examinations that assess language competence.

## Generalized Guidelines

The 1988 publication of the American Council on the Teaching of Foreign Languages (ACTFL) *Provisional Program Guidelines for Foreign Language Teacher Education* represents the profession's attempt to tackle the problem of describing what coursework and experiences should be included in a teacher preparation program for both elementary and secondary foreign language teachers. The elements described by ACTFL fall into traditional categories that could be found in the average university curriculum. They are: general education coursework (defined as personal development); professional education coursework (defined as pedagogy); the future teacher's major field (defined as specialist development); and clinical or field experiences. This proposal is viewed as the first step to help guide the profession along the path toward consensus on teacher preparation. One criticism of the guidelines underscores the weakness in our professional knowledge base: there is no established data base on what currently exists in foreign language teacher education programs in the nation (Hammadou, 1993; Schrier, 1989, 1993).

## Language-Specific Standards

In the second area, specific foreign language associations have undertaken the admirable task of suggesting subject matter specific curricula that would assure language teachers' competence in a target language and culture (e.g., AATF, 1989; Schulz et al., 1993). These curricula contain suggestions for language proficiency levels, criteria for cultural knowledge, and lists containing a variety of pedagogical competencies specific to the target language studied. Hence, it is assumed that if successfully mastered, the foreign language teacher would then have reached an acceptable standard that the corresponding association would certify as competent to teach its language. Both Lafayette (1993) and Schrier (1993) laud the language organizations' interest in teacher development, but as Lafayette so aptly says, "it is somewhat distressing to imagine institutions of higher learning and state departments of education having to deal with documents addressing each of the different languages" (p. 133). The process of creating minimum standards for language teachers is an admirable one because it has helped sensitize the language organizations to the teaching/learning process, but efforts at establishing overall standards for all language teachers are still needed. This newest "frontier" is a critical challenge to our profession. A collaborative effort by ACTFL and by the professional organizations of the three most commonly taught languages (AATF, AATG, and AATSP) is already seeking funding to begin work on such standards for the pre-collegiate levels. Much input will be needed from concerned foreign language educators.

## Language Competence Exams

The last category consists of a selection of objective examinations intended to help states or institutions assess the subject-matter knowledge or language proficiency that their foreign language teachers possess. These examinations are the ACTFL oral proficiency exam, the simulated oral proficiency interview (SOPI) (1989), The Texas Oral Proficiency Test (TOPT) (1991), and the ETS Praxis II exams (Knop, 1991). Chapter Two of this volume includes a detailed description of the tests. Alone, they are unable to provide an assessment that balances, as Shulman (1986) suggested, subject knowledge, skills, and dispositions from both the subject matter and pedagogical domains of knowledge and proficiency. What is necessary is to examine all these domains of teaching toward the goal of being able to predict the success of future foreign language teaching performance.

# Portfolios: An Alternative Approach

Educators have recently been exploring alternative approaches to assessing learning in the various subjects taught in elementary and secondary schools. One strategy, the use of portfolio assessment (Arter and Spandel, 1992; Paulson, Paulson, and Meyer, 1991), may be particularly applicable to assessment of preservice foreign language teachers. Portfolio assessment refers to both a process and a product. Materials that reflect progress toward intended learning goals are collected over time, and specific materials most clearly evidencing learning are reviewed and scored relative to criteria appropriate for the instructional setting. A portfolio is, therefore, a sample set of a student's work judged against predetermined standards of exemplary work. Portfolios are becoming increasingly common in K–12 mathematics and writing and have been suggested for the assessment of teaching at the college level (Seldin, 1991).

A relevant example from preservice teacher training is the experiment at the University of South Carolina (Ryan and Kuhs, 1993) in which the development, presentation, defense, and scoring of a portfolio has replaced traditional written and oral comprehensive examinations in the elementary and early childhood graduate-level teacher-certification program. The goals and objectives of the program are reviewed with students when they begin their studies, and the portfolio procedures and requirements are explained. The portfolio requirements reflect the faculty's beliefs about what an individual must know, care about, and be able to do in order to teach well.

Both the process of developing the portfolio and the product, the final submission, are used for assessment purposes. The process dimension supports on-going, formative assessment and is intended to facilitate supervision as well as self-evaluation and reflection. During courses and field experiences, the prospective teachers collect evidence of their intellectual and professional growth and development for their portfolios. They must eventually select for their final portfolio a limited number of entries or exhibits to document growth and development in the relevant knowledge and skill domains. A rationale for the entries they choose must be included. The final portfolio submission and an oral defense are used for students' final evaluation.

# Framework for Planning Assessment Design: The Construct of Good Teaching

Whether the portfolio approach or some other assessment format is used for the evaluation of preservice foreign language teachers, the system must enable the faculty to evaluate the preservice teachers' knowledge, skills, and dispositions relative to the goals of their specific teacher education program (Ryan and Kuhs, 1993). Six different but highly interrelated components of the desired knowledge base of beginning teachers are proposed below as the appropriate focus for any assessment system designed for evaluating preservice teachers. The six components of the knowledge base are: (a) subject matter knowledge, (b) problem solving skills, (c) pedagogical knowledge and skills, (d) curriculum knowledge and skills, (e) knowledge about learners and learning; and (f) attitudes and dispositions. The discussion of the knowledge base is detailed, since it defines what is expected of preservice teachers. Designers need to be as explicit as possible in their plan about what assessment evidence they expect from each of these areas.

## Knowledge of Subject Matter

One of the challenges to incorporating subject matter knowledge into an assessment system is determining what breadth and depth of knowledge are essential. A review of the literature on the importance of subject matter knowledge to effective teaching (Grossman, Wilson, and Shulman, 1989) revealed that no consistent relationship has been established between traditional indices of teachers' subject matter knowledge (e.g., achievement test scores, courses completed, grade point average) and the achievement of their students. However, the authors describe the effects of what they call "subject matter knowledge for teaching" on such things as teachers' emphasis on topics within a subject, selection of textbooks and other instructional materials, how teachers structure their students' study, and how they organize and conduct instruction.

Despite the difficulty in measuring the impact of subject matter knowledge on teaching performance, it is obviously central to the tasks of teaching. All the myriad of teaching behaviors—planning, motivating, disciplining, sequencing, evaluating—presuppose subject matter knowledge on the part of the teacher. A social worker, counselor and teacher all must be attentive to individual differences and must be effective communicators. Only the teacher, however, has a particular subject matter to impart to learners. Naturally, then, an assessment plan for foreign language teachers must address the issue of language competence. Any successful assessment design will seek documentation of the preservice teachers' depth and breadth of language proficiency. The depth refers to the richness of examples the teacher can offer, for example, and to the diversity of topics and functions available to the teacher. The breadth of knowledge refers to the ability, possibly unique to good teachers, to understand the subject on other people's terms and the teacher's ability to influence other people's understanding of and proficiency in the subject.

This pedagogical dimension of subject matter knowledge recognizes the difference between "subject matter knowledge needed for teaching" and "knowledge of subject matter needed by an expert" in a field or discipline, a distinction many have observed and described (Carlson, 1991; Dewey 1904/1965; Peterson, 1988; Shulman, 1986). The teacher must know the subject and have the ability to see that subject matter from the perspective of the learner. This body of knowledge is what teachers must have beyond the scholar's knowledge of content. The key feature of teachers' understanding that differs from that of other experts is the ability to make their knowledge accessible to students. In order to do so, the teacher segments and structures content to make it accessible to learners. He or she may tailor content in anticipation of learners' preconceptions, aptitudes, interests, age, social class, cultural background, attention span or past difficulties. The teacher may present the new knowledge for students in the form of analogies, metaphors, examples, demonstrations or simulations.

In the foreign language classroom, a teacher might rely more heavily on cognates to increase rapidly beginners' use of the target language, for example. Or the teacher might restrict his/her language use to the limits of novices on some occasions to maximize their comprehension and, at other times, assign them tasks that require only partial comprehension. The teacher might highlight the similar cultural roots to target language customs that appear "different" or "odd" at first glance to students of the language. The teacher might then recycle and expand the learning of culturally different greeting patterns through pen pal letter sources, highlighted video segments, computer simulations, and guest speakers until all culturally authentic uses of the greetings have been used in appropriate settings.

In a portfolio assessment system the following evidence might be evaluated to judge the quality of this aspect of teaching performance as suggested in the AATG Professional Standards: "annotated lesson plans showing the selection and use of instructional strategies and materials relating to specific goals; annotated video segments that illustrate the communicative context of the [language] classroom, and show students engaged in content area learning and critical thinking activities; annotated examples of student portfolios, dialogue journals between teacher and student records of student performance on standardized [German-] language examinations" (Schulz et al., 1993, p. 87). The review of lesson plans, video tapes of teaching, or instructional materials designed or selected for use with real language learners could offer a more credible basis for assessing this important dimension of teacher knowledge than the typical academic test of content knowledge.

## Intellectual Abilities and Problem Solving Skills

Theorists have characterized teachers as decision makers (e.g., Shavelson, 1983) and have described the "professional teacher" (Holmes Group, 1986) as being involved in "deliberate activity" (Kennedy, 1987). Such conceptualizations identify intellectual activity as fundamental to teacher effectiveness. Teachers must have the ability to reflect, analyze critically, select the tools and materials of teaching, and evaluate the products and performance of the learner. They must be continual problem solvers in the workplace.

Additionally, current trends call for teachers to teach critical thinking skills to their students. The work of such professional groups as the National Council of Teachers of Mathematics (1989), the National Council for the Social Studies (1988), the National Science Teachers Association (1987), and various reports written in the past decade (e.g., Education Commission of the States, 1983) call for increased attention to this topic and radical changes in instruction as a result.

Advances in technology and the phenomenon sometimes described as a "knowledge explosion" require teachers themselves to demonstrate critical thinking skills, problem solving ability, and the ability to use modern information technologies. In short, teachers must have the intellectual abilities that we expect them to help develop in their students.

Evidence of the teacher's skills with technology could be judged through annotated lesson plans, unit plans, lists of instructional resources used, a record of annotated readings, personal journal, dialogue journal, reports from professional meetings, or a report of participation in an action research project.

## Pedagogical Skills

The greatest advancement in assessment of teaching has occurred in the area of pedagogical skills, because it is the most basic and fundamental of the professional development areas. The most common tool for evaluation of teachers' pedagogical skills is the observation checklist. A recent review of literature on assessment of teaching (Andrews and Barnes, 1990) identifies the following categories as most common to these checklists: teachers' ability to (a) manage student behavior and the use of time, (b) sustain student involvement and monitor learning, (c) use appropriate curricular materials, and (d) communicate with clarity and correctness. Such systems sometimes incorporate assessment of a teacher's ability to plan instruction by evaluating lesson plans. These checklists are almost always used system- or school-wide, and are therefore generic in nature and rarely look at the teachers' ability to make classroom management decisions appropriate to their subject matter.

Kagan (1992) proposes that the acquisition of teaching skills is a developmental process, "beginning with classroom management and organization, moving to subject matter and pedagogy, and finally to what students are learning from academic tasks" (p. 144). Assessment information from classroom observations is an important part of a system to screen preservice teachers, but it has limited potential for predicting future effectiveness because it focuses only on the lowest level of professional development described by Kagan. However, the accumulation of evidence from observations over time, as is done in portfolio assessment, provides an index of growth as well as a description of current performance, and this might serve as an indicator of potential for continued growth and development by the beginning teacher.

A teacher's ability to assess and monitor pupils' learning is one area of pedagogical performance that should be given more attention. In a portfolio assessment plan, the use of formative assessments by teachers could be documented over time through personal journal entries, annotated lesson plans with notations of changes made according to student assessment information, annotated teacher-made tests, samples of performance-based assessments of students, examples of frequent feedback to students over time, and/or testimonials by students or their parents.

## Curriculum Knowledge, Insight, and Skill

Zumwalt (1989) argues for a broader view of curriculum than has typically been recognized by teacher educators and provides a description of what preservice teachers should learn about curriculum. Zumwalt suggests that the domain of curriculum contains knowledge, insight, and skill components that parallel the need for beginning teachers to explore relationships between what is taught, how it is taught, and what students learn. Thus, preservice teachers must be aware of alternative ways to structure curriculum, be sensitive to different views about the purposes of schooling, and have the ability to plan, deliver, and evaluate instruction that is consistent with a particular curricular approach and philosophical intent.

Reflective teaching experiences provide the basis for future growth in the curriculum domain. The process dimension of portfolio assessment, mentioned earlier, can be particularly useful for encouraging reflection and monitoring students' development in the multi-component curriculum domain. In fact, the portfolio's ability to track this domain of good teaching over time may be the most powerful argument for adopting this assessment design. With a portfolio, students can create, with guidance from faculty mentors, their own assessment documentation to show their reflections over time and even to explore their own concerns—taking some important responsibilities early for the assessment of their own work.

In some portfolio assessment plans, students, with the help of a faculty mentor, identify their own purposes for study by articulating what they believe they need and want to learn. Once they establish these personal goals, they seek out their own activities to meet the needs (e.g., Barton and Collins, 1993). In this model of portfolio assessment, the portfolios change programs in a fundamental way by placing a responsibility on the students to establish a purpose of study. If students are required to integrate theory and practice in their attempts to articulate their own purposes of study, they will become more reflective about issues of student assessment in their own classrooms. This may translate into better assessment and evaluation practices in their own foreign language classes.

## Knowledge about Learners and Learning

The interactive nature of teaching is the primary factor that contributes to the complexity of the work, and this complexity is increased exponentially when anything other than a one-on-one tutorial approach is involved. Knowledge about learners and sensitivity to social context factors that affect learning are essential for effective teaching.

A person who might teach Spanish successfully to highly motivated, academically able 14-year-old suburbanites may be completely ineffective when teaching in a setting where even one of these variables is changed. (Research in the areas of mathematics and English found that teachers shown to be effective with high-ability students, in terms of student achievement, exhibit different teaching behaviors than those shown to be effective with low-ability students. See Medley, 1982; Shavelson and Russo, 1977.) Thus, the pre-service teacher assessment system must recognize not only the existence of essential knowledge about learners but also must determine whether or not preservice teachers can apply this knowledge to the full range of teaching situations in which they may eventually work. At the very least, an accurate and complete description of the students and the school setting should be included. Only then can it be determined whether the entire domain of teaching has been represented. Preservice teachers could demonstrate their expanding sophistication in this area via case studies of individual students, classrooms or schools (see Hammadou, 1991).

## Attitudes and Dispositions

Teachers have certain feelings, beliefs, and emotions that influence their behavior and actions in the classroom. Although attempts to study "teacher attitude" as a variable affecting the quality of teaching has not been fruitful (Borich, 1977), more recent literature on teacher education (e.g., Katz and Raths, 1986) suggests that "dispositions," or tendencies to act in certain ways, may be one dimension of teacher attitude that can be systematically assessed. This dimension is likely to be affected by other aspects of "attitude" that are not easily observed.

For example, the level of a French teacher's appreciation or enthusiasm about a piece of literature may be important only when it affects the teacher's "tendency" to spend more (or less) time discussing the work. The Japanese teacher's sensitivity to the needs of students who have difficulty reading Kanji may be important only if the teacher "tends" to ignore such students during class discussions rather than involving them in reflections and analyses of events described in assigned readings.

Despite the difficulties that have traditionally been associated with assessing attitudes or dispositions, the AATG Task Force's recommendations for professional standards make a number of helpful concrete suggestions for documenting success in this area. In its first standard (commitment to the success of all students. . .), the task force proposes, for example, "letters from students, parents, administrators, colleagues, teacher educators, and others; statistics which indicate continuing study by diverse student groups; description/documentation of service as student mentor" (pp. 84–85). In addition, statements of philosophy or written definitions of what constitutes the subject matter that is being taught could demonstrate the teacher's ability to articulate a position on these important topics.

# Operational Features

Four critical operational features of an assessment system for preservice teachers are: (a) flexibility, (b) the use of information from a variety of sources, (c) collecting assessment information longitudinally, and (d) processing or interpreting the information in an integrated, holistic fashion.

## Flexibility

The flexibility of an assessment system is essential because it must be applicable to preservice teachers preparing for a wide variety of grade level teaching assignments. The FLES preservice teacher should not have the same assessment process as the secondary language teacher. In addition, it must be fair and appropriate when applied to preservice teachers coming from and eventually teaching in diverse settings. It is also critical that important differences among preservice teachers be encouraged and supported by the assessment system, not stifled or constrained by its rigidity.

Isolation is a common dilemma for the foreign language teacher. Many find that they are the only teacher of their language within their building or even within their district. It is critical, therefore, that learning to be responsible for their own professional growth and their own assessment be part of their preservice teaching experience. In order to meet this need it can be built into the portfolio design that some of the evidence will be self-selected by the student as portfolio developer rather than entirely prescribed by the faculty as portfolio designers.

The key to flexibility is a system defined in terms of broad guidelines and examples that are illustrative and suggestive, not prescriptive and restrictive. At least in broad strokes, there must be a careful description of several critical system components: (a) what content and performance domains will be examined: (b) what data collection mechanism will be discouraged, allowed, or encouraged; (c) when data will be collected (at least in terms of time intervals, e.g., with the first 2 weeks, every other week); and (d) what roles various parties involved might play in the system.

Preservice teacher-designed and faculty-developed portfolios can help foreign language teacher educators focus on process as well as product. The table below provides an example of the levels of information that portfolio assessment can supply.

| Table. Possible Portfolio Information | | | |
|---|---|---|---|
| *Type of Information* | *Purpose* | *Traits* | *Contents* |
| Product | Assessment of L$_2$ proficiency and pedagogical skills | Depth and breadth of L$_2$ knowledge | Academic transcripts<br>Selected examples of L$_2$ work (teacher, faculty, or joint selection):<br>oral tapes<br>written papers<br>required projects |
| | | Level of L$_2$ proficiency | OPI (or similar score) |
| | | Pedagogical competencies | Scores from standardized teaching exams<br>Final cooperating-teacher report |
| | | Professional awareness | Participation in professional organizations |
| Process | Assessment of L$_2$ teaching abilities | What I do, know, and think?<br>How do I ...<br>teach?<br>feel about teaching?<br>see myself as a teacher?<br>approach teaching?<br>use/give feedback?<br>challenge myself? | Selected work from professional education coursework<br>microteaching videotapes<br>practicum journals<br>dialogue journals<br>observations of teaching<br>self-evaluations |
| Program | Assessment of the development of an L$_2$ teacher preparation program | Opportunities to experience teaching in:<br>K–6 environment<br>7–12 environment<br>Rural<br>Urban<br>Suburban<br>Entrance into the profession | Selected work from<br>Practicum field work<br>FLES observations<br>Secondary tutorial<br>Job applications and follow-up interviews<br>First-year teaching review |

At the product level, the preservice teachers include evidence of their second language (L2) proficiency and pedagogical knowledge. Traditional evaluation approaches, such as grade point average in required coursework, transcripts of academic work, standardized test scores, and field experience evaluations are included. All of these traits can be evidenced by evaluations of the external human behavior of the preservice teacher. The external products of traditional foreign language education programs, however, are not the only things that teacher educators should evaluate. Teaching abilities and programs must also be examined. Preservice teachers must be screened for future professional development, remedial or advanced. Colleges of education or states must be able to rate the foreign language teacher preparation programs on how well they produce teachers who can effectively teach languages. In both cases, foreign language teaching abilities, and not only language teaching products, need to be examined.

In *Mind in Society* (1978), Lev Vygotsky pointed out that product examinations do not illuminate process. Moreover, Gardner (1983) contended that, to assess *abilities* we must ascertain not only the learners' actions but also their preferences and judgments. Hence, portfolios can help evaluate teaching abilities because they provide insight into the development of the thinking that generates teaching skills. This thinking may be reflected in the order in which preservice teachers select their works (micro teaching tapes, notes, journals) and even the way they label and organize the portfolio. Gardner (1983) and John-Steiner (1985) have used similar materials to trace the intellectual development of artists, scientists, mathematicians, writers, and musicians.

It is true that portfolios contain more than one piece of work by each preservice teacher, and so they are more time-consuming to assess. Because portfolios can include videos, journals, notes, and the student teacher's own evaluations, the information is hard to categorize consistently and inexpensively with large populations. However, because portfolios consist of exactly these components exterior to the finished product but central to the developing processes, they allow valid assessment of teaching programs as well as abilities and products.

The specific details of an assessment protocol for a particular preservice teacher would be the product of a set of negotiations in which the interests of all concerned were considered and represented. Such an approach allows the system to accommodate differences by adjusting how various types of information are selected and used in the assessment process.

A portfolio assessment system can easily accommodate such a need for flexibility. Each program using portfolios can specify broad guidelines or general procedures that assure flexibility in a way that reflects the particular needs of the setting. Such a system might include a "portfolio review committee" empowered to interpret the general guidelines as they apply to particular cases.

## Multiple Data Sources

A listing of potential data sources and mechanisms, along with a procedure for adding others to the list, is essential to provide some structure and direction to the assessment system. Among the data sources that are likely to be considered are: tests and test scores, written work, projects and other products indicative of knowledge and understanding, lesson plans and curriculum designs, reflective journals, observation reports from cooperating and supervising teachers, interview notes, and video and audio tape recordings.

Data sources can be specified in terms of when or how often they might be collected and whether students or others (e.g., faculty, cooperating teacher) provide the information. As was mentioned in the discussion of portfolio evaluation, the role of the students in identifying data sources and selecting material from different points in their programs is not just a procedural feature of the system. This active participation in the selection process also provides evidence of their ability to solve problems and to reflect on and evaluate their own work, and it offers a description of changes in performance over time.

Barton and Collins (1993) report that they have found that "rich portfolios include a combination of some prescribed (designer required) evidence and some elected (developer chosen) evidence" (p. 204). They recommend that when prescribing evidence they, as portfolio "designers," have been "more successful in prescribing form (a video of a lab lesson) than specific content (a lesson on photosynthesis)" in their teacher education programs in literacy and in science education (p. 205).

The use of multiple data sources requires a procedure for identifying a subset of material that best represents the student if the analysis and interpretation of information is to be kept feasible. A distinction between a "working" portfolio and an "assessment" portfolio is helpful in this regard. The working portfolio includes all materials the preservice teacher may accumulate, while the assessment portfolio includes the "best pieces" or the materials that show the student's exemplary works. Guidelines for selecting the material best suited for the assessment portfolio should be explained and discussed throughout the teacher education program. It is essential that the students be involved in the process of selecting this material in response to written guidelines and/or consultation with peers and faculty.

One problem that surfaces immediately is "how much evidence is enough evidence?" Haertel (1991) proposes the value-added principle as a guide for deciding how much evidence to include. The student portfolio developer selects one document that highlights most clearly the meeting of a given goal. As soon as the portfolio developer feels that the next piece of evidence adds nothing new to the portfolio, the portfolio is complete. Barton and Collins (1993) recommend, however, that students continue to consider several pieces until they feel confident about the quality of their portfolios by making the "nothing-new-is-added" decision about several pieces.

## Longitudinal Data Collection

Portfolio assessment provides a natural cumulative record of the preservice teacher's development and achievements. Collecting information about pre-service teachers over time is essential because the longitudinal approach increases the validity of the assessment. This approach minimizes the possibility that information will be collected when students are having a "bad day." Further, it allows for an examination of students' growth in any number of critical areas of the knowledge base. The ability to show growth, as well as current status, is an important consideration in assessing preservice teachers.

Lastly, the use of longitudinal information increases the likelihood that inferences about subsequent classroom teaching performance will be valid. It is difficult to predict how preservice teachers will perform when teaching in their own classrooms, but a record of past behavior is the best predictor of future behavior. The use of preservice teachers' cumulative information data base, reflecting multiple data sources and different dimensions of the students' ability over time, will increase the likelihood that inferences made about the students' subsequent teaching effectiveness will be accurate.

## Integrated Assessment Criteria

It is difficult to interpret comprehensive, multi-dimensional, longitudinal data bases containing both quantitative and qualitative data. Both analytical and holistic approaches can be used to interpret such information. An analytic approach explicates discrete dimensions to be evaluated and employs a quantitative scale on each dimension on which students are rated. The holistic approach to interpreting assessment information is substantially different and offers an integrated interpretation. With this approach, the reviewer or a review committee considers all evidence simultaneously and "compares" the entire corpus of information to a prototype or model and gives it a single score.

A combination of the analytic and holistic approaches is called the modified holistic approach and is especially useful. With modified holistic scoring, certain critical dimensions of the entire body of material are specified and examined. A single, integrated (holistic) score is assigned based on features of the critical dimensions.

The use of a modified holistic approach in the review of preservice teachers' portfolio assessment information is beneficial because it obligates faculty to discuss and agree on what they expect to see when they examine students' assessment information. The modified holistic approach provides an integrated, constructed, more qualitative picture of the prospective teacher's portfolio data rather than reducing each individual to a series of discrete quantitative scales. Such a picture is more faithful to the complexity and integrative nature of teaching and supports the need for flexibility to operate effectively and efficiently a preservice teacher assessment system.

The descriptions of a successful portfolio entry versus a less successful one should not be merely differences of degree (e.g., *excellent* versus *adequate* use of listening comprehension questions); otherwise, students are likely to find themselves compared to each other rather than to the goals being sought. Barton and Collins (1993) report that the two most common reasons that portfolio evidence is found lacking are the following: (a) some entries fail to provide enough evidence of growth, often because the student includes too little information in the entry to document this growth, (b) other entries fail to demonstrate an explicit link between the evidence included and the established goal of the portfolio. A frequent cause of this problem is that the portfolio developer has included too much information and has not reduced the entry to the most relevant elements.

# The Challenges

The strengths of the portfolio system outlined above are also, in many ways, its weaknesses as well. Four major challenges face educators implementing portfolio assessment. First, the system is clearly very time-consuming. It is not surprising, however, that the comprehensive assessment of something as complex and dynamic as teaching would require such an effort. Second, there exists a strong need to demonstrate that a system that allows for individual choices and differences is consistent and equitable to all. Experienced teachers know that to be "fair" to all students does not require rigid adherence to the same answer to each student's questions. On the contrary, fairness usually dictates accommodations to individual cases. This concept of fairness and equity must be made explicit to preservice teachers. Indeed, they need to have a hand in spelling out the parameters for such "different but equitable" portfolios. A subcategory of the fairness problem is the difficulty of choosing and articulating what aspects of good language teaching to look for in the portfolios. This problem of "content validity" is not unique to portfolio assessment. It is the central challenge of all testing, but portfolio assessment makes these decisions much more public.

Thirdly, collaboration between university and school partnerships demands additional efforts to involve all interested parties, including cooperating teachers, supervisors and administrators in the defining of portfolio standards for the teacher education programs in which they participate. The added effort early should pay off with fewer frustrated triangles of student teacher–teacher–university supervisor later.

Finally, there is an ever growing need for foreign language educators to collect and share data about the status of their respective teacher education programs. Too often individual programs are being operated in the dark with little or no information what other programs might have to offer them. Such data collection needs to be complete enough to allow informed comparisons among programs. Assessment and evaluation is one critical area in which data must be shared nationally in order to assist ongoing efforts to improve the status of foreign language teachers and teaching.

# Conclusion

Foreign language teachers know that there is no one "right" method to teach foreign languages. Similarly, there is no one "right" method to evaluate and assess foreign language teachers' competence. Nevertheless, a fair and principled assessment of teaching is possible. Now is an excellent time for foreign language educators to capitalize on the public's interest in teacher education by seeking assistance for the challenges that lie ahead to expand and improve the evaluation of how successful we have been at preparing foreign language teachers for the language classrooms of the '90s and beyond.

The emergence of portfolios as an alternative method of evaluation is not a panacea. They do offer to future teachers, however, increased opportunities to participate actively in their own assessment. It can be difficult at first for faculty and students to agree that students will choose, to a degree, how they want to demonstrate that they have learned what they should have learned. The additional effort to collaborate may pay impressive rewards because, ultimately, the portfolio development process can serve as a powerful lesson for future teachers who, in turn, must decide what students will learn and how students will demonstrate that learning.

# References

American Association of Teachers of French. The teaching of French: A syllabus of competence. *AATF National Bulletin,* October 1989, *15* (Special issue).

American Association of Teachers of Spanish and Portuguese. AATSP program guidelines for the education and training of teachers of Spanish and Portuguese. *Hispania,* 1990, *73,* 785–94.

American Council on the Teaching of Foreign Languages. *Provisional program guidelines for foreign language teacher education,* New York: Author, 1988.

American Council on the Teaching of Foreign Languages. *Proficiency guidelines.* New York: Author, 1986.

Andrews, T.E., and Barnes, S. Assessment of teaching. In W.R. Houston (Ed.), *Handbook of research on teacher education: A project of the Association of Teacher Educators.* New York: Macmillan, 1990.

Arter, J.A., and Spandel, V.A. An NCME instructional module on using portfolios of student work in instruction and assessment. *Educational Measurement: Issues and Practice* 1992, *11,* 36–44.

Ayers, J. *The NTE, PPST, and classroom performance.* Jefferson City. MO: Association of Teacher Educators, 1989. ERIC ED 305 373

Ayers, J., and Qualls, G. Concurrent and predictive validity of the National Teacher Examinations. *Journal of Educational Research,* 1979, *73* (2), 86–92.

Baratz-Snowden, J. Assessment of teachers: A view from the national board for professional teaching standards. In A. D'Costa, and W. Loadman (Eds.), *Assessing tomorrow's teachers* Theory into Practice, Columbus, OH: The Ohio State University, 1993.

Barton, J., and Collins, A. Portfolios in teacher education. *Journal of Teacher Education,* 1993, *44* (3), 200–12.

Borich, G.D. *The appraisal of teaching: Concepts and process.* Reading, MA: Addison Wesley, 1977.

Carlson, W.S. Subject-matter knowledge and science teaching: A pragmatic perspective. In J. Brophy (Ed.), *Teachers' knowledge of subject matter as it relates to their teaching practice.* Greenwich, CT: JAI Press, 1991.

Carnegie Forum on Education and the Economy. Task Force on Teaching as a Profession. *A nation prepared: Teachers for the 21st century.* Washington, DC: Author, 1986.

Cohen, J. Legal challenges to testing for teacher certification: History, impact, and future. *Journal of Law and Education,* 1989, *18,* 229–65.

Costa, A.L. Re-assessing assessment. *Educational Leadership* 1989, *46* (9), 35–37.

Dewey, J. The relation of theory to practice in education. Rpt. in M.L. Borrowman (Ed.), *Teacher education in America: A documentary history.* New York: Teachers College Press, 1965 (Original work published 1904).

Duke, D., and Duke, J. *Predicting PPST scores from ACT scores.* Searcy, AR: Harding University, 1990. ERIC ED 322 185

Dwyer, C.A. and Villegas, A.M. *The praxis series: Foundations for tomorrow's teachers— No. 3. Defining teaching.* Princeton: ETS, 1993.

Education Commission on the States. *A summary of major reports on education*, Denver: Author, 1983.

Ellena, W., Stevenson, M., and Webb, H. *Who's a good teacher?* Washington, DC: American Association of School Administrators, Department of Classroom teachers of the National Education Association, National School Boards Association, 1961.

Gardner, H. *Frames of mind: The theory of multiple intelligences.* New York: Basic Books, 1983.

Goodison, M. *Testing the basic competencies of teacher education candidates with the Pre-Professional Skills Test.* Chicago: American Educational Research Association, 1985. ERIC ED 276 747

Grossman, P.L., Wilson, S.M., and Shulman, L.S. Teacher of substance: Subject matter knowledge for teaching. In M.C. Reynolds (Ed.), *Knowledge base for the beginning teacher.* New York: Pergamon Press, 1989.

Haertel, E.H. Performance tests, simulations, and other methods. In J. Millman and L. Darling-Hammond (Eds.), *The new handbook of teacher evaluation: Assessing elementary and secondary school teachers.* New York: Sage Publications, 1990.

Haertel, E.H. New forms of teacher assessment. In G. Grant (Ed.), *Review of research in education*, 1991, *17*, 23–29. Washington, DC: American Educational Research Association.

Hammadou, J. Beyond language proficiency: The construct of knowledge. In E.S. Silber (Ed.), *Critical issues in foreign language instruction.* New York: Garland, 1991.

Hammadou, J. Inquiry in Language Teacher Education. In G. Guntermann (Ed.), *Developing language teachers for a changing world.* Lincolnwood, IL: National Textbook Company, 1993.

Hancock, C.R. Modest proposals for teacher education in the 1980's. In J. Phillips (Ed.), *Action for the 80's: A political, professional, and public program in foreign language education.* Lincolnwood, IL: National Textbook Company, 1981.

Holmes Group, Inc. *Tomorrow's teachers: A report of the Holmes Group.* East Lansing, MI: Author, 1986.

Jarvis, G.A. Pedagogical knowledge for the second language teacher. In J.E. Alatis, H.H. Stern, and P. Stevens (Eds.) *Applied linguistics and the preparation of second language teachers: Toward a rationale.* Washington, DC: Georgetown University Press, 1983.

John-Steiner, V. *Notebooks of the mind: Exploring thinking.* Albuquerque: University of New Mexico Press, 1985.

Interstate New Teacher Assessment and Support Consortium. *Draft model standards for teacher licensing.* Washington, D.C., Council of Chief State School Officers, 1992.

Kagan, D.M. Professional growth among preservice and beginning teachers. *Review of Educational Research*, 1992, *63*, 129–69.

Katz, L.G., and Raths, J.D. Dispositions as goals for teacher education. *Teaching and Teacher Education*, 1986, *1*, 301–07.

Kennedy, M. *Inexact sciences: Teacher education and learning to teach.* East Lansing: Michigan State University, National Center for Research on Teacher Education, 1987. (Issue Paper 77-2)

Knop, C.K. A report on the ACTFL summer seminar: Teacher education in the 1990s. *Foreign Language Annals*, 1991, *24*, 527–32.

Lafayette, R.C. Subject-matter content: What every foreign language teacher needs to know. In G. Guntermann (Ed.), *Developing language teachers for a changing world.* Lincolnwood, IL: National Textbook Company, 1993.

Lange, D.L. Teacher development and certification in foreign languages: Where is the future? *The Modern Language Journal*, 1993, *67* (4), 374–81.

Medley, D.M. *Teacher competency testing and the teacher educator.* Charlottesville, VA: University of Virginia, Bureau of Educational Research, 1982.

Metcalf, K. The supervision of student teaching: A review of research. *Teacher Educator*, 1991, *26* (4), 27–42.

Millman, J., and Darling-Hammond, L. (Eds.). *The new handbook of teacher evaluation: Assessing elementary and secondary teachers.* New York: Sage Publications, 1990.

Nance, J., and Kinnison, L. An examination of ACT, PPST, and ExCET performance of teacher education candidates. *Teacher Education and Practice*, 1988, *5* (1), 25–30.

National Council for the Social Studies. Standards for the preparation of social studies teachers. *Social Education, 1988, 52,* 10–12.

National Council of Teachers of Mathematics. *Curriculum and evaluation standards for school mathematics.* Reston, VA: Author, 1989.

National Science Teachers Association. *Criteria for excellence.* Washington, DC: Author, 1987.

Paulson, F.L., Paulson, P.R., and Meyer, C.A. What makes a portfolio a portfolio? *Educational Leadership*, 1991, *17* (5), 5–14.

Peterson, P.L. Teachers' and students' cognitional knowledge for classroom teaching and learning. *Educational Researcher*, 1988, *17* (5), 5–14.

President's Commission on Foreign Language and International Studies. *Strength through wisdom: A critique of U.S. capability.* Washington, D.C.: GPO, 1979; Rpt. *The Modern Language Journal*, 1980, *64* (4), 9–57.

Ryan, J.M., and Kuhs, T.M. Assessment of preservice teachers and the use of portfolios. In A. D'Costa, and W. Loadman (Eds.), *Assessing tomorrow's teachers, 1993.* Theory into Practice. Columbus, OH: The Ohio State University, 1993.

Schrier, L.L. A survey of foreign language teacher preparation patterns and procedures in small, private colleges and universities in the United States. Ph.D. diss., The Ohio State University, 1989.

Schrier, L.L. Prospects for the professionalization of foreign language teaching. In G. Guntermann (Ed.), *Developing language teachers for a changing world.* Lincolnwood, IL: National Textbook Company, 1993.

Schulz, R.A., et al. Professional standards for teachers of German: Recommendations of the AATG Task Force on Professional Standards. *Die Unterrichtspraxis*, 1993, *26* (1), 80–96.

Seldin, P. *The teaching portfolio.* Bolton, MA: Anker Publishing, 1991.

Shavelson, R.J. Review of research on teachers' pedagogical judgments, plans, and decisions. *Elementary School Journal*, 1983, *83,* 392–413.

Shavelson, R. and Russo, N. Generalizability of measures of teacher effectiveness. *Educational Research*, 1977, *19,* 171–83.

Shulman, L. Those who understand: Knowledge growth in teaching. *Educational Researcher*, 1986, *15* (2), 4–14.

Silbert, P. *Relationships among the ACT, PPST, NTE, ACT COMP and the GPA* Savannah, GA: Eastern Educational Research Association, 1989. ERIC ED 305 374

Simmons, J. Portfolios for large-scale assessment. In D.H. Graves and B.S. Sunstein (Eds.), *Portfolio portraits* Portsmouth, NH: Heinemann, 1992.

Stansfield, C.W. Simulated oral proficiency interviews. *ERIC Digest.* Washington, DC: Center for Applied Linguistics, December, 1989.

Stocker, W., and Tarrab, M. The relationship between Pre-Professional Skills Test and American College Tests. *Teacher Education and Practice*, 1985, *2* (1), 43–45.

*Texas oral proficiency test 1991–1992: Registration bulletin.* Amherst, MA: National Evaluation Systems, 1991.

TOPT test preparation kit. Preliminary ed. Washington, DC: Center for Applied Linguistics, 1991.

Vygotsky, L. *Mind in society: The development of higher psychological processes.* Cambridge, MA: Harvard University Press, 1978.

Zumwalt, K. Beginning professional teachers: The need for a curriculum vision of teaching. In M.C. Reynolds (Ed.), *Knowledge base for the beginning teacher.* New York: Pergamon Press, 1989.

## Glossary of Selected Terms

Charles R. Hancock

*The Ohio State University*

The following terms related to the theme of the volume and are presented as a tool for readers who want a brief, non-technical, explanation of selected terms frequently encountered in the professional literature.

*Achievement test:*

a test which measures or evaluates what a learner knows from what s/he has been taught; typically it is given at a particular point in time determined by the teacher without or without notice to the learners.

*Alternative assessment:*

an on-going evaluation by a teacher; frequently refers to non-conventional ways (ergo, "alternative") of evaluating what learners know or can do with the foreign language; examples include writing letters, leaving messages on a telephone answering machine, interviewing someone and summarizing interview notes.

*Assessment:*

an on-going evaluation or check by a teacher to determine how a learner is progressing, often for the purpose of making decisions about what instruction is needed by the learner(s).

*Authentic assessment:*

an on-going evaluation based mainly on real-life experiences; having learners show what they have learned by performing tasks similar to those required in real situations; examples include completing an application, giving information about something that one has just witnessed (e.g., an accident), listening to a weather report in order to plan an activity the next day.

*Communicative approach:*

an emphasis in teaching foreign languages in which meaning is more important than form; learners are encouraged to express personal ideas; grammar and other forms of the language are learned primarily "in context" (i.e., as needed for particular situations); it fosters functional, practical outcomes of foreign language study.

*Computer-adaptive testing:*

a procedures in which a computer program presents the items of a test to the learner; in some cases the computer program may keep track of the learner's performance on the test and select particular items (e.g., easier or harder), or "adapt" the next item(s) presented to the learner based on the number of correct or incorrect items s/he has at a particular point during the test; also called computer-assisted testing or computer-administered testing.

*Constructed-response item:*

a type of performance assessment consisting of open-ended written items on a test; learners are required to "construct" an answer to a question or problem, rather than choose an answer from a list (e.g., multiple choice).

*Criterion-referenced testing:*

a learner's performance is compared to some criterion, standard, or skill level (as opposed to comparing the learner's performance with other students' performance).

*Culturally biased test:*

tests or items on a test which favor a particular learner or group of learners and therefore makes the test unfair to other learners; includes the notion of testing learners on content or experiences which may not have been provided for all learners (e.g., including an item on a test dealing with a particular religion when only a few learners are members of that religion).

*Discrete-point testing:*

the type of testing which checks a learner's recognition or ability to use particular aspects of the foreign language (e.g., the third person singular of the verb *to be*); very popular type of test item which is easily scored and for which there is a clearly right or wrong answer.

*Formative evaluation:*

frequent or periodic measurement of a learner's knowledge or skills in the foreign language; its purpose is primarily diagnostic; teachers typically use formative evaluation as a way of deciding how effective a particular lesson was and what, if anything, needs to be re-taught.

*Integrative testing:*

includes the use of testing procedures which require learners to make connections between the discrete points of language; learners are typically required to recognize the interconnectedness of items on a test (e.g., ten separate items in one section of a test tell a story); a type of testing which assumes that contextualized learning is preferred over discrete bits of information.

*Item analysis:*

a procedure in which the items of a test are examined after the test has been given to determine two main points: (1) the level of difficulty of the item(s), and, (2) the degree to which the item discriminates between those who did well on the entire test and those who did poorly on it; a systematic [text missing!]

*Level check:*

a term associated with the ACTFL oral proficiency interview; it refers to the interviewer's attempt to determine the proficiency level (e.g., novice high versus intermediate low) of the person being interviewed.

*Norm-referenced testing:*

refers to interpreting a learner's performance on a particular test in comparison with the performance of other students (e.g., Janine's score on the National Spanish Exam was at the 96th percentile, meaning that she performed better than most of the other students who took the test nationally).

*Oral Proficiency Interview (OPI):*

associated with the ACTFL proficiency scale; it refers to the set procedure (warm-up, level check, probe, wind-down) in which a trained interviewer interacts with a language learner to obtain a good (ratable) sample of the learner's oral use of the foreign language. After the OPI, a separate procedure is followed to determine the ACTFL proficiency level (e.g., novice-high, intermediate-low, etc.) which the language sample matches.

*Performance-based approach:*

refers to language instruction which emphasizes the functional or practical use of the foreign language by the learners; learners demonstrate their knowledge or skills in the language by writing an essay, giving an oral explanation about something, completing a project, or otherwise "using" the language for some identified purpose.

*Portfolio:*

refers to a collection of learner's work assembled for the purpose of determining how much has been learned; it may include examples of the learner's completion of tasks such as reports (both oral and written), creative projects such as artwork, contributions to a group project, writings (essays, poems, written homework), and may include both learner and teacher selection of work to be included.

*Probe:*

a procedure in the Oral Proficiency Interview (OPI) in which the trained interviewer asks questions or makes comments which involve language which is progressively more complex to determine if the person being interviewed can continue to successfully participate in the interview.

*Prochievement:*

a relatively new term referring to the blending of achievement test and proficiency test content and procedures; it assumes that the dichotomy between achievement and proficiency is unrealistic and therefore has to provide for combining the two.

*Prompt:*

typically used in writing and refers to the stimulus or task which the learner is given; a common example of a prompt would be something like: Make a short list of the main suggestions you would offer to someone planning to travel abroad this summer.

*Reliability:*

refers to the consistency of a test or assessment procedure to give trustable results; also refers to generalizability of the results of a particular test; high reliability is typically an indication that a test or testing procedure can be trusted.

*Self-assessment:*

a type of evaluation of learner achievement which involves the individual himself or herself in judging the level of proficiency and/or skill development which has occurred; it relates to the notion of metacognition in which an individual is presumed to know more about how s/he learns than anyone else; some claim that this type of assessment lacks objectivity and reliability.

*Standards:*

refer to goals, desirable behaviors, or levels of achievement which have been established by some individual or agency (e.g., the ACTFL, AATF, AATG, AATSP National Standards in Foreign Languages Project; National Education Goals); a more specific meaning of the term is the level of proficiency expected of students.

*Summative evaluation:*

refers to a test or other evaluation which is given at the end of some particular lesson or unit of instruction; a chapter test or a semester exam is considered to be a summative evaluation because it occurs after instruction and is presumed to measure how much of what was taught has been learned.

*Test:*

a sampling of what a learner knows or can do; it is an estimate of what is known or can be done and, as such, is imprecise; tests have traditionally been used in language programs and will probably continue to be used because they provide valuable information about what a learner knows and can do with the foreign language; caution is warranted, however, in interpreting test results because they may be affected by factors beyond the individual learner's control (classroom climate, parents, learner attitudes, etc.).; they should be used in conjunction with other forms of on-going assessment of learner's achievement and proficiency development.

*Validity:*

traditionally refers to the degree to which a test measures what it is supposed to measure; face validity is the most basic type of validity and refers to whether or not the test "looks like" it does what it is supposed to do (e.g., an OPI seems to be a valid way to test a person's oral proficiency); other types of validity include content, construct, concurrent, predictive, washback validity.

*Warm-up:*

refers to the initial part of the Oral Proficiency Interview (OPI) in which the interviewee is made comfortable by the trained interviewer through non-threatening comments (e.g., Please sit down, Is that chair okay?, How are you today?, etc.); its purpose is to relax the interviewee so that a ratable sample of language may be obtained.

*Washback effect:*

refers to the impact a test or testing program may have on the curriculum in a particular instructional program; it may occur as a direct or an indirect impact; in its most undesirable direct form, the test content is actually taught (sometimes called "teaching to the test").

*Whole-language approach:*

an instructional emphasis on language as part of the overall communicative act; it also refers to the integration of the four skill areas of listening, speaking, reading, and writing as being interdependent; an example might be the reading of an excerpt from literature as the stimulus for a foreign language class activity (group discussions, conducting a survey, reviewing the format for asking questions in the foreign language, interviewing some students who were surveyed, writing a school newspaper article based on the project, etc.).

*Wind-down:*

the final part of the Oral Proficiency Interview (OPI) in which the trained interviewer returns the interview to a level of language use which relaxes the interviewee and brings the iterview to an amiable end.

# *Annotated Bibliography*

Sulaiman Alrarla
Tom Destino
Tona Dickerson
Michelle-Marie Dowell
Liu Jun
Rosalynn Lucas
Lee Wilberscheid-Hull
and Shu-hua Wu[1]

*The Ohio State University*

Apodaca, M. Proficiency sample project, 1990, ERIC ED 332 507.

This document describes a Colorado foreign language proficiency sample project, including directions for administering the sample instrument. When used in Colorado, the project was a voluntary, teacher-designed and administered effort to standardize language proficiency assessment with high school language students. The primary purpose of the instrument is to gather student language samples in the four skill areas (listening, speaking, reading, and writing) and to rate them. A practical article for anyone interested in procedures for collecting student samples but particularly appropriate for those who plan and conduct workshops on this topic.

Bachman, L.F. What does language testing have to offer? *TESOL Quarterly*, 1991, *25*, 671–704.

A review of advances made in language testing during the past decade is presented. After citing specific areas in which improvements have occurred, the author presents an interactional language testing model which considers both the test taker's language ability and the test method. Two types of authenticity are identified: (1) interactional authenticity (degree to which the test evokes the test taker's language ability), and, (2) situational authenticity (degree to which the test method mirrors a specific type of language use appropriate for particular situations). The author concludes with suggestions for increasing the interactional authenticity of testing tasks. An important article for those seeking a deliberative analysis of cutting-edge testing issues.

d'Angeljan, A., Harley, B., and Shapson, S. Student evaluation in a multidimensional core French curriculum. *Canadian Modern Language Review,* 1991, *47* (1), 106–24.

Many basic concepts in evaluation are reviewed as they authors tried to identify the most effective evaluative strategies for core French classes. Formative and summative testing, validity and reliability, and close versus open-ended formats were among the concepts reviewed. The practical nature of the article makes it a useful reference for classroom teachers and curriculum developers.

Halleck, G.B. The oral proficiency interview: Discrete point test or a measure of communicative language ability? *Foreign Language Annals,* 1992, *25,* 227–31.

This article examines the role of discrete-point sentence level grammar in the ratings of individuals in an oral proficiency interview (OPI). The author surveyed trained OPI raters to determine the degree to which specific grammar problems in the OPI sample ratings affected the raters' decisions to rate the candidates at another level (higher or lower) on the ACTFL proficiency scale. According to the findings, the author reported that raters appear to be more concerned with global communicative abilities than with discrete grammar errors. This article would be of particular interest to those who want information about ways to rate students' oral language production. Some familiarity with the ACTFL scale is needed to get the most out of this article.

Heilenman, L.K. Self-assessment and placement: A review of the issues. In R.V. Teschner (Ed.), Assessing foreign language proficiency of undergraduates. Boston: Heinle and Heinle Publishers, 1991.

The author outlines major issues involved in using self-assessment of foreign language students with respect to language proficiency. Placement testing is the focus of the article and the role of undergraduate students in making personal judgments about their language skills. The case is built for self-assessment as one of the types of data which may be used in the placement of students in college classes. This article should be valuable reading for those making decisions about placement and language programs at both the secondary school and college/university levels.

Heining-Boynton, A.L. The development and testing of the FLES program evaluation inventory. *The Modern Language Journal,* 1990, *74,* 432–39.

The author proposes an instrument for evaluating FLES programs by considering both typical historical shortcomings as well as contemporary ones for FLES programs. The instrument known as FPEI includes five forms designed to solicit reactions of key individuals concerned with FLES programs: FLES teachers, regular classroom teachers, students, parents, and administrators. A pilot study using the instrument is described. Sample forms are included. A very useful article for anyone working in or concerned about evaluating a FLES program.

Johnson, H. Defossilizing. *ELT Journal,* 1992, *46* (2), 180–89.

A phenomenon faced by many foreign language students and teachers, fossilization, is defined. The author maintains that communicative interaction should be considered a valid, learning enhancing activity, despite the possibility of fossilization. An action research project is described in which an opportunity is presented for learners to experience an authentic and unpredictable discourse with other students. A relatively short and worth reading article which treats a persistent problem in foreign language education.

Laycock, J., and Bunnag, P. Developing teacher self-awareness: Feedback and the use of video. *ELT Journal,* 1991, *45* (1), 43–53.

As professional development continues to offer opportunities for teachers to grow, technology such as video is a good resource. In the study reported in this article, teachers were provided feedback via video, using viewing guides. The author gives practical examples of how video feedback may effectively be integrated with other types of feedback. A case is built for the positive effect of such viewing on a teacher's self-awareness. An interesting article for those with relatively little recent teacher preparation.

Lee, B. Classroom-based assessment—why and how? *British Journal of Language Teaching,* 1989, *27* (2), 73–76.

The author advocates the integration of classroom assessment with the teaching /learning process. After distinguishing between external (summative) and internal (formative) testing/assessment, the author elaborates the advantages of an integrated approach. Student tasks, assessment criteria and procedures, and ways to make sue of assessment results are described. An interesting article particularly for those interested in practical suggestions and "how to" ideas for developing the match between teaching, testing, and assessment at the classroom level.

Pino, B. G. Prochievement testing of speaking. *Foreign Language Annals,* 1989, *22,* 487–96.

The author describes a relatively new concept known as prochievement testing, which is a blending of achievement and proficiency testing procedures. The focus of Pino's work has been in the area of speaking foreign languages, and she presents information on pilot testing of this approach with university level foreign language students. Specific examples are presented, including practical suggestions for those wishing to implement this type of testing. A useful article for anyone interested in making use of both achievement and proficiency testing data in the foreign language program.

Shohamy, E., Reeves, T., and Bejarano, Y. Introducing a new comprehensive test of oral proficiency. *ELT Journal,* 1987, *40* (3), 212–20.

This article provides an example of research-based testing combined with establishing educational policy. A study is described in which a new oral proficiency test replaces an older one developed by the Israeli Ministry of Education. The authors describes the features which make the newer test better on the basis of selected educational, linguistic, and testing qualities. It is also argued that the test resulted in a broader distribution of scores and assessed a wider range of speech styles. Simple statistics showing important comparisons between the two tests were reported. A useful article for those interested in creating newer tests to replace existing ones.

Stansfield, C.W., and Kenyon, D.M. The development and validation of a simulated oral proficiency interview. *The Modern Language Journal*, 1992, *76*, 129–41.

This article describes the development and validation of the Simulated Oral Proficiency Interview (SOPI), an alternative to the ACTFL oral proficiency interview which normally requires a face-to-face interview. An example of the SOPI using the Indonesian Speaking Test is described. Details of a study using the Indonesian test suggest that this testing alternative is reliable and therefore provides a substitute for the OPI. Additional advantages of the SOPI (versus OPI) are presented. The article describes components of the SOPI (a master audio tape, a test booklet, and a student tape) as well as availability of this resource. This is a very useful article for those who are convinced that OPI is an appropriate testing strategy but, for whatever reason, are looking for an alternative to it.

Wiggins, G. Creating tests worth taking. *Educational Leadership*, 1992, *49* (8), 26–33.

Although this article is not exclusively written for the language profession, the author raises key questions and provides insights which are important for all educators. He makes the statement, for example, that good teaching is inseparable from good assessing, a theme advocated throughout this volume. Based on his work with school districts, Wiggins offers practical suggestions for making tests resemble real world tasks. He argues for a reform in evaluation of student learning, suggesting that the teachers need to "contextualize" the tasks given to students. In his view, testing and assessment ought to be much more authentic than is currently the case. This is an excellent article for anyone interested in creating tests which reflect contemporary thinking about putting the focus on meaningful student tasks.

Zdenek, J.W. Assessment of foreign language majors: an alternative to the ACTFL proficiency tests, 1988, ERIC ED 317 081.

This article describes an alternative approach to testing foreign language majors' language competence. Although it was initially designed as a diagnostic instrument, it was later determined that the test is also appropriate as a screening device for students about to enter student teaching. Another use for the test is to evaluate language competence of French and Spanish majors prior to graduation from college. Advantages of the test as well as a weighted evaluation option are also presented. The article is of particular interest to teacher educators at the college/university level.

# Note

The bibliography items are part of a larger list of references (articles, books, microfiche) read by the doctoral students listed, who were participants in a Foreign Language Education Seminar at The Ohio State University at the time and agreed to read broadly on the topic of this volume and select key references for this annotation.

# Northeast Conference Officers and Directors since 1954

Abbott, Martha G., Fairfax County (VA) Public Schools, Director 1994-97.

Anderson, Nancy E., ETS, Director 1990-93, ACTFL Representative 1994.

Andersson, Theodore, [Yale U]* U of Texas, Director 1954-56.

Andrews, Oliver, Jr., U of Connecticut, Director 1971-74.

Arndt, Richard, Columbia U, Director 1961.

Arsenault, Philip E., Montgomery County (MD) Public S, Local Chair 1967, 1970; Director 1971, 1973-74; Vice Chair 1975; Conference Chair 1976.

Atkins, Jeannette, Staples (Westport, CT) HS, Director 1962-65.

Baird, Janet, U of Maryland, Local Chair 1974.

Baker, Robert M., Middlebury C, Director 1987-90.

Bashour, Dora, [Hunter C], Secretary 1963-1964; Recording Secretary 1965-68.

Baslaw, Annette S., [Teachers C], Hunter C, Local Chair 1973.

Bayerschmidt, Carl F., [Columbia U], Conference Chair 1961.

Bennett, Ruth, Queens C, Local Chair 1975-76.

Bertin, Gerald A., Rutgers U, Local Chair 1960.

Berwald, Jean-Pierre, U of Massachusetts-Amherst, Director 1980-83.

Bird, Thomas E., Queens C, Editor 1967-68; Director 1969.

Bishop, G. Reginald, Jr., Rutgers U, Editor 1960, 1965; Director 1961- 62, 1965,1968; Vice Chair 1966; Conference Chair 1967.

Bishop, Thomas W., New York U, Local Chair 1965.

Born, Warren C., [ACTFL], Editor 1974-79.

Bostroem, Kyra, Westover S, Director 1961.

Bottiglia, William F., MIT, Editor 1957, 1962-63; Director 1964.

Bourque, Jane M., [Stratford (CT) Public S], Mt. Vernon (NY) Public S, Director 1974-75; Vice Chair 1976; Conference Chair 1977.

Bree, Germaine, [New York U, U of Wisconsin], Wake Forest U, Conference Chair 1955; Editor 1955.

Bressler, Julia T., Nashua (NH) Public S, Director 1991-94.

Brod, Richard I., MLA, Consultant to the Chair, 1983; Director 1985-88.

Brooks, Nelson†, [Yale U], Director 1954-57, 1960-61; Vice Chair 1959.

Brooks-Brown, Sylvia R., [Baltimore (MD) City S], Baltimore County (MD) Public S, Director 1988-92; Vice Chair 1993, Conference Chair 1994.

Brown, Christine L., [West Hartford (CT) Public S], Glastonbury (CT) Public S, Director 1982-85; Vice Chair 1986; Conference Chair 1987.

Byrnes, Heidi, Georgetown U, Director 1985-88; Vice Chair 1989; Conference Chair 1990; Editor 1992.

Cadoux, Remunda†, [Hunter C], Vice Chair 1969; Conference Chair 1970.

Campbell, Hugh, [Roxbury Latin S], Rocky Hill Country Day S, Director 1966-67.

Cannon, Adrienne G., Eleanor Roosevelt HS (Greenbelt, MD), Director 1993-96.

Carr, Celestine G., Howard County (MD) Public S, Director 1993-96.

Churchill, J. Frederick, Hofstra U, Director 1966-67; Local Chair 1971- 72.

Ciotti, Marianne C., [Vermont State Department of Education, Boston U], Barre (VT) Public S, Director 1967.

Cincinnato, Paul D., Farmingdale (NY) Public S, Director 1974-77; Vice Chair 1978; Conference Chair 1979.

Cintas, Pierre F., [Dalhousie U], Pennsylvania State U-Ogontz, Director 1976-79.

Cipriani, Anita A., Hunter C Elem S, Director 1986-89.

Clark, John L.D., [CAL], DLI, Director 1976-78; Vice Chair 1979; Conference Chair 1980.

Clark, Richard P., Newton (MA) HS, Director 1967.

Clemens, Brenda Frazier, [Rutgers U, U of Connecticut], Howard U, Director 1972-75.

Cobb, Martha, Howard U, Director 1976-77; Recording Secretary 1978.

Covey, Delvin L., [Montclair State C], Spring Arbor C, Director 1964-65.

Crapotta, James, Barnard C, Director 1992-95.

Crawford, Dorothy B., Philadelphia HS for Girls, Conference Chair 1956.

---

*Where a change of academic affiliation is known, the earlier address appears in brackets.

Crapotta, James, Barnard C, Director 1992-95.

Crawford, Dorothy B., Philadelphia HS for Girls, Conference Chair 1956.

Dahme, Lena F., Hunter C, Local Chair 1958; Director 1959.

Darcey, John M., West Hartford (CT) Public S, Director 1978-81; Vice Chair 1982; Conference Chair 1983; Editor 1987.

Dates, Elaine, Burlington (VT) HS, Recording Secretary 1991.

Del Olmo, Filomena Peloro, [Hackensack (NJ) Public S], Fairleigh Dickinson U, Director 1960-63.

De Napoli, Anthony J., Wantagh (NY) Public S, Local Chair 1980-82, 1987; Director 1982-85.

Di Donato, Robert, MIT, Consultant to the Chair 1986.

Díaz, José M., Hunter C HS, Director 1988-91; Vice Chair 1992; Conference Chair 1993.

Didsbury, Robert, Weston (CT) JHS, Director 1966-69.

Dodge, James W.†, [Middlebury C], Editor 1971-73; Secretary-Treasurer 1973-89.

Dodge, Ursula Seuss, Northeast Conference Secretariat, Interim Secretary-Treasurer 1990.

Donato, Richard, U of Pittsburgh, Director 1993-96.

Dostert, Leon E., [Georgetown U], Occidental C, Conference Chair 1959.

Dufau, Micheline†, U of Massachusetts, Director 1976-79.

Dye, Joan C., Hunter C, Local Chair 1978.

Eaton, Annette, Howard U, Director 1967-70.

Eddy, Frederick D.†, [U of Colorado], Editor 1959; Director 1960.

Eddy, Peter A., [CAL/ERIC], CIA Language S, Director 1977-78.

Edgerton, Mills F., Jr., Bucknell U, Editor 1969; Director 1970; Vice Chair 1971; Conference Chair 1972.

Elkins, Robert, West Virginia U, Director 1991-94.

Elling, Barbara E., SUNY-Stony Brook, Director 1980-83.

Feindler, Joan L., East Williston (NY) Public S, Director 1969-71; Vice Chair 1972; Conference Chair 1973.

Flaxman, Seymour, [New York U], City C of New York, Editor 1961; Director 1962.

Freeman, Stephen A., [Middlebury C], Director 1957-60.

Fulton, Renee J., New York City Board of Education Director 1955.

Gaarder, A. Bruce, [USOE], Director 1971-74.

Galloway, Vicki B., [ACTFL], Georgia Technological U, Consultant to the Chair 1985.

Geary, Edward J., [Harvard U], Bowdoin C, Conference Chair 1962.

Geno, Thomas H., U of Vermont, Director 1975-76; Vice Chair 1977; Conference Chair 1978; Recording Secretary 1979; Editor 1980-81.

Gilman, Margaret†, Bryn Mawr C, Editor 1956.

Glaude, Paul M., New York State Dept of Education, Director 1963-66.

Glisan, Eileen W. Indiana U of Pennsylvania, Director 1992-95.

Golden, Herbert H., Boston U, Director 1962.

Grew, James H., [Phillips Acad], Director 1966-69.

Gutiérrez, John R., Pennsylvania State U, Director 1988-91.

Hancock, Charles R., The Ohio State University, Editor 1994

Hartie, Robert W., Queens C, Local Chair 1966.

Harrison, John S., Baltimore County (MD) Public S, Local Chair 1979, 1983; Director 1983-86; Recording Secretary 1988-89.

Harris-Schenz, Beverly, [U of Pittsburgh], U of Massachusetts-Amherst, Director 1988-91.

Hayden, Hilary, OSB, St. Anselm's Abbey S, Vice Chair 1970; Conference Chair 1971.

Hayes, Alfred S.†, CAL, Vice Chair 1963; Conference Chair 1964.

Hernandez, Juana A., Hood C, Director 1978-81.

Holekamp, Elizabeth L., Executive Director 1990-present.

Holzmann, Albert W.†, Rutgers U, Director 1960.

Hurtgen, André, St. Paul's School (NH), Director 1992-95.

Jalbert, Emile H., [Thayer Acad], Berkshire Comm C, Local Chair 1962.

Jarvis, Gilbert A., Ohio State U, Editor 1984.

Jebe, Suzanne, [Guilford (CT) HS], Minnesota Dept of Education, Director 1975-76; Recording Secretary 1977.

Johnston, Marjorie C., [USOE], Local Chair 1964.

Jones, George W., Jr.†, Norfolk (VA) Public S, Director 1977-80.

Kahn, Timothy M., S Burlington (VT) HS, Director 1979-82.

Keesee, Elizabeth, [USOE], Director 1966-70.

Kellenberger, Hunter†, [Brown U], Conference Chair 1954, Editor 1954.

Kennedy, Dora F., Prince George's County (MD) Public S, Director 1985- 88; Recording Secretary 1990; Consultant to the Chair 1991.

Kesler, Robert, Phillips Exeter Acad, Director 1957.

Kibbe, Doris E., Montclair State C, Director 1968-69.

Kline, Rebecca, [Dickinson C], Pennsylvania State U, Director 1990-93, Vice-Chair 1994; Conference Chair 1995.

Koenig, George, State U of New York-Oswego, Recording Secretary, 1993.

Kramsch, Claire J., [MIT], Cornell, Director 1984-87.

La Follette, James E., Georgetown U, Local Chair 1959.

La Fountaine, Hernan, New York City Board of Education, Director 1972.

Lenz, Harold, Queens C, Local Chair 1961.

Lepke, Helen S., [Kent State U], Clarion U of Pennsylvania, Director 1981-84; Vice Chair 1985; Conference Chair 1986; Editor 1989.

Lester, Kenneth A., Connecticut State Dept of Education, Recording Secretary 1982.

Levy, Harry†, [Hunter C], Fordham U, Editor 1958; Director 1959-61; Conference Chair 1963.

Levy, Stephen L., [New York City Board of Education], Roslyn (NY) Public S, Local Chair 1978, 1980-82, 1984-85, 1987-present; Director 1980-83; Vice Chair 1984; Conference Chair 1985; Consultant to the Chair 1994.

Lieberman, Samuel, Queens C, Director 1966-69.

Lipton, Gladys C., [New York City Board of Education, Anne Arundel County (MD) Public S], U of Maryland-Baltimore County, Director 1973-76; Newsletter Editor 1993-present.

Liskin-Gasparro, Judith E., [ETS], Middlebury C, Recording Secretary 1984; Director

1986-89; Vice Chair 1990; Conference Chair 1991.

Lloyd, Paul M., U of Pennsylvania, Local Chair 1963.

Locke, William N.†, MIT, Conference Chair 1957; Director 1958-59.

MacAllister, Archibald T.†, [Princeton U], Director 1955-57, 1959-61.

Magnan, Sally Sieloff, University of Wisconsin-Madison, Editor 1990.

Masciantonio, Rudolph, School District of Philadelphia, Director 1969- 71.

Mead, Robert G., Jr., U of Connecticut, Director 1955; Editor 1966; Vice Chair 1967; Conference Chair 1968; Editor 1982-83.

Mesnard, Andre, Barnard C, Director 1954-55.

Micozzi, Arthur L., [Baltimore County (MD) Public S], Local Chair 1977, 1979, 1983, 1986; Director 1970-82.

Mirsky, Jerome G. †, [Jericho (NY) SHS], Shoreham-Wading River (NY) HS, Director 1970-73; Vice Chair 1974; Conference Chair 1975.

Nelson, Robert J., [U of Pennsylvania], U of Illinois, Director 1965-68.

Neumaier, Bert J., Timothy Edwards (S Windsor, CT) MS, Director 1988-92.

Neuse, Werner†, [Middlebury C], Director 1954-56.

Nionakis, John P., Hingham (MA) Public S, Director 1984-87; Vice Chair 1988; Conference Chair 1989.

Obstfeld, Roland, Northport (NY) HS, Recording Secretary 1976.

Omaggio, Alice C., U of Illinois, Editor 1985.

Owens, Doris Barry, West Hartford (CT) Public S, Recording Secretary 1983.

Pane, Remigio U., Rutgers U, Conference Chair 1960.

Paquette, Andre, [Middlebury C], Laconia (NH) Public S, Director 1963- 66; Vice Chair 1968; Conference Chair 1969.

Parks, Carolyn, [U of Maryland], French International S, Recording Secretary 1981.

Peel, Emily S., Wethersfield (CT) Public S, Director 1991-94.

Perkins, Jean, Swarthmore C, Treasurer 1963-64; Conference Chair 1966.

Petrosino, Vince J., Baltimore (MD) City S, Local Chair 1986.

Phillips, June K., [Indiana U of Pennsylvania, Tennessee Foreign Language Institute], US Air Force Acad, Director 1979-82; Vice

Chair 1983; Conference Chair 1984; Consultant to the Chair 1986, 1989, 1990, 1992; Editor 1991, 1993.

Prochoroff, Marina, [MLA Materials Center], Director 1974.

Reilly, John H., Queens C, Local Chair 1968-69; Director 1970.

Renjilian-Burgy, Joy, Wellesley C, Director 1987-90; Vice Chair 1991; Chair 1992.

Riley, Kerry, U of Maryland, Consultant to the Chair 1986.

Riordan, Kathleen M., Springfield (MA) Public S, Director 1988-91; Recording Secretary 1992.

Rochefort, Frances A., Cranston (RI) Public S, Director 1986-89.

Rosser, Harry L., Boston College, Director 1994-97.

Russo, Gloria M., [U of Virginia], Director 1983-86.

Sandstrom, Eleanor L., [School District of Philadelphia], Director 1975- 78.

Selvi, Arthur M., Central Connecticut State C, Director 1954.

Senn, Alfred, U of Pennsylvania, Director 1956.

Serafino, Robert, New Haven (CT) Public S, Director 1969-73.

Sheppard, Douglas C., [SUNY-Buffalo], Arizona State U, Director 1968-71.

Shilaeff, Ariadne, Wheaton C, Director 1978-80.

Shuster, George N. †, [U of Notre Dame], Conference Chair 1958.

Simches, Seymour O., Tufts U, Director 1962-65; Vice Chair 1965.

Sims, Edna N., U of the District of Columbia, Director 1981-84.

Singerman, Alan J., Davidson C, Editor 1988.

Sister Margaret Pauline, [Emmanuel C], Director 1957, 1965-68; Recording Secretary 1969-75.

Sister Margaret Therese, Trinity C, Director 1959-60.

Sister Mary Pierre, Georgian Court C, Director 1961-64.

Sousa-Welch, Helen Candi, West Hartford (CT) Public S, Director 1987-90.

Sparks, Kimberly, Middlebury C, Director 1969-72.

Starr, Wilmarth H., [U of Maine], New York U, Director 1960-63, 1966; Vice Chair 1964, Conference Chair 1965.

Steer, Alfred G., Jr., Columbia U, Director 1961.

Stein, Jack M.†, [Harvard U], Director 1962.

Stracener, Rebecca J., Edison (NJ) Public S, Director 1984-87.

Tamarkin, Toby, Manchester (CT) Comm C, Director 1977-80; Vice Chair 1981; Conference Chair 1982; Recording Secretary 1987.

Thompson, Mary P., [Glastonbury (CT) Public S], Director 1957-62.

Trivelli, Remo J., U of Rhode Island, Director 1981-84.

Tursi, Joseph, [SUNY-Stony Brook], Editor 1970; Director 1971-72; Vice Chair 1973; Conference Chair 1974.

Valette, Rebecca, Boston C, Director 1972-75.

Vasquez-Amaral, Jose, Rutgers U, Director 1960.

Walker, Richard H., Bronxville (NY) HS, Director 1954.

Walsh, Donald D.†, [MLA], Director 1954; Secretary-Treasurer 1965-1973.

Walton, A. Ronald, U of Maryland, Director 1990-93.

Warner, Pearl M., New York City Public S, Recording Secretary 1985.

Webb, John, Hunter College HS, Consultant to the Chair, 1993.

White, Emile Margaret, [District of Columbia Public S], Director 1955- 58.

Williamson, Richard C., Bates C, Director 1983-86; Vice Chair 1987; Conference Chair 1988.

Wing, Barbara H., U of New Hampshire, Editor 1986; *Newsletter* Editor 1987-present.

Woodford, Protase E., ETS, Director 1982-85.

Yakobson, Helen B., George Washington U, Director 1959-60.

Yu, Clara, Middlebury College, Director 1994-97.

Zimmer-Loew, Helene, [NY State Education Dept], AATG, Director 1977-79; Vice Chair 1980; Conference Chair 1981.

# Northeast Conference Reports, 1954–1993

**Building Bridges and Making Connections.** June K. Phillips, ed. Eileen W. Glisan and Thekla F. Fall: "Adapting an Elementary Immersion Approach to Secondary and Postsecondary Teaching: The Methodological Connection." Diane Larsen-Freeman: "ESL and FL: Forging Connections." Karen E. Breiner-Sanders: "Higher-Level Language Abilities: The Skills Connection." Barbara Schnuttgen Jurasek and Richard T. Jurasek: "Building Multiple Proficiencies in New Curricular Contexts." Juliette Avots: "Linking the Foreign Language Classroom to the World." Elana Shohamy: "Connecting Testing and Learning in the Classroom and on the Program Level." 1991.

**The Challenge for Excellence in Foreign Language Education.** Gilbert A. Jarvis, ed. Barbara H. Wing: "For Teachers: A Challenge for Competence." Diane W. Birckbichler: "The Challenge of Proficiency: Student Characteristics." Michael Canale: "Testing in a Communicative Approach." Glyn Holmes: "Of Computers and Other Technologies." Christine L. Brown: "The Challenge for Excellence in Curriculum and Materials Development." 1984.

**Culture in Language Learning.** G. Reginald Bishop, Jr., ed.: "An Anthropological Concept of Culture." William E. Welmers: "Language as Culture." Ira Wade: "Teaching of Western European Cultures." Doris E. Kibbe: "Teaching of Classical Cultures." Leon I. Twarog: "Teaching of Slavic Cultures." 1960.

**Culture, Literature, and Articulation.** Germaine Bree, ed.: "The Place of Culture and Civilization in FL Teaching." A.T. MacAllister: "The Role of Literature in Language Teaching." Mary P. Thompson: "FL Instruction in Elementary Schools." Robert G. Mead, Jr.: "FL Instruction in

Secondary Schools." Barbara P. McCarthy: "Classical and Modern FLs: Common Areas and Problems." Nelson Brooks: "Tests: All Skills, Speaking Test." A.G. Grace: "The Preparation of FL Teachers." J.V. Pleasants: "Teaching Aids and Techniques: Principles, Demonstrations." W.H. Starr: "The Role of FLs in American Life." 1955. Out of print.

**Current Issues in Language Teaching.** William F. Bottiglia, ed.: "Linguistics and Language Teaching." Alfred S. Hayes: "Programmed Learning." Nancy V. Alkonis and Mary A. Brophy: "A Survey of FLES Practices." 1962.

**FL Learning: Research and Development.** Thomas E. Bird, ed.: "Innovative FL Programs." Seymour O. Simches: "The Classroom Revisited." Mills F. Edgerton, Jr.: "Liberated Expression." 1968.

**FL Teachers and Tests.** Hunter Kellenberger, ed: "The Qualifications of FL Teachers." Arthur S. Selvi: "FL Instruction in Elementary Schools." Nelson Brooks: "Tests: Listening Comprehension, Other Skills." Norman L. Torrey: "The Teaching of Literature." Theodore Andersson: "The Role of FLs in American Life." Richard H. Walker: "Linguistic Aids." 1954.

**FL Teaching: Challenges to the Profession.** G. Reginald Bishop, Jr., ed.: "The Case for Latin." Stephen A. Freeman: "Study Abroad." A. Bruce Gaarder: "The Challenge of Bilingualism." Micheline Dufau: "From School to College: The Problem of Continuity." 1965.

**FL Teaching: Ideals and Practices.** George F. Jones, ed.: "FL's in the Elementary School." Milton R. Hahn: "FL's in the Secondary School." Roger L. Hadlich: "FL's in Colleges and Universities." 1964.

**FL Tests and Techniques.** Margaret Gilman, ed.: "Teaching Aids and Techniques: The Secondary School Language Laboratory." Stanley M. Sapon: "Tests: Speaking Tests." Mary P. Thompson: "FL Instruction in Elementary Schools." Ruth P. Kroeger: "FL Instruction in Secondary Schools." Josephine P. Bree: "The Teaching of Classical and Modern FLs: Common Areas and Problems." Robert J. Clements: "The Role of Literature in Language Teaching." John B. Carroll and William C. Sayers: "The Place of Culture and Civilization in FL Teaching." Wilmarth H. Starr: "The Role of FLs in American Life." 1956.

**FLs: Reading, Literature, Requirements.** Thomas E. Bird, ed.: "The Teaching of Reading." F.A. Paquette: "The Times and Places for Literature." John F. Gummere: "Trends in FL Requirements and Placement." 1967.

**FLs and The 'New' Student.** Joseph A. Tursi, ed.: "A Relevant Curriculum: An Instrument for Polling Student Opinion." Robert J. Nelson: "Motivation in FL Learning." Eleanor J. Sandstrom: "FLs for All Students?" 1970.

**Foreign Language and International Studies: Toward Cooperation and Integration.** Thomas H. Geno, ed.: "A Chronicle: Political, Professional, and Public Activities Surrounding the President's Commission on Foreign Language and International Studies." Donald H. Bragaw, Helene Z. Loew, and Judith S. Wooster: "Global Responsibility: The Role of the Foreign Language Teacher." Claudia S. Travers: "Exchanges and Travel Abroad in Secondary Schools." Richard C. Williamson: "Toward an International Dimension in Higher Education." Lucia Pierce: "International Training." "Reactions of the Northeast Conference to the Recommendations of the President's Commission on Foreign Language and International Studies." 1981.

**The Foreign Language Teacher: The Lifelong Learner.** Robert G. Mead, Jr., ed. Marilyn J. Conwell and April Nelson: "American Sign Language." David Gidman: "The Chinese Language." Toshiko Phipps and Jean-Pierre Berwald: "Intensive Japanese." Marie Cleary: "Intensive Latin." Rosemarie Pedro Carvalho: "Intensive Portuguese." Robert L. Baker: "Intensive Russian." Pierre Maubrey: "La France Contemporaine." Barbara Elling and Kurt Elling: "Die Bundesrepublik heute." Remo J. Trivelli: "L'Italia Contemporanea." John M. Darcey: "La Espana de Hoy." Frank Dauster: "La Cultura Contemporanea de Hispanoamerica." Elizabeth G. Joiner and June K. Phillips: "Merging Methods and Texts: A Pragmatic Approach." Judith E. Liskin-Gasparro and Protase E. Woodford: "Proficiency Testing in Second Language Classrooms." Carolyn H. Parks: "Audiovisual Materials and Techniques for Teaching Foreign Languages: Recent Trends and Activities." John S. Harrison: "Applications of Computer Technology in Foreign Language Teaching and Learning." 1982. Out of print.

**The Foreign Language Teacher in Today's Classroom Environment.** Warren C. Born, ed.: "Educational Goals: The Foreign Language Teacher's Response." Carol Hosenfeld: "Cindy: A Language Learner in Today's Foreign Language Classroom." Gilbert A. Jarvis: "The Second Language Teacher: A Problem of Reconciling the Vision with the Reality." 1979.

**Foreign Languages: Key Links in the Chain of Learning.** Robert G. Mead, Jr., ed. Myriam Met, et al.: "Elementary School Foreign Language: Key Link in the Chain of Learning." Alice C. Omaggio, et al.: "Foreign Languages in the Secondary Schools: Reconciling the Dream with the Reality." Claire Gaudiani, et al.: "Nurturing the Ties that Bind: Links between Foreign Language Departments and the Rest of the Post-Secondary Educational Enterprise." Vicki Galloway: "Foreign Languages and the 'Other' Student." H.H. Stern: "Toward a Multidimensional Foreign Language Curriculum." Jane McFarland Bourque: "Thirty Years of the Northeast Conference: A Personal Perspective." 1983.

**Goals Clarification: Curriculum, Teaching, Evaluation.** Warren C. Born, ed.: "Goals Clarification: Background" and "Goals Clarification: Implementation." 1975.

**Language: Acquisition, Application, Appreciation.** Warren C. Born, ed.: "Language Acquisition." Kenneth Lester: "Language Application." Germaine Bree: "Language Appreciation." 1977.

**Language and Culture: Heritage and Horizons.** Warren C. Born, ed.: "The French Speaking." Helene Z. Loew: "The German Speaking." Grace Crawford: "Classics in America." 1976.

**The Language Classroom.** William F. Bottiglia, ed.: Blance A. Price: "Teaching Literature for Admission to College with Advanced Standing." Nelson Brooks: "Spoken Language Tests." James H. Grew: "The Place of Grammar and the Use of English in the Teaching of FLs." Renee J. Fulton: "The Drop-Out of Students after the Second Year." John B. Archer: "The Philosophy of the Language Laboratory." Jeanne V. Pleasants: "Teaching Aids and Techniques." 1957.

**The Language Learner.** F.D. Eddy, ed.: "Modern FL Learning: Assumptions and Implications." G.R. Silber: "A Six-Year Sequence." Filomena C. Peloro: "Elementary and Junior High School Curricula." Nelson Brooks: "Definition of Language Competences Through Testing." 1959.

**Language Learning: The Intermediate Phase.** W. F. Bottiglia, ed.: "The Continuum: Listening and Speaking." George Scherer: "Reading for Meaning." Marina

Prochoroff: "Writing as Expression." 1963.

**The Language Teacher.** Harry L. Levy, ed.: "The Teaching of Writing." James H. Grew: "Single vs. Multiple Languages in Secondary Schools." Margaret E. Eaton: "The FL Program, Grades 3-12." Dorothy Brodin: "Patterns as Grammar." Donald D. Walsh: "The Ghosts in the Language Classroom: College FL Departments, College Board Examinations, the Administration, the Textbook." Carolyn E. Bock: "Means of Meeting the Shortage of Teachers." 1958.

**The Language Teacher: Commitment and Collaboration.** John M. Darcey, ed. Claire L. Gaudiani: "The Importance of Collaboration." Humphrey Tonkin: "Grassroots and Treetops: Collaboration in Post-secondary Language Programs." Gordon M. Ambach: "Incorporating an International Dimension in Education Reform: Strategies for Success." Alice G. Pinderhughes: "Baltimore's Foreign Language Mandate: An Experiment That Works." Richard C. Wallace, Jr., Mary Ellen Kirby, and Thekla F. Fall: "Commitment to Excellence: Community Collaboration in Pittsburgh." Carolyn E. Hodych: "Canadian Parents for French: Parent Action and Second Official Language Learning in Canada." Badi G. Foster: "The Role of the Foreign Language Teacher in American Corporate Education." 1987.

**Language Teaching: Broader Contexts.** Robert G. Mead, Jr., ed.: "Research and Language Learning." Brownlee Sands Corrin: "Wider Uses for FLs." Genevieve S. Blew: "Coordination of FL Teaching." 1966.

**Languages for a Multicultural World in Transition.** Heidi Byrnes, ed.: Ofelia García: "Societal Multilingualism in a Multicultural World in Transition." Guadalupe Valdés: "The Role of the Foreign Language Teaching Profession in Maintaining Non-

English Languages in the United States." Claire Gaudiani: "Area Studies for a Multicultural World in Transition." Vicki Galloway: "Toward a Cultural Reading of Authentic Texts." John M. Grandin, Kandace Einbeck, and Walter von Reinhart: "The Changing Goals of Language Instruction." Clara Yu: "Technology at the Cutting Edge: Implications for Second Language Learning." 1992.

**Leadership for Continuing Development.** James W. Dodge, ed.: "Professional Responsibilities." Jerome G. Mirsky: "Inservice Involvement in the Process of Change." Francois Hugot: "Innovative Trends." 1971.

**Listening, Reading, Writing: Analysis and Application.** Barbara H. Wing, ed. Carolyn Gwynn Coakley and Andrew D. Wolvin: "Listening in the Native Language." Elizabeth G. Joiner: "Listening in the Foreign Language." Michael L. Kamil: "Reading in the Native Language." Elizabeth B. Bernhardt: "Reading in the Foreign Language." Trisha Dvorak: "Writing in the Foreign Language." 1986.

**Modern Language Teaching in School and College.** Seymour L. Flaxman, ed.: "Foreword: Learning a Modern FL and Communication." Genevieve S. Blew: "The Preparation of Secondary School Teachers." Jack M. Stein: "The Preparation of College and University Teachers." Evangeline Galas: "The Transition to the Classroom." Guillermo del Olmo: "Coordination between Classroom and Laboratory." 1961.

**New Contents, New Teachers, New Publics.** Warren C. Born, ed.: "New Contents." William E. DeLorenzo: "New Teachers." Joseph A. Tursi: "New Publics." 1978.

**Our Profession: Present Status and Future Directions.** Thomas H. Geno, ed.: "Current Status of Foreign Language

Teaching: A Northeast Conference Survey." Robert C. Lafayette: "Toward an Articulated Curriculum." Mills F. Edgerton, Jr.: "Competence in a Foreign Language: A Valuable Adjunct Skill in the Eighties?" James W. Dodge: "Educational Technology." Helen L. Jorstad: "New Approaches to Assessment of Language Learning." David P. Benseler: "The American Language Association: Toward New Strength, Visibility, and Effectiveness as a Profession." 1980.

**Other Words, Other Worlds: Language in Culture.** James W. Dodge, ed.: "On Teaching Another Language as Part of Another Culture." G.R. Tucker and Wallace E. Lambert: "Sociocultural Aspects of FL Study." Samuel Lieberman: Greece and Rome; Gerard J. Brault: France; Marine Leland: French Canada; Harry F. Young: Germany; Joseph Tursi: Italy; Walter F. Odronic: Japan; Irina Kirk: The Soviet Union; John W. Kronik: Spain; Frank N. Dauster: Spanish America. 1972.

**Proficiency, Curriculum, Evaluation: The Ties that Bind.** Alice C. Omaggio, ed. Frank W. Medley, Jr.: "Designing the Proficiency-Based Curriculum." Jeannette D. Bragger: "The Development of Oral Proficiency." Heidi Byrnes: "Teaching toward Proficiency: The Receptive Skills." Sally Sieloff Magnan: "Teaching and Testing Proficiency in Writing: Skills to Transcend the Second-Language Classroom." Wendy W. Allen: "Toward Cultural Proficiency." J. David Edwards and Melinda E. Hanisch: "A Continuing Chronicle of Professional, Policy, and Public Activities in Foreign Languages and International Studies." 1985.

**Reflecting on Proficiency from a Classroom Perspective.** June K. Phillips, ed.: "Proficiency-OrientedLanguage Learning: Origins, Perspectives, and Prospects." Alice Omaggio Hadley. "Proficiency as a Change Element in Curriula for World Languages in Elementary and Secondary Schools." Robert LaBouve. "Using Foreign Languages to Learn: Rethinking the College Foreign Language Curriculum. Janet Swaffar. "Proficiency as an Inclusive Orientation: Meeting the Challenge of Diversity." Marie Sheppard. "Perspective on Proficiency: Teachers, Students, and the Materials that They Use." Diane W. Birckbichler and Kathryn A. Corl. "On Becoming a Teacher: Teacher Education for the 21st Century." Anne Nerenz. "Forty Years of the Northeast Conference: A Personal Perspective." Stephen L. Levy.

**Sensitivity in the Foreign-Language Classroom.** James W. Dodge, ed.: "Interaction in the Foreign-Language Class." Hernan LaFontaine: "Teaching Spanish to the Native Spanish Speaker." Ronald L. Gougher: "Individualization of Instruction." 1973.

**Shaping the Future Challenges and Opportunities.** Helen S. Lepke, ed. June K. Phillips: "Teacher Education: Target of Reform." Carol Ann Pesola and Helena Anderson Curtain: "Elementary School Foreign Languages: Obstacles and Opportunities." Helen P. Warriner-Burke: "The Secondary Program, 9-12." Dorothy James: "Re-shaping the 'College-Level' Curriculum: Problems and Possibilities." Galal Walker: "The Less Commonly Taught Languages in the Context of American Pedagogy." Emily L. Spinelli: "Beyond the Traditional Classroom." 1989.

**Shifting the Instructional Focus to the Learner.** Sally Sieloff Magnan, ed. Elaine K. Horwitz: "Attending to the Affective Domain in the Foreign Language Classroom." Rebecca L. Oxford: "Language Learning Strategies and Beyond: A Look at Strategies in the Context of Styles." Nancy Rhodes, Helena Curtain, and Mari Haas: "Child Development and Academic Skills in the Elementary School Foreign Language Classroom." Anne G. Nerenz: "The Exploratory Years: Foreign Languages in the Middle-Level Curriculum." Thomas Cooper, Theodore B. Kalivoda, and Genelle

Morain: "Learning Foreign Language in High School and College: Should It Really Be Different?" Katherine M. Kulick: "Foreign Language Proficiency and the Adult Learner." 1990.

**Sight and Sound: The Sensible and Sensitive Use of Audio-Visual Aids.** Mills F. Edgerton, Jr., ed.: "Non-Projected Visuals." Jermaine Arendt: "Sound Recordings." Hilary Hayden: "Slides and Filmstrips." James J. Wrenn: "The Overhead Projector." Allen W. Grundstrom: "Motion Pictures." Joseph H. Sheehan: "Television." 1969.

**Toward A New Integration of Language and Culture.** Alan J. Singerman, ed. Peter Patrikis: "Language and Culture at the Crossroads." Angela Moorjani and Thomas T. Field: "Semiotic and Sociolinguistic Paths to Understanding Culture." Robert C. Lafayette: "Integrating the Teaching of Culture into the Foreign Language Classroom." Claire J. Kramsch: "The Cultural Discourse of Foreign Language Textbooks." Jean-Pierre Berwald: "Mass Media and Authentic Documents: Language in Cultural Context." Seiichi Makino: "Integrating Language and Culture Through Video: A Case Study from the Teaching of Japanese." Aleidine J. Moeller: "Linguistic and Cultural Immersion: Study Abroad for the Younger Student." Norman Stokle: "Linguistic and Cultural Immersion: Study Abroad for the College Student." Barbara Lotito and Mireya Pérez-Erdélyi: "Learning Culture through Local Resources: A Hispanic Model." 1988.

**Toward Student-Centered Foreign-Language Programs.** Warren C. Born, ed.: "Training for Student-Centered Language Programs." Anthony Papalia: "Implementing Student-Centered Foreign-Language Programs." Rene L. Lavergneau: "Careers, Community, and Public Awareness." 1974.

Copies of the Reports may be obtained from Northeast Conference, 29 Ethan Allen Drive, Colchester, VT 05446. Please write for ordering information.